CONTENTS

Records Topple in 1999; North America Hits Highs in Sales and Production as U.S. Economy, Surging Canadian and Mexican Markets Push Industry to New Heights

That 1999 was a good year for the North American automotive industry is an understatement. Sales and production hit all-time highs for the continent — and not by small margins. The U.S. boosted the region, as sales and production hit record levels, but Canada and Mexico also chipped in with major contributions to the industry's rock solid performance. The year was not only a boon for domestic manufacturers, major import retailers also enjoyed considerable growth in both volume and market share. Strong economies — including a near record long expansion in the U.S. — and increasingly intense competition were the spurs behind 1999's excess. Stock markets continued to hit record highs, unemployment remained at record lows and consumer spending appeared to have no boundaries, even as the U.S. Federal Reserve began creeping up interest rates later in the year. Spending on autos was encouraged further by intense competition, as several companies expanded their lineups with new sport/utility vehicles (SUVs) and luxury sedans to lure hungry buyers. This compounded the effects of the strong economy, causing manufacturers to cap prices and offer generous incentives in the form of consumer rebates, low interest rate financing and sweetened lease deals.

Retail Sales

Sales of all vehicles in North America surged to 19.66 million units in 1999, 8.9% above the prior year and by far the highest level ever. Sales by country hit records in the U.S. (17.41 million) and Mexico (706,380), while Canada posted its second best year ever with sales of 1.54 million units. In the U.S. alone, trucks continued to enjoy most of the growth, thanks primarily to consumers' steadily increasing attraction to sport/utility vehicles. But even the low volume heavy-duty (Class 8) commercial vehicle segment posted record sales, as all truck segments enjoyed volume growth in 1999. Resurgence in the luxury sedan and sports car market, as well as an increase in SUV offerings, benefited overseas importers in 1999. And at the entry-level end of the market, South Korean manufacturers began an assault on the small car sector with lower prices and improved quality. Sales of overseas imports in the U.S., alone, totaled 2.51 million in 1999, 22.3% above 1998 and highest since 2.59 million in 1991. The only reason import sales weren't higher was the increased manufacturing presence of overseas-based companies in North America.

North American Production

North American production of all vehicles increased 9.9% from 1998 to 17.62 million — another record chalked up in 1999. All three countries attained individual records, with 13.02 million in the U.S., 3.06 million in Canada and 1.53 million in Mexico.

Vehicles in Operation

Motor vehicles on U.S. roads in 1999 increased from the previous year by 2.2% to 209.5 million units, with trucks accounting for 39.4% of all vehicles on the road, up from 38.6% the previous year. The percentage of trucks on the road hasn't declined on a year-to-year basis since 1961, when they accounted for 15.8% of all vehicles in operation. Individually, the number of cars in operation increased by less than 1% to 126.9 million, and trucks recorded a 4.5% gain to 82.6 million.

In other highlights from Ward's Motor Vehicle Facts & Figures:

■ Export shipments from U.S. plants — including to Canada and Mexico — declined slightly to 1,219,177 units in 1999 from 1,247,814 in 1998, with a decline in trucks more than offsetting an increase in car exports. The dollar value also declined from the prior year to $21.05 billion.

■ U.S. import shipments increased by a noticeable 21% to 6,230,655 from the prior year, while the dollar figure went up by the same percentage to $114.05 billion.

■ The percentage of female buyers for both cars and trucks increased in the 2000 model year from 1999 model levels, while the share of principle buyers under the age of 25 declined.

■ The average interest rate for financing a new or used car purchase in 1999 vs. 1998 increased for new cars and stayed flat for used vehicles. However, the average monthly payment for used cars increased from 1998

■ Expenditures on new cars actually declined for imports in 1999 from 1998, but rose for domestically produced cars. The total average expenditure for a new car increased to $21,020 in 1999, compared to 1998's $20,849.

■ Corporate average fuel economy increased by 1/2 mile for the light-truck fleet in the 2000 model year to 21.2 mpg. CAFE for cars increased too, but by one-tenth of a mile to 28.4 mpg.

U.S. Production and Factory Sales of Passenger Cars, Trucks and Buses

ANNUAL U.S. MOTOR VEHICLE PRODUCTION AND FACTORY SALES

Year	Production			Factory Sales		
	Passenger Cars	Commercial Vehicles	Total	Passenger Cars	Commercial Vehicles	Total
1999	5,637,806	7,387,029	13,024,835	5,427,746	6,699,113	12,126,859
1998	5,554,373	6,448,290	12,002,663	5,676,964	6,435,185	12,112,149
1997	5,927,281	6,191,888	12,119,169	6,069,886	6,152,817	12,222,703
1996	6,083,227	5,749,410	11,832,637	6,140,454	5,775,730	11,916,184
1995	6,350,733	5,634,724	11,985,457	6,309,836	5,713,469	12,023,305
1994	6,613,970	5,648,767	12,262,737	6,548,562	5,640,275	12,188,837
1993	5,981,046	4,916,619	10,897,665	5,961,754	4,895,224	10,856,978
1992	5,664,203	4,037,731	9,701,934	5,685,299	4,062,002	9,747,301
1991	5,438,579	3,371,942	8,810,521	5,407,120	3,387,503	8,794,623
1990	6,077,449	3,705,548	9,782,997	6,049,749	3,725,205	9,774,954
1989	6,823,097	4,050,935	10,874,032	6,807,416	4,061,950	10,869,366
1988	7,113,137	4,100,550	11,213,687	7,104,617	4,120,574	11,225,191
1987	7,098,910	3,825,776	10,924,686	7,085,147	3,821,410	10,906,557
1986	7,828,783	3,505,992	11,334,775	7,516,189	3,500,933	11,017,122
1985	8,184,821	3,467,922	11,652,743	8,002,259	3,464,327	11,466,586
1984	7,773,332	3,151,449	10,924,781	7,621,176	3,175,835	10,797,011
1983	6,781,184	2,443,637	9,224,821	6,739,223	2,433,876	9,173,099
1982	5,073,496	1,912,099	6,985,595	5,049,184	1,906,455	6,955,639
1981	6,253,138	1,689,778	7,942,916	6,255,340	1,700,908	7,956,248
1980	6,375,506	1,634,335	8,009,841	6,400,026	1,667,283	8,067,309
1979	8,433,662	3,046,331	11,479,993	8,419,226	3,036,706	11,455,932
1978	9,176,635	3,722,567	12,899,202	9,165,190	3,706,239	12,871,429
1977	9,213,654	3,489,128	12,702,782	9,200,849	3,441,521	12,642,370
1976	8,497,893	2,999,703	11,497,596	8,500,305	2,979,476	11,479,781
1975	6,716,951	2,269,562	8,986,513	6,712,852	2,272,160	8,985,012
1974	7,324,504	2,746,538	10,071,042	7,331,256	2,727,313	10,058,569
1973	9,667,152	3,014,361	12,681,513	9,657,647	2,979,688	12,637,335
1972	8,828,205	2,482,503	11,310,708	8,823,938	2,446,807	11,270,745
1971	8,583,653	2,088,001	10,671,654	8,584,592	2,053,146	10,637,738
1970	6,550,128	1,733,821	8,283,949	6,546,817	1,692,440	8,239,257
1965	9,335,227	1,785,109	11,120,336	9,305,561	1,751,805	11,057,366
1960	6,703,108	1,202,011	7,905,119	6,674,796	1,194,475	7,869,271
1955	7,950,377	1,253,672	9,204,049	7,920,186	1,249,106	9,169,292
1950	6,628,598	1,377,261	8,005,859	6,665,863	1,337,193	8,003,056
1945	83,786	701,090	784,876	69,532	655,683	725,215
1940	3,728,491	784,404	4,512,895	3,717,385	754,901	4,472,286
1935	3,252,244	694,690	3,946,934	3,273,874	697,367	3,971,241
1930	2,784,745	571,241	3,355,986	2,787,456	575,364	3,362,820
1925	N.A.	N.A.	N.A.	3,735,171	530,659	4,265,830
1920	N.A.	N.A.	N.A.	1,905,560	321,789	2,227,349
1915	N.A.	N.A.	N.A.	895,930	74,000	969,930
1910	N.A.	N.A.	N.A.	181,000	6,000	187,000
1905	N.A.	N.A.	N.A.	24,250	750	25,000
1900	N.A.	N.A.	N.A.	4,192	N.A.	4,192

N.A. - Not available.
SOURCE: Ward's Automotive Reports.

U.S. and Canadian Passenger Car Production by Model

U.S. AND CANADIAN PASSENGER CAR PRODUCTION BY MODEL, 1997-1999

	United States			Canada			U.S. and Canada Total		
	1997	1998	1999	1997	1998	1999	1997	1998	1999
Chrysler 300M	—	—	—	—	51,169	75,191	—	51,169	75,191
Chrysler LHS	—	—	—	26,749	23,097	27,720	26,749	23,097	27,720
Cirrus	38,057	47,246	47,124	—	—	—	38,057	47,246	47,124
Concorde	—	—	—	33,673	87,832	61,403	33,673	87,832	61,403
Total Chrysler	**38,057**	**47,246**	**47,124**	**60,422**	**162,098**	**164,314**	**98,479**	**209,344**	**211,438**
Intrepid	—	—	—	139,558	138,757	174,607	139,558	138,757	174,607
Neon	124,831	124,729	165,229	—	—	—	124,831	124,729	165,229
Stratus	114,437	115,674	100,196	—	—	—	114,437	115,674	100,196
Viper	1,790	1,216	1,600	—	—	—	1,790	1,216	1,600
Total Dodge	**241,058**	**241,619**	**267,025**	**139,558**	**138,757**	**174,607**	**380,616**	**380,376**	**441,632**
Vision	—	—	—	4,008	—	—	4,008	—	—
Total Eagle	**—**	**—**	**—**	**4,008**	**—**	**—**	**4,008**	**—**	**—**
Breeze	74,483	64,270	47,911	—	—	—	74,483	64,270	47,911
Neon	86,656	78,372	66,905	—	—	—	86,656	78,372	66,905
Prowler	463	2,124	2,862	—	—	—	463	2,124	2,862
Total Plymouth	**161,602**	**144,766**	**117,678**	**—**	**—**	**—**	**161,602**	**144,766**	**117,678**
Total Chrysler Corp.	**440,717**	**433,631**	**431,827**	**203,988**	**300,855**	**338,921**	**644,705**	**734,486**	**770,748**
Contour	136,329	129,945	114,897	—	—	—	136,329	129,945	114,897
Crown Victoria	—	—	—	110,163	133,351	124,002	110,163	133,351	124,002
Escort	238,981	198,679	114,171	—	—	—	238,981	198,679	114,171
Focus	—	—	114,682	—	—	—	—	—	114,682
Mustang	119,196	149,129	191,432	—	—	—	119,196	149,129	191,432
Taurus	371,861	400,652	382,858	—	—	—	371,861	400,652	382,858
Thunderbird	47,073	—	—	—	—	—	47,073	—	—
Total Ford	**913,440**	**878,405**	**918,040**	**110,163**	**133,351**	**124,002**	**1,023,603**	**1,011,756**	**1,042,042**
Continental	34,421	36,328	27,121	—	—	—	34,421	36,328	27,121
Lincoln LS	—	—	39,266	—	—	—	—	—	39,266
Mark	17,467	6,103	—	—	—	—	17,467	6,103	—
Town Car	94,594	110,718	81,551	—	—	—	94,594	110,718	81,551
Total Lincoln	**146,482**	**153,149**	**147,938**	**—**	**—**	**—**	**146,482**	**153,149**	**147,938**
Cougar	24,019	—	—	24,019	—	—	—	—	—
Grand Marquis	—	—	—	118,453	135,709	143,627	118,453	135,709	143,627
Mystique	43,501	39,818	38,021	—	—	—	43,501	39,818	38,021
Sable	123,873	111,676	106,427	—	—	—	123,873	111,676	106,427
Tracer	38,473	27,760	14,691	—	—	—	38,473	27,760	14,691
Total Mercury	**229,866**	**179,254**	**159,139**	**118,453**	**135,709**	**143,627**	**348,319**	**314,963**	**302,766**
Total Ford Motor Co.	**1,289,788**	**1,210,808**	**1,225,117**	**228,616**	**269,060**	**267,629**	**1,518,404**	**1,479,868**	**1,492,746**
LeSabre	150,275	142,155	157,501	—	—	—	150,275	142,155	157,501
Park Ave	72,260	65,343	61,009	—	—	—	72,260	65,343	61,009
Regal	—	—	—	180,995	211,715	247,461	180,995	211,715	247,461
Riviera	13,603	6,317	—	—	—	—	13,603	6,317	—
Skylark	51,444	6	—	—	—	—	51,444	6	—
Total Buick	**287,582**	**213,821**	**218,510**	**180,995**	**211,715**	**247,461**	**468,577**	**425,536**	**465,971**
Eldorado	21,783	14,397	17,638	—	—	—	21,783	14,397	17,638
Fleetwood Deville	115,264	105,206	88,922	—	—	—	115,264	105,206	88,922
Seville	32,867	56,429	38,907	—	—	—	32,867	56,429	38,907
Total Cadillac	**169,914**	**176,032**	**145,467**	**—**	**—**	**—**	**169,914**	**176,032**	**145,467**
Camaro	—	—	—	58,010	47,049	44,564	58,010	47,049	44,564
Cavalier	332,189	233,806	269,564	—	—	—	332,189	233,806	269,564
Corvette	24,673	32,046	33,243	—	—	—	24,673	32,046	33,243
Impala	—	—	—	—	—	122,673	—	—	122,673
Lumina	—	—	—	319,421	248,272	76,118	319,421	248,272	76,118
Malibu	233,349	252,479	251,584	—	—	—	233,349	252,479	251,584
Monte Carlo	—	—	—	—	—	69,378	—	—	69,378
Total Chevrolet	**590,211**	**518,331**	**554,391**	**377,431**	**295,321**	**312,733**	**967,642**	**813,652**	**867,124**
Achieva	58,017	6	—	—	—	—	58,017	6	—
Alero	—	56,429	146,329	—	—	—	—	56,429	146,329
Aurora	27,714	21,751	12,260	—	—	—	27,714	21,751	12,260
Cutlass	40,100	50,562	20,784	—	—	—	40,100	50,562	20,784

U.S. and Canadian Passenger Car Production by Model

U.S. AND CANADIAN PASSENGER CAR PRODUCTION BY MODEL, 1997-1999 — continued

	United States			Canada			U.S. and Canada Total		
	1997	1998	1999	1997	1998	1999	1997	1998	1999
Intrigue	54,177	95,255	98,492	—	—	—	54,177	95,255	98,492
Olds 88	74,834	68,140	—	—	—	—	74,834	68,140	—
Supreme	21,518	—	—	—	—	—	21,518	—	—
Total Oldsmobile	**276,360**	**292,143**	**277,865**	—	—	—	**276,360**	**292,143**	**277,865**
Bonneville	75,650	57,516	48,120	—	—	—	75,650	57,516	48,120
Firebird	—	—	—	32,387	33,124	36,581	32,387	33,124	36,581
Grand Am	236,519	184,335	259,471	—	—	—	236,519	184,335	259,471
Grand Prix	163,335	136,948	173,876	—	—	—	163,335	136,948	173,876
Sunfire	122,797	96,851	110,089	—	—	—	122,797	96,851	110,089
Total Pontiac	**598,301**	**475,650**	**591,556**	**32,387**	**33,124**	**36,581**	**630,688**	**508,774**	**628,137**
Saturn	271,471	243,976	238,140	—	—	—	271,471	243,976	238,140
Saturn EV1	404	125	318	—	—	—	404	125	318
Saturn LS	—	—	60,987	—	—	—	—	—	60,987
Total Saturn	**271,875**	**244,101**	**299,445**	—	—	—	**271,875**	**244,101**	**299,445**
Toyota Cavalier	11,940	4,788	6,111	—	—	—	11,940	4,788	6,111
Total General Motors	**2,206,183**	**1,924,866**	**2,093,345**	**590,813**	**540,160**	**596,775**	**2,796,996**	**2,465,026**	**2,690,120**
Ford Probe	9,564	—	—	—	—	—	9,564	—	—
Mazda 626	89,248	94,175	87,065	—	—	—	89,248	94,175	87,065
Mazda Mx6	1,582	—	—	—	—	—	1,582	—	—
Mercury Cougar	—	73,093	78,078	—	—	—	—	73,093	78,078
Total AutoAlliance	**100,394**	**167,268**	**165,143**	—	—	—	**100,394**	**167,268**	**165,143**
BMW Z3	62,943	54,802	48,394	—	—	—	62,943	54,802	48,394
Total BMW	**62,943**	**54,802**	**48,394**	—	—	—	**62,943**	**54,802**	**48,394**
Chevrolet Metro	—	—	—	—	—	—	—	—	—
Suzuki Swift	—	—	—	—	—	—	—	—	—
Total CAMI	—	—	—	—	—	—	—	—	—
Acura CL	31,241	30,480	15,804	—	—	—	31,241	30,480	15,804
Acura EL	—	—	—	10,987	7,925	7,680	10,987	7,925	7,680
Acura TL	—	31,324	78,950	—	—	—	—	31,324	78,950
Total Acura	**31,241**	**61,804**	**94,754**	**10,987**	**7,925**	**7,680**	**42,228**	**69,729**	**102,434**
Accord	415,588	424,660	369,190	—	—	—	415,588	424,660	369,190
Civic	201,439	208,239	221,956	154,194	159,412	168,377	355,633	367,651	390,333
Total Honda	**617,027**	**632,899**	**591,146**	**154,194**	**159,412**	**168,377**	**771,221**	**792,311**	**759,523**
Total Honda	**648,268**	**694,703**	**685,900**	**165,181**	**167,337**	**176,057**	**813,449**	**862,040**	**861,957**
Chrysler Sebring	36,519	36,753	24,853	—	—	—	36,519	36,753	24,853
Dodge Avenger	31,056	23,459	15,801	—	—	—	31,056	23,459	15,801
Eagle Talon	11,069	295	—	—	—	—	11,069	295	—
Mitsubishi Eclipse	67,622	50,715	54,019	—	—	—	67,622	50,715	54,019
Mitsubishi Galant	42,820	45,917	65,029	—	—	—	42,820	45,917	65,029
Total Mitsubishi	**189,086**	**157,139**	**159,702**	—	—	—	**189,086**	**157,139**	**159,702**
Altima	163,934	162,273	152,541	—	—	—	163,934	162,273	152,541
Nissan 200Sx	27,812	6,102	—	—	—	—	27,812	6,102	—
Sentra	87,764	54,358	15,201	—	—	—	87,764	54,358	15,201
Total Nissan	**279,510**	**222,733**	**167,742**	—	—	—	**279,510**	**222,733**	**167,742**
Chevrolet Prizm	60,838	45,284	49,967	—	—	—	60,838	45,284	49,967
Toyota Corolla	149,041	158,180	160,759	—	—	—	149,041	158,180	160,759
Total NUMMI	**209,879**	**203,464**	**210,726**	—	—	—	**209,879**	**203,464**	**210,726**
Legacy	102,180	104,229	93,070	—	—	—	102,180	104,229	93,070
Total Subaru Isuzu	**102,180**	**104,229**	**93,070**	—	—	—	**102,180**	**104,229**	**93,070**
Avalon	79,722	83,718	71,227	—	—	—	79,722	83,718	71,227
Camry	325,251	297,012	285,613	—	—	—	325,251	297,012	285,613
Corolla	—	—	—	108,952	150,413	147,718	108,952	150,413	147,718
Solara	—	—	—	—	21,326	63,364	—	21,326	63,364
Total Toyota	**404,973**	**380,730**	**356,840**	**108,952**	**171,739**	**211,082**	**513,925**	**552,469**	**567,922**
Volvo S70/V70	—	—	—	6,548	8,373	—	6,548	8,373	—
Total Volvo	—	—	—	**6,548**	**8,373**	—	**6,548**	**8,373**	—
Total Passenger Cars	**5,933,921**	**5,554,373**	**5,637,806**	**1,372,588**	**1,481,141**	**1,626,316**	**7,306,509**	**7,035,514**	**7,264,122**

SOURCE: Ward's AutoInfoBank

U.S. Factory Sales of Trucks and Buses by Gross Vehicle Weight Rating

U.S. FACTORY SALES OF TRUCKS AND BUSES BY GROSS VEHICLE WEIGHT RATING, 1980-1999

	Gross Vehicle Weight Rating (Pounds)								
	6,000 & Less	6,001- 10,000	10,001- 14,000	14,001- 16,000	16,001- 19,500	19,501- 26,000	26,001- 33,000	33,001 & Over	Total
U.S. TOTAL									
1999	4,876,534	1,891,397	116,868	44,250	19,699	25,528	122,411	248,332	7,345,059
1998	4,458,970	1,431,110	147,839	33,513	17,441	19,850	116,412	210,050	6,435,185
1997	4,377,340	1,366,899	47,022	32,286	4,056	16,687	128,245	180,282	6,152,817
1996	4,073,778	1,344,826	38,525	32,912	4,127	12,379	106,657	162,526	5,775,730
1995	3,742,739	1,583,878	901	37,073	1,549	16,369	125,703	205,257	5,713,469
1994	3,811,837	1,478,854	848	29,585	550	13,559	115,334	189,708	5,640,275
1993	3,488,278	1,124,106	—	8,149	—	21,943	93,939	158,809	4,895,224
1992	2,978,214	850,876	—	7,193	2	21,993	81,601	122,123	4,062,002
1991	2,533,904	658,425	—	3,820	56	19,498	77,850	93,950	3,387,503
1990	2,574,071	906,423	—	789	1,726	38,123	87,107	116,966	3,725,205
1989	2,657,084	1,130,606	11	146	4,593	37,788	90,440	141,282	4,061,950
1988	2,704,891	1,105,069	—	182	5,618	55,840	97,771	151,203	4,120,574
1987	2,475,402	1,052,958	—	366	6,085	46,473	103,188	136,938	3,821,410
1986	2,238,922	997,272	—	—	5,931	45,333	96,998	116,477	3,500,933
1985	2,095,856	1,057,556	19,463	—	5,345	53,471	98,406	134,230	3,464,327
1984	1,807,811	1,061,974	1,631	4	5,713	60,457	87,396	150,849	3,175,835
1982	917,908	803,639	280	58	1,556	47,330	58,498	77,186	1,906,455
1980	592,339	794,184	5,661	362	2,946	91,119	58,846	121,826	1,667,283
U.S DOMESTIC									
1999	4,453,332	1,723,012	112,349	37,328	17,542	24,362	113,147	218,041	6,699,113
1998	4,053,521	1,303,786	141,781	29,629	15,779	18,989	105,874	177,852	5,847,211
1997	3,894,222	1,236,119	44,893	28,428	3,931	15,609	116,922	149,183	5,489,307
1996	3,699,385	1,225,792	37,559	30,309	4,056	11,717	97,720	141,941	5,248,479
1995	3,405,062	1,458,713	780	35,427	1,471	15,046	114,194	180,652	5,211,345
1994	3,475,044	1,353,576	848	28,437	533	12,123	102,745	165,375	5,138,681
1993	3,187,731	1,031,829	—	7,630	—	19,277	84,779	140,247	4,471,493
1992	2,711,172	785,198	—	6,612	2	19,160	71,899	108,003	3,702,046
1991	2,281,761	594,435	—	3,547	28	16,536	69,703	83,875	3,049,885
1990	2,383,892	848,690	—	693	1,644	34,141	78,553	107,025	3,454,638
1989	2,447,962	1,057,077	11	54	4,234	32,721	81,971	127,880	3,751,910
1988	2,496,648	1,020,515	—	86	5,238	49,670	87,994	135,163	3,795,314
1987	2,270,950	976,573	—	322	5,841	40,502	93,044	121,859	3,509,091
1986	2,072,880	927,462	—	—	5,749	40,353	87,831	103,990	3,238,265
1985	1,962,323	989,633	19,397	—	5,123	46,340	88,784	121,996	3,233,596
1984	1,711,345	997,626	—	4	5,502	52,053	78,977	139,135	2,984,642
1982	870,054	745,208	—	10	1,333	40,165	53,244	69,182	1,779,196
1980	547,426	679,532	4,803	24	1,761	76,208	51,900	102,154	1,463,808

SOURCE: Ward's Communications.

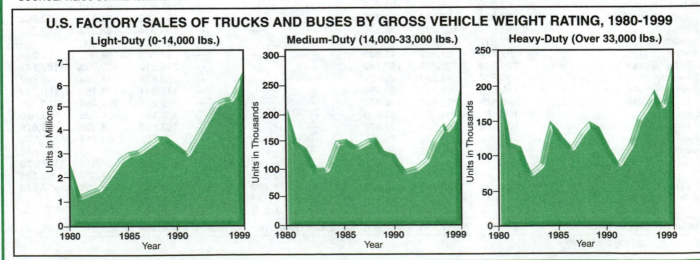

U.S. FACTORY SALES OF TRUCKS AND BUSES BY GROSS VEHICLE WEIGHT RATING, 1980-1999

Light-Duty (0-14,000 lbs.) Medium-Duty (14,000-33,000 lbs.) Heavy-Duty (Over 33,000 lbs.)

U.S. Factory Sales of Diesel Trucks and Motor Vehicle Factory Sales from U.S. and Canadian Plants

U.S. FACTORY SALES OF DIESEL TRUCKS BY GROSS VEHICLE WEIGHT RATING, 1965-1999

| | Gross Vehicle Weight Rating (Pounds) | | | | | | | | |
	6,000 & Less	6,001- 10,000	10,001- 14,000	14,001- 16,000	16,001- 19,500	19,501- 26,000	26,001- 33,000	33,001 & Over	Total
U.S. TOTAL									
1999	2,843	229,401	68,636	27,424	16,846	23,096	90,493	248,372	707,111
1998	2,486	188,027	104,428	24,020	15,792	17,564	84,083	210,050	646,450
1997	3,294	182,170	11,632	19,590	3,640	13,606	89,713	180,281	503,926
1996	3,139	199,079	9,900	21,770	3,811	8,593	72,753	162,526	481,571
1995	5,995	225,968	150	25,241	1,346	11,403	93,237	205,254	568,594
1994	9,468	140,330	—	8,259	550	8,114	83,317	189,692	439,730
1993	9,952	113,935	—	4,894	—	8,346	66,612	158,208	361,947
1992	7,145	106,595	—	1,264	—	7,984	57,025	122,106	302,119
1990	449	102,051	—	81	51	12,567	61,010	116,931	293,140
1985	15,447	132,871	5,870	—	—	16,537	57,238	132,429	360,392
1980	72,501	4,973	—	—	—	15,268	34,544	116,860	244,146
1975	—	1	—	-	159	5,651	11,819	84,878	102,508
1970	8	417	—	168	26	7,875	11,932	85,288	105,714
1965	323	566	146	207	3,739	9,864	16,208	51,098	82,151
U.S DOMESTIC									
1999	2,199	188,823	66,390	24,753	15,025	22,205	83,867	218,041	621,303
1998	261	155,001	99,898	21,597	14,200	16,791	76,200	177,852	561,800
1997	894	153,845	11,340	18,487	3,515	12,686	80,800	149,182	430,749
1996	1,539	167,634	9,516	20,916	3,740	8,125	66,072	141,941	419,483
1995	4,579	191,758	92	23,913	1,272	10,597	84,213	180,652	497,076
1994	7,366	113,358	—	7,689	533	7,107	73,371	165,371	374,795
1993	6,494	94,014	—	4,536	—	6,923	59,172	139,661	310,800
1992	996	94,937	—	1,071	—	6,873	50,273	108,000	262,150
1990	337	94,030	—	55	51	11,458	53,957	107,002	266,890
1985	9,663	123,882	5,870	—	—	14,253	50,492	120,311	324,471
1980	68,868	4,397	—	—	—	12,337	30,958	98,002	214,562
1975	—	1	—	—	159	3,517	8,992	59,936	72,605
1970	—	268	—	165	—	3,158	10,245	77,965	91,801
1965	59	509	123	160	2,715	6,206	14,749	47,836	72,357

MOTOR VEHICLE FACTORY SALES FROM U.S. AND CANADIAN PLANTS,1965-1999

| | U.S. Plants | | | | Canadian Plants* | | | |
	U.S Total	Exports to Canada	Other Exports	U.S. Domestic	Canada Total	Exports to U.S.	Other Exports	Canada Domestic
PASSENGER CARS								
1999	5,427,746	263,160	204,130	4,960,456	1,160,478	1,063,455	15,592	81,431
1998	5,676,964	305,064	176,910	5,194,990	1,109,265	1,017,833	16,216	75,216
1997	6,069,886	342,113	193,853	5,533,920	1,023,828	929,028	18,243	76,557
1996	6,140,454	285,745	238,163	5,616,546	965,849	848,666	23,771	93,412
1995	6,309,839	265,594	256,422	5,787,820	1,028,970	912,939	22,128	93,903
1990	6,049,749	416,459	131,419	5,501,871	901,903	795,621	3,725	102,557
1985	8,002,259	635,546	29,978	7,336,735	1,068,420	878,052	5,878	184,490
1980	6,400,026	488,857	70,864	5,840,305	827,124	539,239	86,297	201,588
1975	6,712,852	549,353	90,199	6,073,300	1,043,245	713,407	58,149	271,689
1970	6,546,817	245,746	113,753	6,187,318	919,232	681,872	30,427	206,933
1965	9,305,561	46,540	158,334	9,100,687	750,777	33,862	39,771	677,144
TRUCKS AND BUSES								
1999	7,345,059	416,010	229,936	6,699,113	1,241,442	1,017,982	11,814	211,646
1998	6,435,185	364,865	223,109	5,847,211	1,041,626	814,961	10,223	216,442
1997	6,152,817	402,138	261,372	5,489,307	1,153,540	924,837	11,329	217,374
1996	5,775,730	327,701	199,550	5,248,479	1,058,106	891,117	11,772	155,217
1995	5,713,469	318,470	183,654	5,211,345	1,004,717	871,134	5,180	128,403
1990	3,725,205	207,559	63,008	3,454,638	8,124,697	660,176	26,441	125,850
1985	3,464,327	197,903	32,828	3,233,596	853,974	677,998	7,706	168,270
1980	1,667,283	86,420	117,055	1,463,808	525,968	290,529	47,228	188,211
1975	2,272,160	133,701	135,701	2,002,758	390,065	181,165	47,742	161,158
1970	1,692,440	53,646	73,125	1,565,669	252,079	157,532	32,429	962,118
1965	1,751,805	9,550	126,311	1,615,944	151,214	7,001	15,525	128,688

* Reporting firms do not represent the entire industry.
SOURCE: Ward's Communications.

Passenger Car Production by City and State

PASSENGER CAR PRODUCTION BY CITY AND STATE, 1999

State/City	Model	Units	Percent
CALIFORNIA		**210,726**	**3.7**
Fremont	Corolla	160,759	2.9
	Prizm	49,967	0.9
	Total NUMMI	**210,726**	**3.7**
DELAWARE		**83,942**	**1.5**
Wilmington	Malibu	22,955	0.4
	Saturn LS	60,987	1.1
	Total General Motors	**83,942**	**1.5**
GEORGIA		**243,842**	**4.3**
Atlanta	Sable	52,629	0.9
	Taurus	191,213	3.4
	Total Ford	**243,842**	**4.3**
ILLINOIS		**637,279**	**11.3**
Belvidere	Dodge Neon	165,229	2.9
	Plymouth Neon	66,905	1.2
	Total Chrysler	**232,134**	**4.1**
Chicago	Sable	53,798	1.0
	Taurus	191,645	3.4
	Total Ford	**245,443**	**4.4**
Normal	Chrysler Sebring	24,853	0.4
	Dodge Avenger	15,801	0.3
	Mitsubishi Eclipse	54,019	1.0
	Mitsubishi Galant	65,029	1.2
	Total Mitsubishi	**159,702**	**2.8**
INDIANA		**93,070**	**1.7**
Lafayette	Legacy	93,070	1.7
	Total Subaru	**93,070**	**1.7**
KANSAS		**272,368**	**4.8**
Fairfax	Grand Prix	173,876	3.1
	Intrigue	98,492	1.7
	Total General Motors	**272,368**	**4.8**
KENTUCKY		**390,083**	**6.9**
Bowling Green	Corvette	33,243	0.6
	Total General Motors	**33,243**	**0.6**
Georgetown	Avalon	71,227	1.3
	Camry	285,613	5.1
	Total Toyota	**356,840**	**6.3**
MICHIGAN		**1,794,270**	**31.8**
Flat Rock	Cougar	78,078	1.4
	Mazda 626	87,065	1.5
	Total AutoAlliance	**165,143**	**2.9**
Detroit	Prowler	2,862	0.1
	Viper	1,600	0.0
Sterling Heights	Breeze	47,911	0.8
	Cirrus	47,124	0.8
	Stratus	100,196	1.8
	Total Chrysler	**199,693**	**3.5**
Dearborn	Mustang	191,432	3.4
Wayne	Escort	114,171	2.0
	Focus	114,682	2.0
	Tracer	14,691	0.3
Wixom	Continental	27,121	0.5
	Lincoln LS	39,266	0.7

State/City	Model	Units	Percent
	Town Car	81,551	1.4
	Total Ford	**582,914**	**10.3**
Craft Center	Saturn EV1	318	0.0
Flint	Bonneville	28,040	0.5
	LeSabre	38,738	0.7
Hamtramck	Eldorado	17,638	0.3
	Fleetwood Deville	88,922	1.6
	LeSabre	68,906	1.2
	Seville	38,907	0.7
Lansing	Alero	146,329	2.6
	Cavalier	9,274	0.2
	Grand Am	259,471	4.6
	Sunfire	6,771	0.1
Orion	Aurora	12,260	0.2
	Bonneville	20,080	0.4
	LeSabre	49,857	0.9
	Park Ave	61,009	1.1
	Total General Motors	**846,520**	**15.0**
MISSOURI		**152,918**	**2.7**
Kansas City	Contour	114,897	2.0
	Mystique	38,021	0.7
	Total Ford	**152,918**	**2.7**
OHIO		**1,055,619**	**18.7**
East Liberty	Acura CL	15,661	0.3
	Civic	221,956	3.9
Marysville	Accord	369,333	6.6
	Acura TL	78,950	1.4
	Total Honda	**685,900**	**12.2**
Lordstown	Cavalier	260,290	4.6
	Sunfire	103,318	1.8
	Toyota Cavalier	6,111	0.1
	Total General Motors	**369,719**	**6.6**
OKLAHOMA		**249,413**	**4.4**
Oklahoma City	Cutlass	20,784	0.4
	Malibu	228,629	4.1
	Total General Motors	**249,413**	**4.4**
SOUTH CAROLINA		**48,394**	**0.9**
Spartanburg	BMW Z3	48,394	0.9
	Total BMW	**48,394**	**0.9**
TENNESSEE		**405,882**	**7.2**
Smyrna	Altima	152,541	2.7
	Sentra	15,201	0.3
	Total Nissan	**167,742**	**3.0**
Spring Hill	Saturn	238,140	4.2
	Total General Motors	**238,140**	**4.2**
TOTAL		**5,637,806**	**100.0**

Top States in Calendar 1999 U.S. Production

Cars		Trucks	
1. Michigan	1,794,270	1. Michigan	1,329,974
2. Ohio	1,055,619	2. Missouri	1,068,191
3. Illinois	637,279	3. Ohio	918,210
4. Tennessee	405,882	4. Kentucky	844,548
5. Kentucky	390,083	5. New Jersey	427,719

SOURCE: *Ward's AutoInfoBank.*

Truck Production by City and State

TRUCK PRODUCTION BY CITY AND STATE, 1999

State/City	Model	Units	Percent
ALABAMA		**77,696**	**1.1**
Vance	Mercedes M Class ...	77,696	1.1
	Total Mercedes	**77,696**	**1.1**
CALIFORNIA		**156,395**	**2.1**
Fremont	Tacoma	156,395	2.1
	Total NUMMI	**156,395**	**2.1**
DELAWARE		**220,097**	**3.0**
Newark	Durango	220,097	3.0
	Total Chrysler	**220,097**	**3.0**
GEORGIA		**285,871**	**3.9**
Doraville	Montana	95,693	1.3
	Opel Sintra	7,932	0.1
	Silhouette	51,239	0.7
	Venture	131,007	1.8
	Total General Motors	**285,871**	**3.9**
INDIANA		**356,790**	**4.8**
Fort Wayne	Chevy Silverado	190,168	2.6
	GMC Sierra	67,492	0.9
	Total General Motors	**257,660**	**3.5**
Lafayette	Honda Passport	23,112	0.3
	Isuzu Amigo	9,890	0.1
	Isuzu Rodeo	66,128	0.9
	Total Subaru-Isuzu ..	**99,130**	**1.3**
KENTUCKY		**844,548**	**11.4**
Kentucky Truck	Excursion	29,685	0.4
	Ford F Series	363,016	4.9
Louisville	Explorer	257,391	3.5
	Mountaineer	51,628	0.7
	Ranger	22,142	0.3
	Total Ford	**723,862**	**9.8**
Georgetown	Sienna	120,686	1.6
	Total Toyota	**120,686**	**1.6**
LOUISIANA		**210,863**	**2.9**
Shreveport	Chevy S-10	152,844	2.1
	GMC Sonoma	51,395	0.7
	Isuzu Hombre	6,624	0.1
	Total General Motors	**210,863**	**2.9**
MARYLAND		**168,057**	**2.3**
Baltimore	Astro	123,510	1.7
	Safari	44,547	0.6
	Total General Motors	**168,057**	**2.3**
MICHIGAN		**1,329,974**	**18.0**
Detroit	Grand Cherokee	343,536	4.7
Warren	Dakota	170,949	2.3
	Dodge Ram	86,006	1.2
	Total Chrysler	**600,491**	**8.1**
Wayne	Expedition	256,562	3.5
	Navigator	42,689	0.6
	Total Ford	**299,251**	**4.1**
Flint	Chevy C/K	87,696	1.2
	GMC Sierra	32,626	0.4
Pontiac East	Chevy Silverado	221,966	3.0
	GMC Sierra	87,944	1.2
	Total General Motors	**430,232**	**5.8**
MINNESOTA		**213,836**	**2.9**
Twin Cities	Ford Ranger	213,836	2.9
	Total Ford	**213,836**	**2.9**
MISSOURI		**1,068,191**	**14.5**
St. Louis North	Dodge Ram	160,162	2.2
St. Louis South	Caravan	136,704	1.9
	Town & Country	83,664	1.1
	Voyager	40,103	0.5

State/City	Model	Units	Percent
	Total Chrysler	**420,633**	**5.7**
Kansas City	Ford F Series	224,637	3.0
St. Louis	Explorer	249,700	3.4
	Total Ford	**474,337**	**6.4**
Wentzville	Express	121,818	1.6
	Savana	51,403	0.7
	Total General Motors	**173,221**	**2.3**
NORTH CAROLINA		**2,412**	**0.0**
Spartanburg	BMW X5	2,412	0.0
	Total BMW	**2,412**	**0.0**
NEW JERSEY		**427,719**	**5.8**
Edison	Ford Ranger	119,443	1.6
	Mazda Pickup	49,587	0.7
	Total Ford	**169,030**	**2.3**
Linden	Chevy Blazer	80,204	1.1
	Chevy S-10	98,625	1.3
	GMC Jimmy	11,121	0.2
	GMC Sonoma	12,563	0.2
	Total General Motors	**202,513**	**2.7**
Princeton	Toyota Tundra	56,176	0.8
	Total Toyota	**56,176**	**0.8**
OHIO		**918,210**	**12.4**
Toledo	Cherokee	186,116	2.5
	Wrangler	100,946	1.4
	Total Chrysler	**287,062**	**3.9**
Avon Lake	Mercury Villager	45,597	0.6
	Nissan Quest	49,061	0.7
Lorain Truck	Econoline	233,178	3.2
	Total Ford	**327,836**	**4.4**
Moraine	Bravada	28,547	0.4
	Chevy Blazer	192,653	2.6
	GMC Jimmy	82,112	1.1
	Total General Motors	**303,312**	**4.1**
TENNESSEE		**156,903**	**2.1**
Smyrna	Nissan Frontier	99,117	1.3
	Nissan Xterra	57,786	0.8
	Total Nissan	**156,903**	**2.1**
TEXAS		**123,608**	**1.7**
Arlington	Chevy C/K	39,039	0.5
	Escalade	28,846	0.4
	GMC Sierra	12,486	0.2
	Tahoe	22,523	0.3
	Yukon	20,714	0.3
	Total General Motors	**123,608**	**1.7**
VIRGINIA		**237,142**	**3.2**
Norfolk	Ford F Series	237,142	3.2
	Total Ford	**237,142**	**3.2**
WISCONSIN		**244,203**	**3.3**
Janesville	Chevy CT Series	9,548	0.1
	Chevy Suburban	45,269	0.6
	Chevy Tahoe	97,133	1.3
	Chevy W4 Tiltmaster .	563	0.0
	GMC CT Series	26,298	0.4
	GMC Suburban	20,023	0.3
	GMC W4 Forward	1,086	0.0
	GMC Yukon	37,856	0.5
	GMC Yukon XL	106	0.0
	Isuzu Medium Duty ...	1,622	0.0
	Isuzu NPR	4,699	0.1
	Total General Motors	**244,203**	**3.3**
Other		**344,514**	**4.7**
TOTAL		**7,387,029**	**100.0**

SOURCE: *Ward's AutoInfoBank.*

Factory Installations of Selected Passenger Car and Light Truck Equipment

FACTORY INSTALLATIONS OF SELECTED EQUIPMENT, 1996-1999 MODEL YEARS*

	1996		1997		1998		1999	
	Units (000)	% of Total	Units (000)	% of Total	Units (000)	% of Total	Units (000)	% of Total
PASSENGER CARS								
AutomaticTransmission	5,958	87.5	6,238	88.7	5,933	89.4	6,392	90.2
5-Speed Transmission	826	12.1	777	11.0	689	10.3	665	9.4
6-Speed Transmission	19	0.3	15	0.2	18	0.3	31	0.4
Four-Wheel Drive	86	1.3	96	1.4	93	1.4	89	1.3
3-Cylinder Engine	25	0.4	18	0.3	12	0.2	8	0.1
4-Cylinder Engine	3,341	49.2	3,699	52.6	3,451	52.0	3,335	47.7
6-Cylinder Engine	2,629	38.7	2,573	36.6	2,571	38.7	2,976	42.6
8-Cylinder Engine	796	11.7	739	10.5	605	9.1	667	9.6
Traction Control	1,014	14.9	1,271	18.1	1,342	20.2	1,848	26.1
Anti-Lock Brakes	3,939	57.8	3,970	56.5	3,930	59.2	4,612	65.1
Power Door Locks	5,447	80.0	5,573	79.3	5,466	82.3	6,072	85.7
Power Seats, 4 or 6 way	2,380	34.9	2,683	38.2	2,472	37.2	3,047	42.0
Power Windows	4,969	73.0	5,296	75.3	5,195	78.2	5,857	82.6
Sun Roof	792	11.6	891	12.7	1,194	18.0	1,437	20.3
Side Air Bags	NA.	NA.	100	1.4	428	6.4	639	9.0
Windshield Wiper Delay	6,594	96.8	6,849	97.4	6,523	98.2	7,029	99.2
Trip Computer	301	4.4	433	6.2	346	5.2	625	8.8
Keyless Remote	1,967	28.9	2,875	40.9	3,280	49.4	4,080	57.6
Air Conditioning,Automatic Temp. Cont	722	10.6	852	12.1	1,069	16.1	1,243	17.5
Air Conditioning, Manual Temp. Contro	5,841	85.8	5,877	83.6	5,400	81.3	5,692	80.3
Limited Slip Differential	171	2.5	120	1.7	114	1.7	165	2.3
Styled Wheels	2,714	39.8	3,113	44.3	3,078	46.4	3,528	49.8
Adjustable Steering Column	5,822	85.5	6,027	85.7	5,928	89.3	6,537	92.2
Rear Window Defogger	6,419	94.3	6,655	94.7	8,332	95.4	6,749	95.2
Cruise Control	5,250	77.1	5,519	78.5	5,228	78.7	5,611	79.2
Anti-Theft Device	614	9.0	1,655	23.5	2,012	30.3	2,019	28.5
Mobile Phone	29	0.4	41	0.6	28	0.4	24	0.3
LIGHT TRUCKS (0-10,000 lbs. G.V.W.R.)								
AutomaticTransmission	4,627	82.5	5,340	83.8	5,694	87.2	6,587	89.2
Four Wheel Anti-Lock Brakes	3,559	63.4	3,863	60.6	4,393	67.2	5,270	71.4
Rear Anti-Lock Brakes	1,569	28.0	2,044	32.1	1,610	24.6	1,491	20.6
Keyless Entry	1,942	34.6	2,757	43.3	3,335	51.0	4,458	60.4
Anti-Theft Device	900	13.2	832	13.1	1,484	22.7	1,949	26.4
Side Air Bag	NA.	NA.	NA.	NA.	232	3.6	304	4.1
Four-Wheel Drive	2,075	37.0	2,526	39.6	2,705	41.4	3,195	43.3
Diesel Engine	208	3.7	304	4.8	112	1.7	435	5.9
4-Cylinder Gasoline Engine	722	12.9	703	11.0	203	10.8	557	7.5
6-Cylinder Gasoline Engine	2,974	53.0	2,761	43.3	3,345	51.2	3,478	47.1
8-Cylinder Gasoline Engine	1,690	30.1	2,562	40.2	2,462	37.7	3,220	43.6
Air Conditioning	5,162	92.0	6,007	94.3	6,320	96.7	7,219	96.8
Cruise Control	4,211	75.0	4,870	76.4	5,168	79.1	6,003	81.3
Limited Slip Differential	1,218	21.7	1,817	28.5	1,762	27.0	2,234	30.2

*Based on production in the United States, Canada and Mexico for the United States market.
N.A.-Not available.
SOURCE: Ward's Communications.

Recreational Vehicle Shipments

U.S. RECREATIONAL VEHICLE SHIPMENTS BY TYPE, 1976-1999

Year	Total All Types	Travel Trailers Conven- tional	Travel Trailers Fifth Wheel[1]	Folding Camping Trailers	Truck Campers	Motor Homes Type A Conven- tional	Motor Homes Type B Van Campers[2]	Motor Homes Type C Chopped Vans[3]	Multi-use Van Con- versions
1999	481,200	117,500	60,500	60,100	11,500	49,400	3,600	18,600	104,100
1998	441,300	98,600	56,500	63,300	10,800	42,900	3,600	17,000	104,600
1997	438,800	78,800	52,800	57,600	10,300	37,600	3,800	13,600	122,300
1996	466,800	75,400	48,500	57,300	11,000	36,500	4,100	14,700	144,000
1995	475,200	75,300	45,900	61,100	11,900	33,000	4,100	15,700	151,100
1994	518,800	79,100	48,900	61,700	11,400	37,300	3,500	17,300	181,800
1993	420,200	69,700	43,900	51,900	10,900	31,900	3,000	16,500	192,400
1992	382,700	63,600	38,900	43,300	10,600	27,300	2,900	16,800	179,300
1991	293,700	49,300	28,300	33,900	9,600	23,500	3,500	15,200	130,400
1990	347,300	52,500	27,900	30,700	9,700	29,000	5,900	17,400	174,200
1989	388,300	53,500	29,400	33,900	9,900	35,400	5,000	20,800	200,400
1988	420,000	58,300	31,300	42,300	11,000	41,500	5,200	26,200	204,200
1987	393,600	59,100	27,100	41,600	10,100	40,800	6,600	26,400	181,900
1986	371,700	55,100	23,100	36,500	7,400	33,300	6,200	28,200	181,900
1985	351,700	54,700	20,700	35,900	6,900	33,600	6,700	28,400	104,800
1984	391,000	65,600	19,600	40,900	7,600	42,100	7,100	32,800	175,300
1983	350,800	64,700	18,100	37,500	6,800	34,400	5,600	30,500	154,200
1982	251,900	47,700	11,700	34,300	5,700	19,300	3,900	18,000	111,300
1981	233,400	48,500	9,600	35,000	5,100	14,300	3,800	17,300	99,800
1980	178,500	42,700	6,300	24,500	5,000	9,800	2,400	16,400	71,400
1979	307,700	74,700	15,500	31,300	13,800	21,500	3,400	39,200	108,500
1978	526,300	132,700	27,100	48,200	24,700	46,600	19,500	91,100	136,400
1977	533,900	145,900	22,000	53,900	31,900	43,000	40,800	76,400	120,000
1976	541,100	168,300	21,400	53,300	42,000	45,200	36,100	74,800	100,000

(1) To be towed by pickup truck with fifth-wheel hitch mounted on the truck bed.
(2) Panel-type trucks with interior converted to living area.
(3) Chopped Vans: (Mini)-unit over 8' high attaches to van chassis of 6,500 lbs. GVWR or more; (Low Profile)-unit less than 8' high attaches to van chassis of 6,500 lbs. GVWR or more: (Compact)-unit attaches to van chassis less than 6,500 lbs. GVWR.

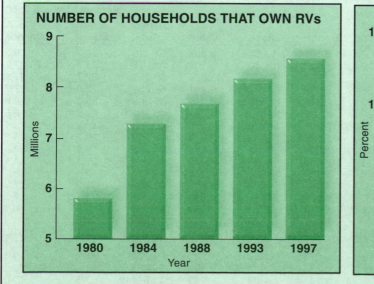

NUMBER OF HOUSEHOLDS THAT OWN RVs

RV OWNERSHIP RATES BY AGE

SOURCE: Recreation Vehicle Industry Association. Permission for further use must be obtained from the Recreation Vehicle Industry Association.

World Motor Vehicle Production by Country

WORLD MOTOR VEHICLE PRODUCTION BY COUNTRY, 1999

Region/Country	Passenger Cars	Commercial Vehicles	Total
North America	8,258,226	9,357,385	17,615,611
Canada	1,626,316	1,430,300	3,056,616
Mexico	994,104	540,056	1,534,160
U.S.A.	5,637,806	7,387,029	13,024,835
Western Europe	14,416,852	2,144,232	16,561,084
Austria	123,586	15,674	139,260
Belgium	217,919	73,563	291,482
Finland	30,000	472	30,472
France	2,675,892	357,073	3,032,965
Germany	5,309,524	378,066	5,687,590
Italy	1,410,317	290,797	1,701,114
Netherlands	262,242	25,073	287,315
Portugal	186,996	65,294	252,290
Spain	2,028,708	643,681	2,672,389
Sweden	385,044	108,632	493,676
United Kingdom	1,786,624	185,907	1,972,531
Eastern and Central Europe .	2,277,799	319,610	2,597,409
Czech Republic	348,479	27,115	375,594
Hungary	121,475	2,500	123,975
Poland	650,700	44,000	694,700
Romania	88,313	18,584	106,897
Russia	946,084	226,018	1,172,102
Serbia	4,616	1,393	6,009
Slovenia	118,132	0	118,132
South America	1,327,258	322,143	1,649,401
Argentina	224,825	80,088	304,913
Brazil	1,102,433	242,055	1,344,488
Asia-Oceania	12,299,081	3,888,973	16,188,054
Australia	293,587	17,444	311,031
China	570,000	1,234,500	1,804,500
India	518,590	260,915	779,505
Japan	8,100,169	1,805,307	9,905,476
Malaysia	200,000	5,000	205,000
South Korea	2,361,735	470,516	2,832,251
Taiwan	255,000	95,291	350,291
Africa	236,992	99,162	336,154
South Africa	236,992	99,162	336,154
Total	**38,816,208**	**16,131,505**	**54,947,713**

WORLD MOTOR VEHICLE PRODUCTION BY REGION 1999

Africa 0.6%
Eastern & Central Europe 4.7%
South America 3.1%
Asia-Oceania 29.4%
Western Europe 30.1%
North America 32.1%

WORLD MOTOR VEHICLE PRODUCTION, 1950-1999 (In Thousands)

Year	United States	Canada	U.S. & Canada Total	Europe	Japan	Other	World Total	Percent of World Total United States	U.S. & Canada
1999	13,025	3,057	16,082	19,158	9,905	9,803	54,948	23.7	29.3
1998	12,006	2,173	14,179	18,137	10,050	9,732	52,098	23.1	27.2
1997	12,119	2,571	14,690	17,773	10,975	10,024	53,463	22.7	27.5
1996	11,799	2,397	14,196	17,550	10,346	9,241	51,332	22.0	27.7
1995	11,985	2,408	14,393	17,045	10,196	8,349	49,983	23.0	28.8
1994	12,263	2,321	14,583	16,195	10,554	8,167	49,500	24.8	29.5
1993	10,898	2,246	13,144	15,208	11,228	7,205	46,785	23.3	28.1
1992	9,729	1,961	11,692	17,628	12,499	6,269	48,088	20.2	24.3
1991	8,811	1,888	10,699	17,804	13,245	5,180	46,928	18.8	22.8
1990	9,783	1,928	11,711	18,866	13,487	4,496	48,554	20.1	24.1
1989	10,874	2,002	12,876	19,126	13,026	4,220	49,248	22.1	26.1
1988	11,214	1,949	13,163	18,383	12,700	4,113	48,359	23.2	27.2
1987	10,925	1,635	12,560	17,686	12,249	3,546	46,041	23.7	27.3
1985	11,653	1,933	13,586	16,113	12,271	2,939	44,909	25.9	30.3
1980	8,010	1,324	9,334	15,496	11,043	2,692	38,565	20.8	24.2
1975	8,987	1,385	10,372	13,581	6,942	2,211	33,106	27.1	31.3
1970	8,284	1,160	9,444	13,049	5,289	1,637	29,419	28.2	32.1
1965	11,138	847	11,985	9,576	1,876	834	24,271	45.9	49.4
1960	7,905	398	8,303	6,837	482	866	16,488	47.9	50.4
1955	9,204	452	9,656	3,741	68	163	13,628	67.5	70.9
1950	8,006	388	8,394	1,991	32	160	10,577	75.7	79.4

SOURCE: Compiled by Ward's Communications from various sources.

World Motor Vehicle Production by Manufacturer

WORLD MOTOR VEHICLE PRODUCTION BY MANUFACTURER, 1999 (In Thousands)

Manufacturer	Passenger Cars	Light Trucks	Heavy Trucks	Buses	Total
General Motors	5,281	2,951	4	0	8,235
Ford	3,499	3,108	58	0	6,664
Toyota-Daihatsu	4,341	1,118	34	3	5,496
DaimlerChrysler	2,081	2,416	287	38	4,823
Volkswagen	4,548	225	11	2	4,786
Fiat	2,227	283	107	7	2,624
PSA Peugeot Citroen	2,182	333	0	0	2,515
Nissan	1,911	524	21	1	2,457
Honda	2,249	176	0	0	2,425
Renault	1,982	276	87	0	2,345
Hyundai	1,552	414	4	0	1,970
Mitsubishi	1,108	401	44	2	1,555
Suzuki-Maruti	1,214	307	0	0	1,521
BMW Rover	1,123	24	0	0	1,147
Mazda	816	148	3	0	967
Daewoo	913	44	8	2	967
Avtovaz	680	0	0	0	680
Fuji-Subaru	491	87	0	0	577
Isuzu	38	421	59	2	520
Volvo	409	0	85	10	**504**
Proton	275	0	0	0	275
GAZ	103	108	0	0	211
Tata	71	111	0	0	182
Navistar	0.0	0	118	20	138
PACCAR	0.0	0	108	0	108
Dacia	70	16	0	0	86
MAN	0.0	0	56	4	60
Scania	0.0	0	46	5	51
Porsche	46	0	0	0	46

SOURCE: OICA.

Motor Vehicle Production in Mexico

MOTOR VEHICLE PRODUCTION IN MEXICO, 1998-1999

	For Domestic Market		For Export		Total	
	1998	1999	1998	1999	1998	1999
BMW 3 Series	1,601	1,401	0	0	1,601	1,401
BMW 5 Series	331	194	0	0	331	194
BMW 7 Series	0	1	0	0	0	1
Porsche 911	13	9	0	0	13	9
Total BMW	**1,945**	**1,605**	**0**	**0**	**1,945**	**1,605**
Chrysler RT	72	0	0	0	72	0
Cirrus	2,944	2,416	0	0	2,944	2,416
Neon (Chrysler)	21,824	0	0	0	21,824	0
Neon (Dodge)	0	0	16,719	10,356	16,719	10,356
Neon (Plym)	0	0	17,087	5,824	17,087	5,824
Sebring	0	0	55,494	56,123	55,494	56,123
Stratus	18,584	17,905	0	0	18,584	17,905
Total Chrysler	**43,424**	**20,321**	**89,300**	**72,303**	**132,724**	**92,624**
Contour	7,703	7,105	10,908	7,644	18,611	14,749
Escort	6,759	4,495	129,985	108,546	136,744	113,041
Focus	0	0	0	12,924	0	12,924
Mystique	2,305	3,475	4,235	1,847	6,540	5,322
Tracer	0	0	1,872	975	1,872	975
Total Ford Motor Co. ..	**16,767**	**15,075**	**147,000**	**131,936**	**163,767**	**147,011**
Cavalier	11,414	12,513	66,962	53,815	78,376	66,328
Joy/Swing	55,240	55,868	1,208	1,540	56,448	57,408
Monza	22,015	27,655	3,163	2,407	25,178	30,062
Sunfire	6,193	7,440	1,019	23,444	7,212	30,884
Total General Motors ..	**94,862**	**103,476**	**72,352**	**81,206**	**167,214**	**184,682**
Accord	7,194	8,446	0	1,795	7,194	10,241
Total Honda	**7,194**	**8,446**	**0**	**1,795**	**7,194**	**10,241**
Mercedes C Class	457	107	0	0	457	107
Mercedes E Class	265	83	0	0	265	83
Total Mercedes Benz ..	**722**	**190**	**0**	**0**	**722**	**190**
Lucino	1,477	1,208	0	0	1,477	1,208
Sentra	28,171	28,568	34,068	46,369	62,239	74,937
Tsubame	2,683	2,069	443	274	3,126	2,343
Tsuru	67,053	66,396	9,934	2,559	76,987	68,955
Total Nissan	**99,384**	**98,241**	**44,445**	**49,202**	**143,829**	**147,443**
Beetle	3,563	1,483	103,064	158,664	106,627	160,147
Golf	21,146	209	38,920	3	60,066	212
Jetta	31,371	31,317	91,666	165,670	123,037	196,987
Sedan	35,280	35,993	1,212	453	36,492	36,446
VW Cabrio	0	0	12,737	16,516	12,737	16,516
Total Volkswagen	**91,360**	**69,002**	**247,599**	**341,306**	**338,959**	**410,308**
Total Passenger Cars ...	**355,658**	**316,356**	**600,696**	**677,748**	**956,354**	**994,104**
Chrysler Corp.	16,897	16,714	212,393	223,448	229,290	240,162
Dina Camiones	3,596	1,973	0	0	3,596	1,973
Ford Motor Co..	22,912	30,339	30,401	46,852	53,313	77,191
General Motors	21,061	21,489	128,241	124,850	149,302	146,339
Kenworth	6,153	7,233	830	0	6,983	7,233
Mercedes Benz	9,783	21,751	0	0	9,783	21,751
Navistar	3,322	6,418	0	0	3,322	6,418
Nissan	34,444	32,297	11,514	5,834	45,958	38,131
Oshmex	753	542	0	0	753	542
Scania Heavy Truck	233	316	0	0	233	316
Trailers De Monterrey	1,004	0	0	0	1,004	0
Total Trucks	**120,158**	**139,072**	**383,379**	**400,984**	**503,537**	**540,056**
Total Cars and Trucks ..	**475,816**	**455,428**	**984,075**	**1,078,732**	**1,459,891**	**1,534,160**

SOURCE: AMIA, ANPACT.

U.S. Retail Sales of Cars and Trucks

ANNUAL U.S. MOTOR VEHICLE RETAIL SALES (In Thousands)

Year	Passenger Cars			Trucks			Motor Vehicles		
	Domestic	Import	Total	Domestic	Import	Total	Domestic	Import	Total
1999	6,979	1,719	8,698	7,922	795	8,716	14,901	2,513	17,415
1998	6,762	1,380	8,142	7,151	674	7,826	13,913	2,054	15,967
1997	6,917	1,355	8,272	6,632	593	7,226	13,549	1,949	15,498
1996	7,255	1,271	8,526	6,478	452	6,929	13,732	1,723	15,455
1995	7,129	1,506	8,635	6,064	417	6,481	13,193	1,923	15,116
1994	7,255	1,735	8,990	5,995	426	6,421	13,250	2,161	15,411
1993	6,742	1,776	8,518	5,287	394	5,681	12,029	2,170	14,199
1992	6,277	1,937	8,214	4,481	422	4,903	10,758	2,359	13,117
1991	6,137	2,038	8,175	3,813	551	4,364	9,950	2,589	12,539
1990	6,897	2,403	9,300	4,215	631	4,846	11,112	3,034	14,146
1989	7,073	2,699	9,772	4,403	538	4,941	11,476	3,237	14,713
1988	7,526	3,004	10,530	4,508	641	5,149	12,034	3,645	15,679
1987	7,081	3,196	10,277	4,055	858	4,913	11,136	4,054	15,190
1986	8,215	3,245	11,460	3,921	941	4,862	12,136	4,186	16,322
1985	8,205	2,838	11,043	3,902	779	4,681	12,107	3,617	15,724
1984	7,952	2,439	10,391	3,475	618	4,093	11,427	3,057	14,484
1983	6,795	2,387	9,182	2,658	471	3,129	9,453	2,858	12,311
1982	5,759	2,224	7,983	2,146	414	2,560	7,905	2,638	10,543
1981	6,209	2,327	8,536	1,809	451	2,260	8,018	2,778	10,796
1980	6,581	2,398	8,979	2,001	487	2,488	8,582	2,885	11,467
1979	8,341	2,332	10,673	3,010	470	3,480	11,351	2,802	14,153
1978	9,312	2,002	11,314	3,773	336	4,109	13,085	2,338	15,423
1977	9,109	2,074	11,183	3,352	323	3,675	12,461	2,397	14,858
1976	8,611	1,499	10,110	2,944	237	3,181	11,555	1,736	13,291
1975	7,053	1,571	8,624	2,249	229	2,478	9,302	1,800	11,102
1974	7,454	1,399	8,853	2,512	176	2,688	9,966	1,575	11,541
1973	9,676	1,748	11,424	2,916	233	3,149	12,592	1,981	14,573
1972	9,327	1,614	10,941	2,486	143	2,629	11,813	1,757	13,570
1971	8,681	1,561	10,242	2,011	85	2,096	10,692	1,646	12,338
1970	7,119	1,280	8,399	1,746	65	1,811	8,865	1,345	10,210
1969	8,464	1,118	9,582	1,936	34	1,970	10,400	1,152	11,552
1958	8,625	1,031	9,656	1,807	24	1,831	10,432	1,055	11,487
1967	7,568	769	8,337	1,524	21	1,545	9,092	790	9,882
1966	8,377	651	9,028	1,619	17	1,636	9,996	668	10,664
1965	8,763	569	9,332	1,539	14	1,553	10,302	583	10,885
1964	7,617	484	8,101	1,351	42	1,393	8,968	526	9,494
1963	7,334	386	7,720	1,230	40	1,270	8,564	426	8,990
1962	6,753	339	7,092	1,068	32	1,100	7,821	371	8,192
1961	5,556	379	5,935	908	29	937	6,464	408	6,872
1959	5,486	614	6,100	928	37	965	6,414	651	7,065
1957	5,826	207	6,033	878	16	894	6,704	223	6,927
1955	7,408	58	7,466	1,012	3	1,015	8,420	61	8,481
1953	5,775	33	5,808	965	N.A.	965	6,740	33	6,773
1951	5,143	21	5,164	1,111	N.A.	1,111	6,254	21	6,275
1942-1950	N.A.	N.A.	N.A.	N.A.	N.A.	N.A.	N.A.	N.A.	N.A.
1941	3,763	N.A.	3,763	902	N.A.	902	4,665	N.A.	4,665
1939	2,724	N.A.	2,724	521	N.A.	521	3,245	N.A.	3,245
1937	3,508	N.A.	3,508	645	N.A.	645	4,153	N.A.	4,153
1935	2,867	N.A.	2,867	552	N.A.	552	3,419	N.A.	3,419
1933	1,526	N.A.	1,526	261	N.A.	261	1,787	N.A.	1,787
1931	1,903	N.A.	1,903	328	N.A.	328	2,231	N.A.	2,231

N.A.-Not available.
SOURCE: Ward's Communications.

U.S. Retail Sales of Passenger Cars

U.S. RETAIL SALES OF PASSENGER CARS, 1995-1999

Model	1995	1996	1997	1998	1999
BMW 3 Series	6,194	5,468	824	0	0
BMW 3 Series*	48,526	44,779	51,648	57,520	77,138
BMW 5 Series*	22,636	22,775	31,347	35,100	38,218
BMW 7 Series*	15,005	17,174	18,273	18,309	18,233
BMW 8 Series*	948	525	648	17	7
BMW Z3	0	15,040	19,760	20,613	20,062
Total BMW	**93,309**	**105,761**	**122,500**	**131,559**	**153,658**
Chrysler 300M	0	0	0	30,765	55,966
Chrysler LHS	29,677	34,659	30,189	16,753	24,307
Cirrus	60,554	36,007	31,549	38,504	31,859
Concorde	49,521	52,106	38,772	64,912	59,855
Lebaron	30,189	1,062	0	0	0
New Yorker	16,785	2,554	0	0	0
Sebring Coupe	24,562	31,781	35,365	33,584	25,581
Sebring Convertible	3,876	53,852	53,054	51,342	51,750
Total Chrysler	**215,164**	**212,021**	**188,929**	**235,860**	**249,318**
Avenger	34,757	35,774	31,943	24,084	17,658
Colt*	611	0	0	0	0
Intrepid	147,576	145,402	118,537	110,499	144,355
Neon	133,984	139,831	121,854	117,964	112,236
Spirit	6,158	0	0	0	0
Stealth*	4,087	1,276	0	0	0
Stratus	75,439	98,065	99,040	106,434	94,413
Viper	1,227	1,597	1,458	1,248	1,315
Total Dodge	**403,839**	**421,945**	**372,832**	**360,229**	**369,977**
Summit*	4,383	1,365	0	0	0
Summit Wagon*	5,060	2,051	0	0	0
Talon	20,824	13,842	10,206	2,957	0
Vision	23,345	11,437	5,146	501	0
Total Eagle	**53,612**	**28,695**	**15,352**	**3,458**	**0**
Acclaim	6,457	0	0	0	0
Breeze	221	64,500	72,499	59,543	52,054
Colt*	682	0	0	0	0
Neon	106,205	105,472	86,798	78,533	71,561
Prowler	0	0	120	1,594	2,365
Total Plymouth	**113,565**	**169,972**	**159,417**	**139,670**	**125,980**
Total Chrysler Corp.	**786,180**	**832,633**	**736,530**	**739,217**	**745,275**
Lanos	0	0	0	388	9,321
Leganza	0	0	0	1,331	12,913
Nubira	0	0	0	523	8,553
Total Daewoo	**0**	**0**	**0**	**2,242**	**30,787**
Alfa Romeo 164*	384	0	0	0	0
Alfa Spider*	30	0	0	0	0
Total Alfa Romeo	**414**	**0**	**0**	**0**	**0**
Aspire*	59,191	37,359	33,243	4,917	0
Contour	174,214	174,187	151,060	139,838	134,487
Crown Victoria	98,163	108,789	107,872	111,531	114,669
Escort	285,570	284,644	283,898	291,936	260,486
Focus	0	0	0	0	55,846
Mustang	136,962	122,674	116,610	144,732	166,915
Probe	52,696	32,505	16,361	3,058	0
Taurus	366,266	401,049	357,162	371,074	368,327
Tempo	1,780	0	0	0	0
Thunderbird	104,254	79,721	66,334	2,243	0

U.S. Retail Sales of Passenger Cars

U.S. RETAIL SALES OF PASSENGER CARS, 1995-1999 — continued

Model	1995	1996	1997	1998	1999
Total Ford	**1,279,096**	**1,240,928**	**1,132,540**	**1,069,329**	**1,100,730**
Jaguar Vanden Plas*	3,463	4,383	3,174	4,789	4,438
Jaguar S-Type*	0	0	0	0	15,541
Jaguar XJ12*	410	374	48	0	0
Jaguar XJ6*	9,120	7,583	8,598	10,191	7,366
Jaguar XJS Coupe*	415	3	0	0	0
Jaguar XJS Sc*	4,120	2,867	49	0	0
Jaguar XK8*	0	2,050	6,864	5,861	6,154
Jaguar XJR Sedan*	557	618	768	1,662	1,540
Total Jaguar	**18,085**	**17,878**	**19,501**	**22,503**	**35,039**
Continental	40,708	32,019	31,220	35,210	26,246
Lincoln LS	0	0	0	0	26,368
Mark	17,433	15,859	16,023	10,505	0
Town Car	92,673	93,598	92,297	97,547	84,629
Total Lincoln	**150,814**	**141,476**	**139,540**	**143,262**	**137,243**
Cougar	53,387	36,015	30,516	38,216	56,831
Grand Marquis	90,367	99,770	109,539	114,162	122,776
Mystique	62,609	57,102	41,038	38,274	39,531
Sable	102,565	114,164	112,400	100,367	101,120
Topaz	399	0	0	0	0
Tracer	51,988	47,797	43,589	33,077	23,146
Total Mercury	**361,315**	**354,848**	**337,082**	**324,096**	**343,404**
Volvo 200*	7	0	0	0	0
Volvo 40*	0	0	0	0	11,988
Volvo 80*	0	0	0	6,071	33,549
Volvo 800*	60,391	68,403	20,184	410	18
Volvo 90*	0	0	9,017	7,894	32
Volvo 900*	28,107	20,178	8,698	0	0
Volvo S70 V70*	0	0	52,995	86,797	71,105
Total Volvo	**88,505**	**88,581**	**90,894**	**101,172**	**116,692**
Total Ford Motor Co.	**1,897,815**	**1,843,711**	**1,719,557**	**1,660,362**	**1,733,108**
Impreza*	24,415	24,687	24,242	19,041	19,356
Legacy	74,151	94,950	92,913	88,660	87,267
Legacy*	40	0	0	0	0
SVX*	1,801	1,111	640	0	0
Total Subaru	**100,407**	**120,748**	**117,795**	**107,701**	**106,623**
Century	93,361	72,433	91,232	126,220	157,035
Lesabre	141,410	131,316	150,744	136,551	149,445
Park Ave	53,045	47,732	68,777	58,187	62,868
Regal	90,896	86,847	50,691	65,979	74,016
Riviera	23,350	20,641	14,089	9,390	2,247
Roadmaster	25,235	17,112	3,200	82	0
Skylark	44,522	51,269	59,331	1,747	0
Total Buick	**471,819**	**427,350**	**438,064**	**398,156**	**445,611**
Catera*	0	1,676	25,411	24,635	15,068
Eldorado	23,200	20,964	20,609	15,598	15,255
Fleetwood Brougham	13,698	10,200	2,024	22	0
Fleetwood Deville	106,581	103,730	104,743	100,513	90,755
Seville	37,025	33,809	29,837	38,713	33,532
Total Cadillac	**180,504**	**170,379**	**182,624**	**179,481**	**154,610**
Camaro	97,525	66,866	55,973	47,577	40,726
Caprice	78,890	46,261	11,583	67	0
Cavalier	212,767	277,222	302,161	256,099	272,122
Corsica Beretta	192,361	149,117	4,844	58	0
Corvette	18,966	17,805	22,724	29,208	29,963
Impala	0	0	0	0	81,247

U.S. Retail Sales of Passenger Cars

U.S. RETAIL SALES OF PASSENGER CARS, 1995-1999 — continued

Model	1995	1996	1997	1998	1999
Lumina	214,595	237,973	228,451	177,631	97,607
Malibu	0	2,274	164,654	223,703	218,540
Metro	75,697	88,773	55,629	28,515	31,989
Monte Carlo	75,924	79,593	71,543	64,022	68,309
Prizm	87,295	79,288	62,992	49,552	44,246
Storm/Spectrum*	51	0	0	0	0
Total Chevrolet	**1,054,071**	**1,045,172**	**980,554**	**876,432**	**884,749**
Achieva	44,787	40,344	63,196	888	34
Alero	0	0	0	28,134	118,907
Aurora	26,544	23,717	25,404	21,374	16,321
Ciera	128,860	89,577	4,322	63	0
Cutlass	0	434	26,708	53,438	32,677
Intrigue	0	0	23,460	90,563	90,057
Olds 88	61,897	58,525	67,223	65,877	23,915
Olds 98	20,008	12,626	633	48	0
Supreme	89,629	81,263	40,717	1,601	78
Total Oldsmobile	**371,725**	**306,486**	**251,663**	**261,986**	**281,989**
Bonneville	83,364	73,849	75,882	59,638	45,111
Firebird	42,302	32,622	32,524	31,692	33,850
Grand Am	234,226	222,477	204,078	180,428	234,936
Grand Prix	131,747	104,979	142,018	122,915	148,197
Sunbird	763	0	0	0	0
Sunfire	74,424	95,783	102,160	82,748	90,256
Total Pontiac	**566,826**	**529,710**	**556,662**	**477,421**	**552,350**
Saab 9-3*	0	0	0	12,826	22,473
Saab 9-5*	0	0	0	7,928	16,778
Saab 900*	19,557	22,436	23,049	9,009	238
Saab 9000*	6,035	6,003	5,404	993	52
Total Saab	**25,592**	**28,439**	**28,453**	**30,756**	**39,541**
Saturn EV1	0	0	289	264	137
Saturn LS	0	0	0	0	24,456
Saturn S	285,674	278,574	250,810	231,522	207,977
Total Saturn	**285,674**	**278,574**	**251,099**	**231,786**	**232,570**
Total General Motors	**2,956,211**	**2,786,110**	**2,689,119**	**2,456,018**	**2,591,420**
Acura CL	0	16,740	28,939	26,644	20,968
Acura NSX*	884	460	415	303	238
Acura RL*	0	15,948	16,004	15,024	13,366
Acura TL	0	0	0	16,718	56,556
Acura TL*	16,539	24,700	23,151	15,165	0
Integra*	61,316	46,966	38,331	34,904	26,184
Legend*	18,159	629	4	0	0
Vigor*	253	0	0	0	0
Total Acura	**97,151**	**105,443**	**106,844**	**108,758**	**117,312**
Accord	293,898	381,912	363,016	370,984	316,339
Accord*	47,486	386	21,593	30,087	87,853
Civic	217,146	266,859	273,356	317,134	308,807
Civic*	58,268	11,673	42,190	17,428	9,501
Del Sol*	14,021	7,818	5,598	548	1
Honda EV Plus*	0	0	105	133	62
Honda S2000*	0	0	0	0	3,400
Insight*	0	0	0	0	17
Prelude*	12,517	12,063	16,678	15,399	11,378
Total Honda	**643,336**	**680,711**	**722,536**	**751,713**	**737,358**
Total Honda	**740,487**	**786,154**	**829,380**	**860,471**	**854,670**
Accent*	45,574	53,230	40,355	30,231	41,235
Elantra*	37,653	39,801	41,303	37,501	83,292

U.S. Retail Sales of Passenger Cars

U.S. RETAIL SALES OF PASSENGER CARS, 1995-1999 — continued

Model	1995	1996	1997	1998	1999
Excel*	2,334	22	0	0	0
Scoupe*	4,762	458	9	0	0
Sonata	7	0	0	0	0
Sonata*	17,048	14,616	22,128	14,144	30,022
Tiburon*	0	341	9,391	8,341	9,641
Total Hyundai	**107,378**	**108,468**	**113,186**	**90,217**	**164,190**
Impulse*	1	0	0	0	0
Isuzu Stylus*	15	1	0	0	0
Total Isuzu	**16**	**1**	**0**	**0**	**0**
Sephia*	16,725	26,366	35,494	54,311	82,211
Total Kia Motors	**16,725**	**26,366**	**35,494**	**54,311**	**82,211**
Mazda 323*	27	0	0	0	0
Mazda 626	89,699	79,354	75,800	91,147	86,735
Mazda 929*	3,773	1,232	7	0	0
Mazda MX6	16,153	6,550	3,546	443	14
Mazda RX7*	1,399	369	12	0	0
Miata*	20,174	18,408	17,218	19,845	17,738
Millenia*	21,561	13,019	18,020	16,717	19,198
MX3*	8,076	2,399	7	0	0
Protégé*	62,849	59,644	53,930	58,349	65,242
Total Mazda	**223,711**	**180,975**	**168,540**	**186,501**	**188,927**
Mercedes C Class*	27,119	28,715	32,543	34,487	29,770
Mercedes CL*	0	0	0	0	367
Mercedes CLK*	0	0	1,236	11,622	16,714
Mercedes E Class*	24,915	37,956	42,883	47,563	50,214
Mercedes S Class*	17,754	17,317	16,119	15,010	28,713
Mercedes SL Class*	6,964	6,856	8,025	7,809	7,853
Mercedes SLK*	0	0	6,890	10,620	10,600
Total Mercedes Benz	**76,752**	**90,844**	**107,696**	**127,111**	**144,231**
Diamante*	10,335	2,718	11,402	8,563	9,921
Eclipse	52,555	63,116	58,569	57,955	61,874
Expo*	3,761	2	1	0	0
Galant	48,478	62,518	42,588	44,201	74,782
Galant*	6,806	3,174	19	1	0
Mirage*	42,902	30,338	31,717	33,072	47,136
Mitsubishi 3000 GT*	10,430	8,317	6,086	4,164	3,419
Total Mitsubishi	**175,267**	**170,183**	**150,382**	**147,956**	**197,132**
Infiniti G20*	16,818	13,467	419	7,217	16,108
Infiniti I30*	16,096	27,057	31,303	26,350	31,042
Infiniti J30*	17,899	7,564	4,594	1,783	17
Infiniti Q45*	7,803	5,896	10,443	8,244	6,271
Total Infiniti	**58,616**	**53,984**	**46,759**	**43,594**	**53,438**
Altima	148,172	147,910	144,483	144,451	153,525
Altra EV*	0	0	0	0	30
Maxima*	128,599	128,395	123,215	113,843	131,182
Nissan 200SX	32,663	31,388	26,032	18,734	1,193
Nissan 240SX*	13,175	7,029	3,533	2,266	954
Nissan 300ZX*	4,176	2,074	1,010	124	15
Nissan NX*	1	1	0	0	0
Sentra	119,049	129,593	122,468	88,363	63,134
Sentra*	15,805	3	0	0	0
Stanza*	2	0	0	0	0

U.S. Retail Sales
of Passenger Cars

U.S. RETAIL SALES OF PASSENGER CARS, 1995-1999 — continued

Model	1995	1996	1997	1998	1999
Total Nissan	461,642	446,393	420,741	367,781	350,033
Total Nissan	520,258	500,377	467,500	411,375	403,471
Boxster*	0	0	6,989	9,696	12,681
Porsche 911*	5,311	7,141	5,977	7,547	8,194
Porsche 928*	95	5	0	0	0
Porsche 968*	365	6	10	0	0
Total Porsche	5,771	7,152	12,976	17,243	20,875
Esteem*	3,219	6,996	6,968	13,915	12,320
Swift	4,126	3,379	1,615	2,254	2,290
Swift*	1,166	13	1	0	0
Total Suzuki	8,511	10,388	8,584	16,169	14,610
Lexus ES300*	41,508	44,773	58,428	48,644	45,860
Lexus GS300*	6,449	2,044	3,823	20,696	24,990
Lexus GS400*	0	0	3,890	9,926	6,894
Lexus LS400*	23,657	22,237	19,618	20,790	16,357
Lexus SC300*	3,356	2,390	2,999	1,766	1,731
Lexus SC400*	4,364	2,557	2,042	1,243	826
Total Lexus	79,334	74,001	90,800	103,065	96,658
Avalon	66,445	73,308	71,309	77,752	68,038
Camry	248,188	280,021	305,416	295,108	320,156
Camry*	80,412	79,412	91,740	134,467	128,006
Celica*	21,386	14,343	9,021	4,290	16,418
Corolla	184,002	202,417	217,207	250,500	249,127
Corolla*	29,638	6,631	1,254	1	1
Cressida*	2	0	0	0	0
Echo*	0	0	0	0	10,490
Paseo*	5,618	6,069	2,786	200	5
Supra*	2,273	861	1,389	688	24
Tercel*	76,289	56,492	31,651	1,743	46
Toyota MR2*	387	37	9	0	0
Total Toyota	714,640	719,591	731,782	764,749	792,311
Total Toyota	793,974	793,592	822,582	867,814	888,969
Audi 100*	6,358	0	0	0	0
Audi 80*	1	0	0	0	0
Audi A4*	7,467	15,319	20,871	26,635	32,137
Audi A6*	2,261	9,908	9,949	18,050	26,131
Audi A8*	0	559	2,085	2,172	2,481
Audi Cabrio*	1,088	1,183	1,255	660	71
Audi S4*	948	410	0	0	0
Audi TT*	0	0	0	0	5,139
Audi V8*	1	0	0	0	0
Total Audi	18,124	27,379	34,160	47,517	65,959
Beetle	0	0	0	55,842	83,434
Corrado*	172	2	1	0	0
Golf	18,429	24,208	20,702	18,282	0
Golf*	0	0	0	0	18,990
Jetta	75,393	85,022	90,984	89,311	130,054
Passat*	14,010	19,850	14,868	39,272	68,151
VW Cabrio	0	975	9,538	15,230	11,539
VW Cabrio*	5,538	4,853	0	0	0
VW Fox	112	2	0	0	0
Total Volkswagen	113,654	134,912	136,093	217,937	312,168
Total Volkswagen	131,778	162,291	170,253	265,454	378,127
Total Passenger Cars	8,634,964	8,525,754	8,272,074	8,141,721	8,698,284

*Units imported from outside North America.
SOURCE: Ward's AutoInfoBank.

U.S. Retail Sales of Passenger Cars by Country of Origin, Market Class and Purchasing Sector

U.S. RETAIL SALES OF PASSENGER CARS, 1971-1999

Year	Domestic	Imports From Japan	Imports From Germany	Imports From Other Countries	Total Imports	U.S. Total	Import Percent Total	Import Percent Japan	Import Percent Germany
1999	6,979,357	757,568	466,870	494,489	1,718,927	8,698,284	19.8	8.7	5.4
1998	6,761,940	691,162	366,724	321,895	1,379,781	8,141,721	16.9	8.5	4.5
1997	6,916,769	726,104	297,028	332,173	1,355,305	8,272,074	16.4	8.8	3.6
1996	7,253,582	726,940	237,984	308,247	1,273,171	8,526,753	14.9	8.5	2.8
1995	7,128,707	981,506	207,482	317,269	1,506,257	8,634,964	17.4	11.4	2.4
1994	7,255,303	1,239,450	192,275	303,489	1,735,214	8,990,517	19.3	13.8	2.1
1993	6,741,667	1,328,445	186,177	261,570	1,776,192	8,517,859	20.9	15.6	2.2
1992	6,276,557	1,451,766	200,851	283,938	1,936,555	8,213,112	23.6	17.7	2.4
1991	6,136,757	1,500,309	192,776	344,814	2,037,899	8,174,656	24.9	18.4	2.4
1990	6,896,888	1,719,384	265,116	418,823	2,403,323	9,300,211	25.8	18.5	2.9
1989	7,072,902	1,897,143	248,561	553,660	2,699,364	9,772,266	27.6	19.4	2.5
1988	7,526,038	2,022,602	280,099	700,991	3,003,692	10,529,730	28.5	19.2	2.7
1987	7,080,858	2,190,405	347,881	657,465	3,195,751	10,276,609	31.1	21.3	3.4
1986	8,214,897	2,382,614	443,721	418,286	3,244,621	11,459,518	28.3	20.8	3.9
1985	8,204,542	2,217,837	423,983	195,925	2,837,745	11,042,287	25.7	20.1	3.8
1984	7,951,523	1,906,206	344,416	188,220	2,438,842	10,390,365	23.5	18.3	3.3
1983	6,795,295	1,915,621	279,748	191,403	2,386,772	9,182,067	26.0	20.9	3.1
1982	5,758,586	1,801,969	247,080	174,508	2,223,557	7,982,143	27.9	22.6	3.1
1981	6,208,760	1,858,896	282,881	185,502	2,327,279	8,536,039	27.3	21.8	3.3
1979	8,341,139	1,755,818	366,084	209,727	2,331,629	10,672,768	21.8	16.5	3.4
1977	9,109,022	1,387,856	459,707	226,827	2,074,390	11,183,412	18.5	12.4	4.1
1975	7,053,016	807,931	492,507	271,034	1,571,472	8,624,488	18.2	9.4	5.7
1973	9,675,790	742,621	787,562	217,878	1,748,061	11,423,851	15.3	6.5	6.9
1971	8,681,409	578,977	769,457	212,362	1,560,796	10,242,205	15.2	5.7	7.5

SOURCE: Ward's Communications.

U.S. CAR SALES BY MARKET CLASS, 1983-1999

Year	Small	Middle	Large	Luxury	Total
1999	23.2%	52.7%	7.6%	16.5%	100.0%
1998	24.7	51.1	8.2	16.0	100.0
1997	26.8	49.0	9.5	14.8	100.0
1996	27.3	49.4	9.9	13.5	100.0
1995	27.1	48.5	10.8	13.6	100.0
1993	32.8	43.3	11.1	12.8	100.0
1991	33.0	44.9	8.3	13.9	100.0
1989	36.6	41.9	11.9	11.6	100.0
1987	38.4	42.3	9.1	10.2	100.0
1985	37.9	42.1	9.8	10.2	100.0
1983	38.8	40.6	10.7	9.9	100.0

SOURCE: Ward's Communications.

U.S. CAR SALES BY SECTOR, 1960-1999

Year	Units by Consuming Sector (000) Consumer	Units by Consuming Sector (000) Business	Units by Consuming Sector (000) Government	Units by Consuming Sector (000) Total	% of Total Sales Consumer	% of Total Sales Business
1999	4,364	4,137	194	8,695	50.2%	47.6%
1998	3,988	3,992	161	8,142	48.0	49.0
1997	3,910	4,216	147	8,273	47.3	50.0
1996	4,079	4,273	176	8,527	47.8	50.1
1995	4,351	4,186	151	8,687	50.1	48.2
1994	4,600	4,268	124	8,991	51.2	47.5
1993	4,657	3,748	113	8,518	54.7	44.0
1992	4,566	3,529	119	8,214	55.6	42.0
1991	4,424	3,648	103	8,175	54.1	44.6
1990	5,677	3,477	147	9,301	61.0	37.4
1989	6,288	3,362	127	9,777	64.3	34.4
1988	6,746	3,669	131	10,546	63.0	34.8
1987	6,625	3,416	130	10,171	65.1	33.6
1986	7,579	3,701	126	11,406	66.4	32.4
1985	7,092	3,754	132	10,978	64.6	34.2
1980	6,100	2,758	124	8,982	67.9	30.7
1975	5,907	2,508	123	8,538	69.2	29.4
1970	6,252	2,056	94	8,403	74.4	24.5
1965	7,106	2,149	89	9,344	76.1	22.0
1960	4,950	1,616	66	6,632	74.6	24.4

SOURCE: U.S. Department of Commerce, Bureau of Economic Analysis.

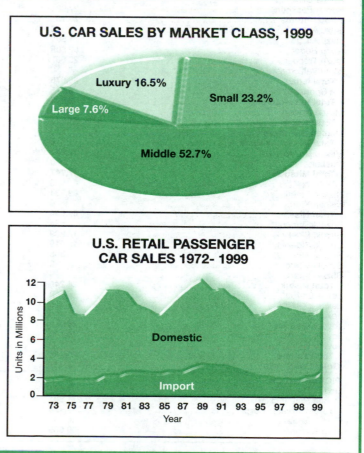

U.S. CAR SALES BY MARKET CLASS, 1999

Luxury 16.5%
Large 7.6%
Small 23.2%
Middle 52.7%

U.S. RETAIL PASSENGER CAR SALES 1972- 1999

Domestic
Import

U.S. Light Truck Sales by Segment

U.S. LIGHT TRUCK SALES BY SEGMENT, 1995-1999

Model	1995	1996	1997	1998	1999
SPORT UTILITY VEHICLES					
BMW X5	0	0	0	0	1,312
Rover Defender*	1,571	606	2,501	122	0
Rover Discovery*	11,570	15,491	14,703	14,230	21,931
Range Rover*	6,885	7,085	6,621	7,070	7,449
Total BMW	**20,026**	**23,182**	**23,825**	**21,422**	**30,692**
Dodge Durango	0	0	20,263	156,923	189,840
Jeep Cherokee XJ	110,552	148,544	130,041	146,298	165,261
Jeep Grand Cherokee	252,186	279,195	260,875	229,135	300,031
Jeep Wrangler	63,890	81,444	81,956	83,861	89,174
Total Chrysler Corp.	**426,628**	**509,183**	**493,135**	**616,217**	**744,306**
Ford Bronco	34,210	36,833	0	0	0
Ford Excursion	0	0	0	0	18,315
Ford Expedition	0	45,974	214,524	225,703	233,125
Ford Explorer	395,227	402,663	383,852	431,488	428,772
Lincoln Navigator	0	0	26,831	43,859	39,250
Mercury Mountaineer	0	26,700	45,363	47,595	49,281
Total Ford Motor Co.	**429,437**	**512,170**	**670,570**	**748,645**	**768,743**
Subaru Forester*	0	0	15,988	40,132	50,183
Total Subaru	**0**	**0**	**15,988**	**40,132**	**50,183**
Cadillac Escalade	0	0	0	3,089	23,897
Chevrolet Blazer	327	23	0	0	0
Chevrolet Suburban	78,544	94,010	99,068	108,933	138,977
Chevrolet S Blazer	214,661	246,307	221,400	219,710	232,140
Chevrolet Tahoe	80,704	124,038	124,125	133,235	122,213
Chevrolet Tracker	41,643	47,188	33,354	20,296	40,024
GMC Suburban	30,435	43,161	43,137	42,423	44,886
GMC S Jimmy	71,807	77,838	75,817	72,301	79,375
GMC Yukon	29,049	36,566	41,072	49,355	53,280
GMC Yukon XL	0	0	0	0	1,857
Oldsmobile Bravada	3,946	15,471	28,481	30,202	29,258
Total General Motors	**551,116**	**684,602**	**666,454**	**679,544**	**765,907**
Acura SLX*	200	2,565	1,299	1,634	694
Honda CRV*	0	0	66,752	100,582	120,754
Honda Passport	27,981	28,184	22,622	26,094	22,974
Total Honda	**28,181**	**30,749**	**90,673**	**128,310**	**144,422**
Isuzu Amigo	0	0	0	7,088	8,298
Isuzu Amigo*	1,561	35	0	0	0
Isuzu Rodeo	60,908	61,073	63,597	59,889	64,771
Isuzu Trooper*	23,607	18,495	10,956	18,191	20,755
Isuzu Vehicross*	0	0	0	0	1,271
Total Isuzu	**86,076**	**79,603**	**74,553**	**85,168**	**95,095**
Kia Sportage*	8,015	9,908	19,831	28,582	52,383
Total Kia Motors	**8,015**	**9,908**	**19,831**	**28,582**	**52,383**
Mazda Navajo	1,813	68	4	0	0
Total Mazda	**1,813**	**68**	**4**	**0**	**0**
Mercedes M Class	0	0	14,569	43,134	45,206
Total Mercedes Benz	**0**	**0**	**14,569**	**43,134**	**45,206**
Mitsubishi Montero*	17,747	12,083	6,915	4,120	5,115
Mitsubishi Montero Sport*	0	232	31,659	38,439	59,007
Total Mitsubishi	**17,747**	**12,315**	**38,574**	**42,559**	**64,122**
Infiniti Qx4*	0	1,983	18,793	20,055	19,199
Nissan Pathfinder*	69,934	73,686	73,365	68,003	65,968
Nissan Xterra	0	0	0	0	47,806
Total Nissan	**69,934**	**75,669**	**92,158**	**88,058**	**132,973**
Suzuki Samurai*	624	22	0	0	0
Suzuki Sidekick	13,209	11,476	6,307	5,316	224
Suzuki Sidekick*	10,019	11,222	11,757	9,619	621
Suzuki X90*	388	3,602	2,625	591	35
Suzuki Vitara	0	0	0	3	6,948
Suzuki Vitara*	0	0	0	5,910	27,450
Total Suzuki	**24,240**	**26,322**	**20,689**	**21,439**	**35,278**
Lexus LX450*	0	7,528	6,785	312	0
Lexus LX470*	0	0	0	10,692	15,734
Lexus RX300*	0	0	0	42,191	73,498
Toyota 4Runner Pass*	75,962	99,597	128,496	118,484	124,221
Toyota Land Cruiser*	14,240	12,850	11,510	14,327	18,602
Toyota RAV4*	2	56,709	67,487	64,990	57,138
Total Toyota	**90,204**	**176,684**	**214,278**	**250,996**	**289,193**
Total Sport Utility	**1,753,417**	**2,140,455**	**2,435,301**	**2,794,206**	**3,218,503**
PICKUP TRUCKS					
Dodge Dakota	111,677	104,754	131,961	152,629	144,148
Dodge Ram Pickup	271,501	383,960	350,257	410,130	428,930
Total Chrysler Corp.	**383,178**	**488,714**	**482,218**	**562,759**	**573,078**
Ford F Series	658,202	744,189	710,156	787,552	806,579
Ford Ranger	309,085	288,393	298,796	328,136	348,358

U.S. Light Truck Sales by Segment

U.S. LIGHT TRUCK SALES BY SEGMENT, 1995-1999 — continued

Model	1995	1996	1997	1998	1999
Total Ford Motor Co.	**967,287**	**1,032,582**	**1,008,952**	**1,115,688**	**1,154,937**
Chevrolet CK Pickup	505,464	519,106	527,842	454,311	98,285
Chevrolet S10 Pickup	207,193	190,178	192,314	228,093	233,669
Chevrolet Silverado	0	0	0	78,866	530,106
GMC Sierra	172,457	169,054	168,478	156,244	204,128
GMC Sonoma	50,517	44,629	41,714	54,819	57,992
Total General Motors	**935,631**	**922,967**	**930,348**	**972,333**	**1,124,180**
Isuzu Hombre	0	10,165	13,975	14,991	7,766
Isuzu Pickup	348	0	0	0	0
Isuzu Pickup*	14,422	1,993	12	0	0
Total Isuzu	**14,770**	**12,158**	**13,987**	**14,991**	**7,766**
Mazda Pickup	43,434	42,815	37,697	41,620	38,726
Mazda Pickup*	3	0	0	0	0
Total Mazda	**43,437**	**42,815**	**37,697**	**41,620**	**38,726**
Mitsubishi Pickup*	5,045	3,629	207	0	0
Total Mitsubishi	**5,045**	**3,629**	**207**	**0**	**0**
Nissan Frontier	0	0	25,249	91,629	96,301
Nissan Pickup	126,662	127,081	96,612	0	0
Total Nissan	**126,662**	**127,081**	**121,861**	**91,629**	**96,301**
Toyota Tacoma	88,967	142,356	145,870	152,770	155,476
Toyota Pickup	23,635	0	0	0	0
Toyota Pickup*	30,870	640	41	0	0
Toyota T100*	37,467	37,926	28,381	7,959	225
Toyota Tundra	0	0	0	0	42,769
Total Toyota	**180,939**	**180,922**	**174,292**	**160,729**	**198,470**
Total Pickup	**2,656,949**	**2,810,868**	**2,769,562**	**2,959,749**	**3,193,458**
VANS					
Chrysler Town & Country	50,733	84,828	76,653	71,981	71,957
Chrysler Voyager	0	0	0	0	129
Dodge Caravan	267,020	300,117	285,736	293,819	293,100
Dodge Ram Van	72,277	81,489	73,460	69,047	72,072
Plymouth Voyager	178,327	153,862	156,056	156,971	138,644
Total Chrysler Corp.	**568,357**	**620,296**	**591,905**	**591,818**	**575,902**
Ford Aerostar	87,547	73,685	44,829	1,060	0
Ford Econoline	195,035	176,480	186,690	206,026	202,024
Ford Windstar	222,147	209,033	205,356	190,173	213,844
Mercury Villager	75,052	65,587	55,168	38,495	45,315
Total Ford Motor Co.	**579,781**	**524,785**	**492,043**	**435,754**	**461,183**
Chevrolet Astro	119,510	125,962	111,390	95,977	102,427
Chevrolet Van	93,928	77,510	77,667	73,812	92,627
Chevrolet Express	0	2,693	5,975	8,658	13,214
Chevrolet Lumina Van	47,428	27,442	1,243	12	0
Chevrolet Venture	0	3,788	76,171	97,362	96,643
GMC Safari	40,085	39,999	35,787	30,921	31,840
GMC Savana	0	16,171	33,951	35,656	39,058
GMC Vandura Rally	34,570	13,486	488	0	0
Oldsmobile Silhouette	11,874	9,330	24,615	37,554	40,950
Pontiac Montana	0	0	0	10,819	62,547
Pontiac Trans Sport	32,297	21,397	51,961	48,229	1,516
Total General Motors	**379,692**	**337,778**	**419,248**	**439,000**	**480,822**
Honda Odyssey	0	0	0	7,154	77,626
Honda Odyssey*	25,911	27,025	20,333	13,665	175
Total Honda	**25,911**	**27,025**	**20,333**	**20,819**	**77,801**
Isuzu Oasis*	0	2,128	2,943	1,671	1,076
Total Isuzu	**0**	**2,128**	**2,943**	**1,671**	**1,076**
Mazda MPV*	14,784	14,427	15,599	12,425	16,055
Total Mazda	**14,784**	**14,427**	**15,599**	**12,425**	**16,055**
Nissan Quest	54,050	46,636	46,858	30,466	44,467
Total Nissan	**54,050**	**46,636**	**46,858**	**30,466**	**44,467**
Toyota Previa*	18,234	8,520	3,780	95	0
Toyota Sienna	0	0	15,180	81,391	98,809
Total Toyota	**18,234**	**8,520**	**18,960**	**81,486**	**98,809**
Volkswagen Eurovan*	1,460	995	1,792	1,742	3,395
Total Volkswagen	**1,460**	**995**	**1,792**	**1,742**	**3,395**
Total Van	**1,642,269**	**1,582,590**	**1,609,681**	**1,615,181**	**1,759,510**
COMMERCIAL CHASSIS					
General Motors	32,406	29,333	26,833	22,489	12,247
Isuzu Truck*	5,604	5,252	6,312	6,648	7,593
Freightliner Truck*	10	164	143	670	945
Mitsu-Fuso Truck*	2,429	1,768	1,815	2,270	2,210
Nissan Diesel Truck*	0	0	0	73	788
Total Commercial Chassis	**40,449**	**36,517**	**35,103**	**32,150**	**23,783**
TOTAL LIGHT TRUCKS	**6,093,084**	**6,570,430**	**6,849,647**	**7,401,286**	**8,195,254**

*Units imported from outside North America.
SOURCE: Ward's AutoInfoBank.

U.S. Retail Sales of Trucks by Manufacturer and Gross Vehicle Weight Rating

U.S. RETAIL SALES OF TRUCKS BY MANUFACTURER AND GROSS VEHICLE WEIGHT RATING, 1999

	Gross Vehicle Weight Rating (Pounds)								
	6,000 & Less	6,001-10,000	10,000-14,000	14,001-16,000	16,001-19,500	19,501-26,000	26,001-33,000	33,001 & Over	Total
DOMESTIC*									
BMW	1,312	0	0	0	0	0	0	0	1,312
Chrysler	1,202,444	653,089	37,753	0	0	0	0	0	1,893,286
Ford	1,288,361	1,029,180	67,322	21,862	22,323	21,702	7,306	146	2,458,202
Freightliner	0	0	945	5,143	1,214	13,244	28,181	97,881	146,608
General Motors	1,693,964	683,395	1,688	12,324	0	6,964	23,084	0	2,421,419
Honda	100,600	0	0	0	0	0	0	0	100,600
Isuzu Truck	0	0	2,411	1,408	0	1,640	86	0	5,545
Kenworth	0	0	0	0	0	0	2,026	28,637	30,663
Mack	0	0	0	0	0	0	0	34,264	34,264
Mazda	38,726	0	0	0	0	0	0	0	38,726
Mercedes-Benz	45,206	0	0	0	0	0	0	0	45,206
Navistar	0	0	0	0	633	1,351	67,633	41,648	111,265
Nissan	188,574	0	0	0	0	0	0	0	188,574
Peterbilt	0	0	0	0	0	0	1,437	26,725	28,162
Subaru-Isuzu	80,835	0	0	0	0	0	0	0	80,835
Suzuki	7,172	0	0	0	0	0	0	0	7,172
Toyota	297,054	0	0	0	0	0	0	0	297,054
Volvo	0	0	0	0	0	0	1	28,177	28,178
Western Star	0	0	0	0	0	0	0	3,550	3,550
Other Domestic	0	0	0	0	0	0	0	1,288	1,288
Total Domestic	**4,944,248**	**2,365,664**	**110,119**	**40,737**	**24,170**	**44,901**	**129,754**	**262,316**	**7,921,909**
IMPORT									
General Motors	0	0	4,109	0	202	0	0	0	4,311
Hino	0	0	0	270	412	684	198	0	1,564
Honda	121,623	0	0	0	0	0	0	0	121,623
Isuzu	23,102	0	0	0	0	0	0	0	23,102
Isuzu Truck	0.0	0.0	5182	6245	3122	0.0	0.0	0.0	14,549
Kia	52,383	0	0	0	0	0	0	0	52,383
Land Rover	29,380	0	0	0	0	0	0	0	29,380
Mack	0.0	0.0	0.0	0.0	0.0	828	683	0.0	1,511
Mazda	16,055	0	0	0	0	0	0	0	16,055
Mitsubishi	64,122	0	0	0	0	0	0	0	64,122
Mitsubishi Fuso	0	0	2,210	1,387	1,259	917	237	0	6,010
Nissan	85,167	0	0	0	0	0	0	0	85,167
Nissan Diesel	0	0	788	784	1,188	785	111	0	3,656
Subaru-Isuzu	50,183	0	0	0	0	0	0	0	50,183
Suzuki	28,106	0	0	0	0	0	0	0	28,106
Toyota	289,418	0	0	0	0	0	0	0	289,418
Volkswagen	3,395	0	0	0	0	0	0	0	3,395
Total Import	**762,934**	**0**	**12,289**	**8,686**	**6,183**	**3,214**	**1,229**	**0**	**794,535**
Total Trucks	**5,707,182**	**2,365,664**	**122,408**	**49,423**	**30,353**	**48,115**	**130,983**	**262,316**	**8,716,444**

*Units produced in the United States, Canada and Mexico.
NOTE: Includes school bus chassis.
SOURCE: Ward's AutoInfoBank

U.S. Retail Sales of Trucks by Gross Vehicle Weight Rating and Body Type

U.S. RETAIL SALES OF DOMESTIC LIGHT TRUCKS BY GROSS VEHICLE WEIGHT RATING AND BODY TYPE, 1994-1999

GVWR/Body type	1994	1995	1996	1997	1998	1999
0-6,000 Lbs.						
Utility	1,130,183	1,257,823	1,391,565	1,368,240	1,428,600	1,610,855
Compact Pickup	1,097,578	961,518	984,957	984,203	1,058,425	1,082,436
Mini Van	82,234	73,302	63,878	64,008	43,876	46,364
Van	12,406	12,293	18,369	47,410	39,035	42,662
Conventional Pickup	677,436	613,649	840,361	924,412	896,143	885,198
Mini Passenger Carrier	1,132,214	1,112,768	1,097,788	1,123,014	1,146,438	1,273,450
Passenger Carrier	18	17	971	2,407	2,659	3,283
Total 0-6,000 lbs.	**4,132,069**	**4,031,370**	**4,397,889**	**4,513,694**	**4,615,176**	**4,944,248**
6,001-10,000 Lbs.						
Utility	72,007	144,290	243,434	426,815	614,267	670,920
Van	274,792	274,190	253,777	230,194	252,639	282,808
Van Cutaway	55,853	46,167	36,676	38,264	36,883	25,412
Conventional Pickup	882,605	966,874	935,994	792,634	903,121	1,120,524
Station Wagon	124,960	108,979	137,171	142,205	151,356	185,720
Passenger Carrier	66,072	63,143	57,703	59,945	61,983	64,830
Multi-Stop	29,610	27,660	24,984	21,986	17,491	6,450
Total 6,001-10,000 lbs.	**1,505,899**	**1,631,303**	**1,689,739**	**1,712,043**	**2,037,740**	**2,365,664**
10,001 - 14,000 lbs.						
Conventional Pickup	19,666	27,101	39,954	39,687	89,989	105,075
Other Body Types	0	1,129	4,064	5,281	2,699	5,044
Total 10,001-14,000 lbs.	**19,666**	**28,230**	**44,018**	**44,968**	**92,688**	**110,119**
Total Domestic Light Trucks	**5,657,634**	**5,690,903**	**6,131,646**	**6,270,705**	**6,745,604**	**7,420,031**

*Units produced in U.S., Canada and Mexico.

U.S. RETAIL SALES OF DOMESTIC AND IMPORTED TRUCKS, 1985-1999

Year	Domestic				Imports		Total U.S. Sales
	Gross Vehicle Weight Rating						
	0-14,000 lbs.	14,001-33,000 lbs.	33,001 lbs. & Over	Total Domestic	From Japan	Total Imports	
1999	7,420,031	239,562	262,316	7,921,909	707,866	794,535	8,716,444
1998	6,745,284	196,321	209,483	7,151,088	621,187	674,478	7,825,566
1997	6,270,705	183,800	178,551	6,633,056	546,015	592,755	7,225,811
1996	6,131,646	176,147	170,009	6,477,802	416,211	451,789	6,929,591
1995	5,690,903	171,948	201,303	6,064,154	393,573	417,203	6,481,357
1994	5,657,634	151,897	185,696	5,995,227	406,682	425,630	6,420,857
1993	5,000,430	129,063	157,886	5,287,379	381,433	393,615	5,680,994
1992	4,247,097	115,198	119,030	4,481,325	412,961	422,037	4,903,362
1991	3,605,779	108,751	98,643	3,813,173	539,556	551,499	4,364,672
1990	3,956,835	137,031	121,137	4,215,003	610,688	631,159	4,846,162
1989	4,113,467	145,104	144,728	4,403,299	514,532	537,921	4,941,220
1988	4,199,643	160,544	147,872	4,508,059	623,540	640,905	5,148,964
1987	3,790,606	133,872	130,260	4,054,738	840,297	857,636	4,912,374
1986	3,676,129	133,465	111,814	3,921,408	926,729	941,309	4,862,717
1985	3,629,080	139,756	133,581	3,902,417	768,625	779,281	4,681,698

SOURCE: Ward's AutoInfoBank.

Annual and Monthly Records for U.S. Production and Sales

RECORD U.S. PRODUCTION YEARS

Passenger Cars		Trucks	
Year	Units	Year	Units
1973	9,667,152	1999	7,387,029
1965	9,335,227	1998	6,448,290
1977	9,213,654	1997	6,196,654
1978	9,176,635	1996	5,747,322
1968	8,848,620	1995	5,655,281
1972	8,828,205	1994	5,638,068
1966	8,604,712	1993	4,873,342

RECORD U.S. RETAIL SALES YEARS

Passenger Cars		Trucks	
Year	Units	Year	Units
1986	11,459,518	1999	8,716,444
1973	11,423,851	1998	7,825,566
1978	11,314,079	1997	7,225,786
1977	11,183,412	1996	6,929,359
1985	11,042,287	1995	6,481,361
1972	10,940,482	1994	6,420,857
1979	10,672,768	1993	5,680,995

RECORD U.S. PRODUCTION BY MONTH

Month	Year	Units
Passenger Cars		
January	1973	917,273
February	1973	856,117
March	1965	963,101
April	1978	870,689
May	1973	941,019
June	1977	949,440
July	1965	740,576
August	1950	684,970
September	1972	758,578
October	1973	951,434
November	1965	913,146
December	1964	866,632
Trucks		
January	1999	534,620
February	1999	626,171
March	1999	717,743
April	1999	639,703
May	1999	658,772
June	1999	659,878
July	1999	365,279
August	1999	687,772
September	1999	647,573
October	1999	685,153
November	1999	613,129
December	1999	551,236

RECORD U.S. RETAIL SALES BY MONTH

Month	Year	Units
Passenger Cars		
January	1973	874,084
February	1973	918,681
March	1973	1,140,386
April	1978	1,043,341
May	1978	1,159,996
June	1978	1,138,504
July	1973	958,270
August	1986	1,000,658
September	1987	1,217,171
October	1972	1,068,400
November	1972	1,029,689
December	1987	995,415
Trucks		
January	1999	576,396
February	1999	654,429
March	1999	791,629
April	1999	714,842
May	1999	802,429
June	1999	820,446
July	1999	758,093
August	1999	724,960
September	1999	726,552
October	1999	708,264
November	1999	677,843
December	1999	760,561

U.S. FACTORY SALES MILESTONES

Passenger Cars		Trucks		Total Motor Vehicles	
Year	Units	Year	Units	Year	Units
1912	1 millionth	1915	100,000th	1906	100,000th
1920	10 millionth	1920	1 millionth	1912	1 millionth
1925	25 millionth	1929	5 millionth	1920	10 millionth
1935	50 millionth	1938	10 millionth	1931	50 millionth
1952	100 millionth	1949	20 millionth	1948	100 millionth
1960	150 millionth	1957	30 millionth	1955	150 millionth
1967	200 millionth	1965	40 millionth	1962	200 millionth
1973	250 millionth	1971	50 millionth	1968	250 millionth
1979	300 millionth	1979	75 millionth	1972	300 millionth
1986	350 millionth	1988	100 millionth	1982	400 millionth
1994	400 millionth	1998	150 millionth	1992	500 millionth

SOURCE: Ward's Communications.

Top Selling Vehicles and Automotive Color Popularity

TOP 20 SELLING PASSENGER CARS IN THE U.S., 1997-1999

1997		1998		1999	
Toyota Camry	397,156	Toyota Camry	429,575	Toyota Camry	448,162
Honda Accord	384,609	Honda Accord	401,071	Honda Accord	404,192
Ford Taurus	357,162	Ford Taurus	371,074	Ford Taurus	368,327
Honda Civic	315,546	Honda Civic	334,562	Honda Civic	318,308
Chevrolet Cavalier	302,161	Ford Escort	291,936	Chevrolet Cavalier	272,122
Ford Escort	283,898	Chevrolet Cavalier	256,099	Ford Escort	260,486
Saturn S	250,810	Toyota Corolla	250,501	Toyota Corolla	249,128
Chevrolet Lumina	228,451	Saturn S	231,522	Pontiac Grand Am	234,936
Toyota Corolla	218,461	Chevrolet Malibu	223,703	Chevrolet Malibu	218,540
Pontiac Grand Am	204,078	Pontiac Grand Am	180,428	Saturn S	207,977
Chevrolet Malibu	164,654	Chevrolet Lumina	177,631	Ford Mustang	166,915
Ford Contour	151,060	Ford Mustang	144,732	Buick Century	157,035
Buick Lesabre	150,744	Nissan Altima	144,451	Nissan Altima	153,525
Nissan Altima	144,483	Ford Contour	139,838	Buick Lesabre	149,445
Pontiac Grand Prix	142,018	Buick Lesabre	136,551	Pontiac Grand Prix	148,197
Nissan Maxima	123,215	Buick Century	126,220	Dodge Intrepid	144,355
Nissan Sentra	122,468	Pontiac Grand Prix	122,915	Ford Contour	134,487
Dodge Neon	121,854	Dodge Neon	117,964	Nissan Maxima	131,182
Dodge Intrepid	118,537	Mercury Grand Marquis	114,162	Volkswagen Jetta	130,054
Ford Mustang	116,610	Nissan Maxima	113,843	Mercury Grand Marquis	122,776

TOP 10 SELLING LIGHT TRUCKS IN THE U.S., 1997-1999

1997		1998		1999	
Ford F Series	710,156	Ford F Series	787,552	Ford F Series	806,579
Chevrolet C/K Pickup	527,842	Chevy C/K Pickup/Silverado	533,177	Chevy C/K Pickup/Silverado	628,391
Ford Explorer	383,852	Ford Explorer	431,488	Dodge Ram Pickup	428,930
Dodge Ram Pickup	350,257	Dodge Ram Pickup	410,130	Ford Explorer	428,772
Ford Ranger	298,796	Ford Ranger	328,136	Ford Ranger	348,358
Dodge Caravan	285,736	Dodge Caravan	293,819	Jeep Grand Cherokee	300,031
Jeep Grand Cherokee	260,875	Jeep Grand Cherokee	229,135	Dodge Caravan	293,100
Chevrolet S Blazer	221,400	Chevrolet S10 Pickup	228,093	Chevrolet S10 Pickup	233,669
Ford Expedition	214,524	Ford Expedition	225,703	Ford Expedition	233,125
Ford Windstar	205,356	Chevrolet S Blazer	219,710	Chevrolet S Blazer	232,140

Source: Ward's AutoInfoBank.

AUTOMOTIVE PAINT COLOR POPULARITY BY VEHICLE TYPE, 1999 MODEL YEAR

Luxury Cars		Full Size/Intermediate Cars		Compact/Sports Cars		Light Trucks	
Color	Percent	Color	Percent	Color	Percent	Color	Percent
Silver	14.8	White	15.4	Silver	16.2	White	26.2
Light Brown	12.9	Silver	14.1	Black	14.7	Black	11.2
White	10.3	Light Brown	14.0	White	14.0	Medium/Dark Green	11.0
Black	9.4	Medium/Dark Green	13.9	Medium/Dark Green	12.4	Medium/Dark Blue	8.4
Medium/Dark Gray	8.3	Black	11.7	Light Brown	8.5	Silver	7.7
Gold	7.0	Medium/Dark Blue	6.4	Medium/Dark Blue	8.5	Medium Red	7.4
Medium/Dark Green	6.1	Medium Red	5.7	Bright Red	7.5	Light Brown	6.2
Medium Red	6.0	Bright Red	4.9	Medium Red	7.0	Bright Red	6.1
White Metallic	5.8	Medium/Dark Gray	4.3	Dark Red	4.5	Medium/DarkGrey	3.2
Medium/Dark Blue	4.9	Gold	1.8	Light Green	1.7	Dark Red	3.1
Other	14.5	Other	7.8	Other	5.0	Other	9.5

Source: Du Pont Automotive Products.

Motor Vehicle Sales and Registrations in Canada

NEW MOTOR VEHICLE SALES IN CANADA, 1972-1999

Year	Passenger Cars			Commercial Vehicles			Total Vehicles
	Domestic[1]	Imports	Total	Domestic[1]	Imports	Total	
1999	620,880	185,560	806,440	676,243	57,696	733,939	1,540,379
1998	591,272	150,775	742,047	684,592	55,954	704,546	1,446,593
1997	629,488	109,062	738,550	628,214	57,616	685,830	1,424,380
1996	572,581	88,188	660,769	517,738	26,050	543,788	1,204,557
1995	553,265	116,925	670,190	469,590	26,755	496,345	1,166,535
1994	573,361	175,305	748,666	475,444	35,946	511,390	1,260,056
1993	493,759	245,290	739,049	402,112	51,773	453,885	1,192,934
1992	503,460	294,563	798,023	370,422	58,974	429,396	1,227,419
1991	573,297	299,887	873,184	347,671	66,935	414,606	1,287,790
1990	580,397	304,167	884,564	361,403	71,902	433,305	1,317,869
1989	675,340	312,794	988,134	422,398	73,343	495,741	1,483,875
1988	724,733	331,577	1,056,310	459,777	49,414	509,191	1,565,501
1987	700,930	364,163	1,065,093	417,189	51,355	468,544	1,533,637
1986	761,169	334,144	1,095,313	368,423	52,184	420,607	1,515,920
1985	794,965	342,251	1,137,216	344,871	48,323	393,194	1,530,410
1984	724,932	246,278	971,210	273,604	38,688	312,292	1,283,502
1983	625,088	218,230	843,318	192,609	45,161	237,770	1,081,088
1982	489,435	224,046	713,481	166,986	40,435	207,421	920,902
1981	646,942	257,253	904,195	250,775	35,912	288,687	1,190,882
1980	740,767	191,293	932,060	310,273	21,474	331,747	1,263,807
1979	863,554	139,454	1,003,008	381,562	11,832	393,394	1,396,402
1978	815,994	172,896	988,890	364,241	13,413	377,654	1,366,544
1977	797,752	193,646	991,398	337,914	15,647	353,561	1,344,959
1976	793,201	153,287	946,488	331,027	13,948	344,975	1,291,463
1975	835,679	153,601	989,280	310,590	16,759	327,349	1,316,629
1972	653,933	205,026	858,959	189,577	17,085	206,662	1,065,621

TOTAL REGISTRATIONS BY PROVINCE, 1998

Province	Total Registrations by Type			
	Passenger Cars	Trucks	Vehicles Buses	Total
Newfoundland	219,143	91,002	2,568	312,713
Prince Edward Island	57,505	25,486	439	83,430
Nova Scotia	356,544	177,562	1,785	535,891
New Brunswick	336,028	141,721	2466	480,215
Quebec	3,285,742	539,189	16,491	3,841,422
Ontario	5,369,972	1,159,878	27,474	6,557,324
Manitoba	437,527	178,704	112	616,343
Saskatchewan	481,830	316,753	4,160	802,743
Alberta	1,669,952	380,809	12,529	2,063,290
British Columbia	1,647,900	597,319	0.0	2,245,219
Yukon	8,383	16,236	218	24,837
Northwest Territories	15,063	771	56	15,890
Nunavut	1,681	388	9	2,078
Total	13,887,270	3,625,818	68,307	17,581,395

TOTAL REGISTRATIONS IN CANADA, 1974-1998

Year	Passenger Cars (000)	Commercial Vehicles (000)	Total (000)
1998	13,887	3,694	17,581
1997	13,487	3,591	17,078
1996	13,217	3,644	16,861
1995	13,183	3,485	16,668
1994	13,122	3,466	16,588
1992	12,781	3,413	16,194
1990	12,622	3,931	16,553
1988	12,086	3,766	15,852
1986	11,586	3,213	14,799
1984	10,781	3,099	13,880
1982	10,530	3,293	13,823
1980	10,256	2,955	13,211
1978	9,745	2,771	12,516
1976	9,016	2,319	11,335
1974	8,472	2,028	10,500

(1) Units produced in the United States, Canada and Mexico.
SOURCE: Statistics Canada.

Motor Vehicle Sales in Canada and Mexico

MOTOR VEHICLE SALES IN CANADA, 1999

	Passenger Cars			Commercial Vehicles			Total		
	Domestic*	Import	Total	Domestic*	Import	Total	Domestic*	Import	Total
Auto Vaz	0	38	38	0	73	73	0	111	111
BMW	654	8,268	8,922	89	1,210	1,299	743	9,478	10,221
Chrysler Corp.	84,616	0	84,616	180,201	0	180,201	264,817	0	264,817
Daewoo	0	2,504	2,504	0	0	0	0	2,504	2,504
Ford Motor Co.	88,311	9,745	98,056	194,623	0	194,623	282,934	9,745	292,679
Fuji	6,481	2,440	8,921	0	4,097	4,097	6,481	6,537	13,018
General Motors	257,746	1,929	259,675	216,003	0	216,003	473,749	1,929	475,678
Honda	90,044	14,383	104,427	12,465	14,511	26,976	102,509	28,894	131,403
Hyundai	0	30,367	30,367	0	0	0	0	30,367	30,367
Isuzu	0	0	0	1,054	191	1,245	1,054	191	1,245
Kia Motors	0	851	851	0	566	566	0	1,417	1,417
Mack	0	0	0	2,858	120	2,978	2,858	120	2,978
Mazda	4,643	27,312	31,955	4,690	4,034	9,324	9,333	31,946	41,279
Mercedes Benz	0	7,448	7,448	16,179	0	16,179	16,179	7,448	23,627
Navistar	0	0	0	9,940	0	9,940	9,940	0	9,940
Nissan	12,223	9,364	21,587	4,679	11,634	16,313	16,902	20,998	37,900
PACCAR	0	0	0	5,511	0	5,511	5,511	0	5,511
Porsche	0	1,021	1,021	0	0	0	0	1,021	1,021
Suzuki	1,544	3,411	4,955	2,102	4,155	6,257	3,646	7,566	11,212
Toyota	46,016	48,198	94,214	19,306	16,344	35,650	65,322	64,542	129,864
Volkswagen	28,602	18,281	46,883	0	161	161	28,602	18,442	47,044
Volvo Truck	0	0	0	4,426	0	4,426	4,426	0	4,426
Western Star	0	0	0	2,117	0	2,117	2,117	0	2,117
Total	**620,880**	**185,560**	**806,440**	**676,243**	**57,696**	**733,939**	**1,297,123**	**243,256**	**1,540,379**

MOTOR VEHICLE SALES IN MEXICO, 1999

	Passenger Cars			Commercial Vehicles			Total		
	Domestic*	Import	Total	Domestic*	Import	Total	Domestic*	Import	Total
BMW	1,987	537	2,524	0	272	272	1,987	809	2,796
Chrysler Corp.	47,472	0	47,472	42,967	0	42,967	90,439	0	90,439
Dina Camiones	0	0	0	1,838	0	1,838	1,838	0	1,838
Ford Motor Co.	38,863	9,221	48,084	67,461	0	67,461	106,324	9,221	115,545
General Motors	116,820	363	117,183	59,066	5,160	64,226	175,886	5,523	181,409
Honda	18,219	602	18,821	370	0	370	18,589	602	19,191
Mercedes Benz	723	1,809	2,532	8,651	2	8,653	9,374	1,811	11,185
Navistar	0	0	0	5,349	0	5,349	5,349	0	5,349
Nissan	103,871	2,496	106,367	34,286	3,449	37,735	138,157	5,945	144,102
Oshmex Truck	0	0	0	526	0	526	526	0	526
PACCAR	0	0	0	4,887	0	4,887	4,887	0	4,887
Porsche	9	0	9	0	0	0	9	0	9
Scania AB	0	0	0	288	0	288	288	0	288
Volkswagen	78,332	42,234	120,566	0	5,516	5,516	78,332	47,750	126,082
Volvo Truck	0	0	0	1,229	0	1,229	1,229	0	1,229
Total	**406,296**	**57,262**	**463,558**	**226,918**	**14,399**	**241,317**	**633,214**	**71,661**	**704,875**

*Units produced in U.S., Canada and Mexico.
SOURCE: Ward's AutoInfoBank, AMIA, ANPACT.

New Passenger Car and Truck Registrations by State

NEW PASSENGER CAR AND TRUCK REGISTRATIONS BY STATE, 1998-1999

State	Passenger Cars		Trucks		Total	
	1998	1999	1998	1999	1998	1999
Alabama	98,989	104,320	119,226	129,370	218,215	233,690
Alaska	10,335	11,024	19,608	20,990	29,943	32,014
Arizona	122,541	136,856	145,315	164,976	267,856	301,832
Arkansas	48,572	54,451	83,838	92,711	132,410	147,162
California	914,376	994,487	755,606	867,184	1,669,982	1,861,671
Colorado	111,669	125,700	143,838	173,248	255,507	298,948
Connecticut	116,681	117,752	78,105	86,810	194,786	204,562
Delaware	30,719	30,292	29,936	31,428	60,655	61,720
Florida	740,223	760,686	487,096	524,497	1,227,319	1,285,183
Georgia	216,098	245,935	240,101	297,492	456,199	543,427
Hawaii	40,248	41,140	25,717	30,263	65,965	71,403
Idaho	16,558	17,518	31,658	36,932	48,216	54,450
Illinois	415,045	410,130	334,787	348,020	749,832	758,150
Indiana	146,440	154,578	158,658	184,866	305,098	339,444
Iowa	54,583	59,603	75,458	83,384	130,041	142,987
Kansas	56,082	58,322	72,338	78,153	128,420	136,475
Kentucky	82,677	83,567	91,871	92,459	174,548	176,026
Louisianna	108,054	112,496	135,598	141,903	243,652	254,399
Maine	24,622	25,049	31,802	34,764	56,424	59,813
Maryland	207,143	223,951	150,407	168,020	357,550	391,971
Massachusetts	204,030	217,151	144,306	167,052	348,336	384,203
Michigan	373,043	378,368	438,916	499,635	811,959	878,003
Minnesota	130,692	141,677	153,004	171,905	283,696	313,582
Mississippi	51,182	52,011	71,854	72,590	123,036	124,601
Missouri	154,593	152,791	176,346	161,691	330,939	314,482
Montana	12,800	12,935	26,454	27,646	39,254	40,581
Nebraska	35,049	37,543	49,787	53,275	84,836	90,818
Nevada	66,331	62,858	61,189	62,992	127,520	125,850
New Hampshire	41,910	44,849	45,136	50,101	87,046	94,950
New Jersey	348,559	361,413	220,432	239,375	568,991	600,788
New Mexico	39,907	41,023	51,738	50,570	91,645	91,593
New York	485,436	508,876	344,747	396,155	830,183	905,031
North Carolina	211,070	219,470	230,442	255,499	441,512	474,969
North Dakota	9,181	9,570	17,779	19,300	26,960	28,870
Ohio	398,906	426,350	351,658	400,328	750,564	826,678
Oklahoma	62,342	64,760	98,424	112,929	160,766	177,689
Oregon	79,272	78,992	101,247	104,919	180,519	183,911
Pennsylvania	359,824	401,637	291,025	341,037	650,849	742,674
Rhode Island	31,043	30,655	17,944	19,206	48,987	49,861
South Carolina	91,527	98,345	102,126	117,634	193,653	215,979
South Dakota	11,821	11,825	21,067	22,977	32,888	34,802
Tennessee	143,639	145,521	159,887	165,333	303,526	310,854
Texas	549,276	570,811	698,656	754,221	1,247,932	1,325,032
Utah	43,789	44,787	61,132	60,529	104,921	105,316
Vermont	17,033	17,473	20,815	22,569	37,848	40,042
Virginia	208,519	236,087	161,753	185,879	370,272	421,966
Washington	116,230	121,371	137,440	143,941	253,670	265,312
West Virginia	37,804	39,679	47,031	48,879	84,835	88,558
Wisconsin	135,708	140,874	165,007	175,976	300,715	316,850
Wyoming	6,656	6,733	15,498	14,753	22,154	21,486
District of Colombia	10,421	11,537	4,106	4,599	14,527	16,136
Federal Government*	13,488	16,249	33,608	18,597	47,096	34,846
Total	8,042,736	8,472,078	7,731,517	8,529,562	15,774,253	17,001,640

*Federal government registrations not included in any state.
Source: The Polk Company. Permission for further use must be obtained from The Polk Company.

New Passenger Car Registrations by Manufacturer and State

NEW PASSENGER CAR REGISTRATIONS BY MANUFACTURER AND STATE, 1999

STATE	Chrysler	Dodge	Eagle	Plymouth	Total DCC	Ford	Lincoln	Mercury	Total Ford
Alabama	2,482	3,847	2	1,099	7,430	14,197	2,055	4,215	20,467
Alaska	208	668	0	329	1,205	1,905	71	444	2,420
Arizona	3,629	8,330	3	2,251	14,213	16,648	1,964	5,752	24,364
Arkansas	1,686	2,813	2	716	5,217	7,281	1,117	2,705	11,103
California *	23,298	32,336	4	9,507	65,145	111,167	10,063	27,716	148,946
Colorado	2,627	5,896	1	1,687	10,211	16,537	1,080	4,739	22,356
Connecticut	2,982	3,338	2	1,027	7,349	9,437	1,060	3,222	13,719
Delaware	1,359	1,563	3	653	3,578	3,353	388	1,179	4,920
Florida	21,592	26,327	1	9,043	56,963	74,284	17,023	33,164	124,471
Georgia	7,014	8,942	5	3,019	18,980	37,736	4,947	10,320	53,003
Hawaii	1,076	3,707	0	1,901	6,684	4,886	488	1,078	6,452
Idaho	434	810	0	340	1,584	2,281	217	506	3,004
Illinois	15,482	21,626	1	5,115	42,224	52,851	6,424	18,572	77,847
Indiana	6,428	7,832	3	2,622	16,885	19,723	2,318	6,676	28,717
Iowa	2,241	3,207	0	765	6,213	8,376	848	2,905	12,129
Kansas	2,426	3,001	1	770	6,198	9,760	1,089	2,432	13,281
Kentucky	2,018	3,853	1	1,148	7,020	12,369	1,258	3,681	17,308
Louisianna	2,572	4,662	2	1,173	8,409	15,769	2,544	5,809	24,122
Maine	535	1,052	2	226	1,815	3,378	161	1,138	4,677
Maryland	5,873	13,067	2	3,520	22,462	27,919	2,515	7,942	38,376
Massachusetts	5,039	6,277	7	2,140	13,463	21,672	2,311	9,149	33,132
Michigan	19,762	19,364	2	5,531	44,659	62,221	15,089	24,904	102,214
Minnesota	3,946	8,165	2	1,512	13,625	17,322	1,259	5,080	23,661
Mississippi	1,288	1,660	1	399	3,348	7,935	1,172	2,719	11,826
Missouri	5,086	9,664	12	3,186	17,948	26,285	2,374	7,165	35,824
Montana	335	666	0	159	1,160	2,104	92	431	2,627
Nebraska	1,432	2,016	0	715	4,163	4,908	453	1,276	6,637
Nevada	1,834	3,334	1	901	6,070	7,311	1,049	2,716	11,076
New Hampshire	902	1,623	0	477	3,002	5,099	388	1,726	7,213
New Jersey	8,783	9,745	3	3,940	22,471	40,734	6,528	17,965	65,227
New Mexico	1,015	2,166	0	742	3,923	5,965	521	1,754	8,240
New York	13,659	18,192	4	6,086	37,941	47,629	9,511	16,919	74,059
North Carolina	5,923	8,936	1	2,301	17,161	34,169	2,910	6,718	43,797
North Dakota	320	595	0	301	1,216	1,237	119	633	1,989
Ohio	15,067	18,046	5	5,587	38,705	58,021	6,211	18,105	82,337
Oklahoma	2,060	3,665	3	1,085	6,813	9,842	1,588	3,386	14,816
Oregon	1,787	2,836	0	1,315	5,938	10,992	644	2,347	13,983
Pennsylvania	14,331	18,535	9	7,439	40,314	47,714	4,439	14,996	67,149
Rhode Island	786	1,285	0	332	2,403	3,053	308	1,377	4,738
South Carolina	2,687	4,008	2	1,118	7,815	14,996	1,899	3,917	20,812
South Dakota	440	538	0	133	1,111	1,622	148	379	2,149
Tennessee	3,406	6,328	1	1,901	11,636	19,012	2,427	6,194	27,633
Texas	13,567	23,701	9	8,233	45,510	88,634	9,423	25,492	123,549
Utah	963	2,414	2	622	4,001	5,679	399	1,543	7,621
Vermont	263	611	0	274	1,148	2,099	95	637	2,831
Virginia	6,023	10,086	5	3,726	19,840	29,420	2,379	9,032	40,831
Washington	2,461	3,824	0	1,097	7,382	16,239	916	3,279	20,434
West Virginia	1,359	1,968	1	936	4,264	5,772	310	1,157	7,239
Wisconsin	5,441	7,733	1	2,465	15,640	17,639	1,557	5,659	24,855
Wyoming	225	293	0	112	630	734	79	284	1,097
District of Colombia	302	238	0	84	624	763	240	390	1,393
Federal Government	104	288	0	6,527	6,919	8,016	104	177	8,297
TOTAL	246,558	355,677	106	118,287	720,628	1,074,695	134,572	341,701	1,550,968

SOURCE: The Polk Company. Permission for further use must be obtained from The Polk Company.

New Passenger Car Registrations by Manufacturer and State

NEW PASSENGER CAR REGISTRATIONS BY MANUFACTURER AND STATE, 1999 — continued

STATE	Buick	Cadillac	Chevrolet	Oldsmobile	Pontiac	Saturn	Total GM	Acura	Honda	Total Honda
Alabama	6,615	2,513	12,039	3,491	6,504	2,221	33,383	1,250	9,545	10,795
Alaska	309	63	1,052	209	969	404	3,006	60	529	589
Arizona	5,931	3,464	12,572	3,208	6,230	3,185	34,590	1,626	12,770	14,396
Arkansas	3,167	1,456	6,626	1,769	4,308	1,172	18,498	436	5,143	5,579
California *	26,994	13,158	61,050	20,307	34,321	26,586	182,416	19,950	135,848	155,798
Colorado	4,938	1,790	12,471	2,844	7,756	5,745	35,544	1,775	9,827	11,602
Connecticut	4,856	1,290	8,071	2,643	3,670	2,374	22,904	2,841	12,255	15,096
Delaware	1,295	359	2,734	959	1,775	651	7,773	440	2,800	3,240
Florida	47,670	18,029	89,898	29,146	37,117	16,654	238,514	10,781	50,670	61,451
Georgia	9,410	4,132	19,329	6,034	14,359	4,935	58,199	4,163	25,093	29,256
Hawaii	1,173	189	3,775	1,317	2,589	854	9,897	510	4,154	4,664
Idaho	886	238	1,820	371	1,356	529	5,200	126	1,442	1,568
Illinois	25,967	8,026	48,688	16,289	36,981	11,002	146,953	4,019	24,416	28,435
Indiana	12,491	3,440	22,000	8,317	17,595	5,347	69,190	702	9,339	10,041
Iowa	6,097	1,081	8,997	3,076	5,732	1,580	26,563	257	3,004	3,261
Kansas	3,662	991	5,912	2,072	4,910	1,765	19,312	980	4,850	5,830
Kentucky	4,864	1,584	10,007	2,760	5,222	1,853	26,290	555	5,708	6,263
Louisianna	5,564	1,940	11,919	3,524	7,638	3,164	33,749	998	10,251	11,249
Maine	1,334	168	2,265	718	1,343	708	6,536	43	1,599	1,642
Maryland	8,753	2,777	23,180	5,802	12,608	5,667	58,787	3,817	19,598	23,415
Massachusetts	9,122	2,727	14,841	5,033	7,505	5,891	45,119	2,979	20,213	23,192
Michigan	27,875	14,166	46,733	25,054	45,102	11,466	170,396	1,321	12,931	14,252
Minnesota	13,570	1,974	18,109	9,221	13,865	4,912	61,651	1,136	7,393	8,529
Mississippi	3,156	1,281	5,463	1,965	3,953	964	16,782	397	3,089	3,486
Missouri	9,305	2,679	19,412	6,425	13,520	4,052	55,393	1,321	8,712	10,033
Montana	907	207	1,257	507	1,026	82	3,986	39	773	812
Nebraska	3,472	613	4,486	2,346	3,179	1,008	15,104	301	2,563	2,864
Nevada	2,587	1,249	6,179	2,509	3,073	2,752	18,349	591	3,683	4,274
New Hampshire	1,576	394	3,740	958	2,009	858	9,535	441	3,951	4,392
New Jersey	14,146	6,297	26,617	10,226	16,191	9,190	82,667	7,864	28,439	36,303
New Mexico	2,026	576	4,777	1,767	3,597	973	13,716	296	3,052	3,348
New York	21,748	7,355	44,403	17,096	22,895	14,875	128,372	8,552	48,474	57,026
North Carolina	12,317	3,893	20,598	5,006	11,565	4,786	58,165	3,169	22,819	25,988
North Dakota	1,083	221	1,392	573	1,014	243	4,526	11	561	572
Ohio	26,958	8,660	55,900	17,965	38,383	10,885	158,751	3,784	35,748	39,532
Oklahoma	3,833	1,449	7,551	1,737	5,958	1,413	21,941	535	5,357	5,892
Oregon	2,863	1,053	4,679	1,697	2,984	1,574	14,850	1,721	9,799	11,520
Pennsylvania	21,513	6,233	47,424	14,739	28,823	10,186	128,918	5,437	29,162	34,599
Rhode Island	1,175	303	1,705	685	1,442	1,101	6,411	466	2,966	3,432
South Carolina	6,134	2,010	9,376	3,100	6,070	2,341	29,031	932	10,245	11,177
South Dakota	1,413	237	1,578	665	1,280	296	5,469	18	862	880
Tennessee	8,375	3,374	15,370	4,285	9,316	4,606	45,326	1,520	11,144	12,664
Texas	24,123	11,316	62,362	13,934	35,978	14,293	162,006	7,682	50,492	58,174
Utah	1,693	504	4,160	1,082	2,885	1,496	11,820	412	4,425	4,837
Vermont	749	99	1,610	463	805	392	4,118	123	1,639	1,762
Virginia	10,023	3,238	22,829	9,050	15,285	4,957	65,382	3,844	22,206	26,050
Washington	4,769	1,266	9,776	2,679	5,241	4,406	28,137	2,429	13,441	15,870
West Virginia	2,548	573	6,517	1,424	3,630	713	15,405	123	2,267	2,390
Wisconsin	11,540	2,335	18,555	5,875	14,855	5,140	58,300	1,160	8,386	9,546
Wyoming	533	170	736	273	644	475	2,831	16	462	478
District of Colombia	250	204	825	136	141	218	1,774	207	1,214	1,421
Federal Government	68	14	173	49	70	1	375	5	157	162
TOTAL	433,426	153,358	853,538	283,380	535,267	222,941	2,481,910	114,161	725,466	839,627

SOURCE: The Polk Company. Permission for further use must be obtained from The Polk Company.

New Passenger Car Registrations by Manufacturer and State

NEW PASSENGER CAR REGISTRATIONS BY MANUFACTURER AND STATE, 1999 — continued

STATE	Infiniti	Nissan	Total Nissan	Lexus	Toyota	Total Toyota	Mazda	Mitsubishi	Mercedes	Others	TOTAL
Alabama	632	4,317	4,949	1,030	10,605	11,635	3,156	2,800	1,507	8,198	104,320
Alaska	4	161	165	25	618	643	160	72	79	2,685	11,024
Arizona	1,937	10,356	12,293	1,953	12,630	14,583	2,421	2,134	1,870	15,992	136,856
Arkansas	255	1,940	2,195	453	4,513	4,966	1,168	793	426	4,506	54,451
California *	10,027	37,828	47,855	20,399	140,761	161,160	19,650	22,721	31,803	158,993	994,487
Colorado	545	4,946	5,491	1,133	9,118	10,251	2,639	2,409	1,018	24,179	125,700
Connecticut	685	7,787	8,472	1,294	10,676	11,970	2,375	3,741	2,659	29,467	117,752
Delaware	124	1,522	1,646	258	2,060	2,318	1,039	369	570	4,839	30,292
Florida	5,085	36,723	41,808	10,212	78,338	88,550	19,443	36,041	14,470	78,975	760,686
Georgia	1,753	12,735	14,488	2,792	25,772	28,564	6,595	6,046	4,128	26,676	245,935
Hawaii	194	2,989	3,183	468	4,366	4,834	676	110	606	4,034	41,140
Idaho	8	529	537	104	1,387	1,491	422	270	143	3,299	17,518
Illinois	2,297	13,437	15,734	4,358	28,674	33,032	6,048	6,159	5,120	48,578	410,130
Indiana	376	3,330	3,706	798	8,294	9,092	1,718	2,770	1,010	11,449	154,578
Iowa	116	1,359	1,475	295	3,470	3,765	922	769	262	4,244	59,603
Kansas	252	1,196	1,448	457	5,249	5,706	1,186	830	451	4,080	58,322
Kentucky	434	2,800	3,234	608	11,233	11,841	1,873	2,033	751	6,954	83,567
Louisianna	664	4,665	5,329	1,143	12,755	13,898	4,323	3,720	1,270	6,427	112,496
Maine	58	758	816	98	2,217	2,315	723	290	153	6,082	25,049
Maryland	815	9,443	10,258	2,124	23,623	25,747	5,598	5,405	3,669	30,234	223,951
Massachusetts	1,243	10,698	11,941	2,291	27,379	29,670	4,220	3,561	3,527	49,326	217,151
Michigan	355	3,713	4,068	1,670	11,051	12,721	3,772	1,766	2,319	22,201	378,368
Minnesota	286	2,685	2,971	753	8,382	9,135	2,749	1,949	891	16,516	141,677
Mississippi	300	2,781	3,081	386	5,125	5,511	2,623	1,120	538	3,696	52,011
Missouri	889	4,738	5,627	872	9,672	10,544	2,977	2,245	1,140	11,060	152,791
Montana	6	304	310	34	730	764	156	240	73	2,807	12,935
Nebraska	69	1,105	1,174	297	2,292	2,589	1,208	569	232	3,003	37,543
Nevada	523	3,154	3,677	635	6,146	6,781	1,056	2,215	794	8,566	62,858
New Hampshire	72	2,600	2,672	237	5,335	5,572	746	596	505	10,616	44,849
New Jersey	3,904	20,573	24,477	5,589	34,320	39,909	8,111	7,264	10,209	64,775	361,413
New Mexico	225	1,233	1,458	309	2,904	3,213	784	934	248	5,159	41,023
New York	4,587	32,568	37,155	7,260	44,870	52,130	8,040	11,354	11,785	91,014	508,876
North Carolina	825	10,631	11,456	2,156	21,119	23,275	8,287	4,945	3,268	23,128	219,470
North Dakota	1	136	137	24	458	482	102	42	33	471	9,570
Ohio	2,205	10,169	12,374	3,380	37,432	40,812	5,814	6,681	3,608	37,736	426,350
Oklahoma	313	2,609	2,922	739	4,520	5,259	1,530	1,062	627	3,898	64,760
Oregon	232	1,880	2,112	688	8,874	9,562	1,903	1,111	1,049	16,964	78,992
Pennsylvania	1,389	15,443	16,832	2,893	30,340	33,233	7,058	5,594	5,108	62,832	401,637
Rhode Island	245	1,816	2,061	263	3,326	3,589	875	603	445	6,098	30,655
South Carolina	585	3,715	4,300	919	9,238	10,157	3,506	2,076	1,549	7,922	98,345
South Dakota	6	167	173	30	673	703	209	142	73	916	11,825
Tennessee	838	9,142	9,980	1,478	13,097	14,575	4,847	3,524	1,570	13,766	145,521
Texas	4,699	24,706	29,405	8,770	49,261	58,031	18,013	12,818	8,593	54,712	570,811
Utah	204	1,812	2,016	303	3,868	4,171	1,177	1,019	265	7,860	44,787
Vermont	44	684	728	14	1,561	1,575	345	115	98	4,753	17,473
Virginia	960	11,080	12,040	2,024	22,057	24,081	6,542	4,782	3,363	33,176	236,087
Washington	464	4,130	4,594	1,404	10,962	12,366	3,025	1,943	1,620	26,000	121,371
West Virginia	16	1,052	1,068	128	3,120	3,248	383	520	312	4,850	39,679
Wisconsin	344	2,234	2,578	724	10,847	11,571	2,247	1,405	909	13,823	140,874
Wyoming	2	198	200	17	447	464	61	46	30	896	6,733
District of Colombia	43	524	567	121	1,293	1,414	577	152	365	3,250	11,537
Federal Government	4	28	32	4	107	111	17	7	39	290	16,249
TOTAL	52,139	347,129	399,268	96,414	787,165	883,579	185,095	181,882	137,150	1,091,971	8,472,078

SOURCE: The Polk Company. Permission for further use must be obtained from The Polk Company.

New Truck Registrations by Manufacturer and State

NEW TRUCK REGISTRATIONS BY MANUFACTURER AND STATE, 1999

State	Chrysler	Dodge	Jeep	Plymouth	Total DCC	Ford	Lincoln	Mercury
Alabama	695	13,048	6,309	1,017	**21,069**	35,429	580	1,146
Alaska	49	2,860	826	203	**3,938**	6,464	46	160
Arizona	857	21,740	7,031	1,724	**31,352**	42,569	684	731
Arkansas	446	15,932	4,221	597	**21,196**	22,474	339	582
California	4,175	96,405	41,451	11,092	**153,123**	243,222	5,085	6,649
Colorado	799	20,464	13,802	1,363	**36,428**	55,262	532	1,406
Connecticut	982	11,819	10,637	2,153	**25,591**	17,602	312	801
Delaware	282	4,534	2,828	719	**8,363**	7,058	110	346
Florida	4,513	63,213	24,925	11,460	**104,111**	141,468	3,633	5,587
Georgia	2,733	31,687	16,427	3,624	**54,471**	99,731	2,002	3,309
Hawaii	55	2,955	1,848	868	**5,726**	6,635	66	265
Idaho	156	5,705	1,152	364	**7,377**	11,309	103	153
Illinois	4,368	55,715	24,999	6,552	**91,634**	82,662	1,697	4,647
Indiana	1,759	24,789	9,901	2,886	**39,335**	46,284	582	2,352
Iowa	1,335	13,050	3,378	1,109	**18,872**	21,746	170	955
Kansas	1,019	11,022	4,684	1,578	**18,303**	23,400	291	691
Kentucky	620	13,419	4,926	1,043	**20,008**	24,999	356	816
Louisiana	407	18,785	5,308	1,524	**26,024**	38,803	860	1,176
Maine	208	4,969	2,430	270	**7,877**	8,592	64	239
Maryland	1,399	25,839	12,764	3,835	**43,837**	42,139	656	1,395
Massachusetts	1,510	24,192	16,225	3,549	**45,476**	38,571	606	2,010
Michigan	5,547	61,045	48,508	8,282	**123,382**	146,353	2,834	14,212
Minnesota	2,119	24,064	9,092	3,783	**39,058**	48,725	435	1,681
Mississippi	283	8,114	2,888	536	**11,821**	21,972	348	755
Missouri	1,385	23,365	8,002	2,526	**35,278**	48,151	602	1,634
Montana	110	4,968	858	232	**6,168**	7,857	65	151
Nebraska	688	6,704	2,270	1,125	**10,787**	14,726	123	443
Nevada	202	8,534	3,355	673	**12,764**	17,045	374	674
New Hampshire	343	7,078	4,562	842	**12,825**	12,953	121	410
New Jersey	2,352	28,053	22,406	5,108	**57,919**	61,056	1,272	4,326
New Mexico	207	6,766	2,537	451	**9,961**	15,037	160	357
New York	3,886	51,585	46,401	10,071	**111,943**	85,381	1,898	5,594
North Carolina	2,628	32,037	14,868	3,614	**53,147**	71,627	1,019	1,344
North Dakota	233	2,630	682	219	**3,764**	5,538	36	237
Ohio	4,652	51,100	27,605	8,787	**92,144**	105,807	1,580	6,025
Oklahoma	675	15,091	3,151	1,231	**20,148**	26,423	420	689
Oregon	619	14,945	5,838	2,164	**23,566**	32,635	317	553
Pennsylvania	3,790	48,516	31,942	8,499	**92,747**	84,718	1,361	3,636
Rhode Island	122	3,046	1,352	556	**5,076**	4,850	59	295
South Carolina	828	14,570	6,174	1,990	**23,562**	32,917	512	1,016
South Dakota	305	3,074	1,010	264	**4,653**	7,182	42	165
Tennessee	983	18,698	8,741	2,062	**30,484**	42,326	627	1,491
Texas	3,147	92,874	29,488	9,161	**134,670**	242,243	4,375	6,070
Utah	203	9,570	4,604	375	**14,752**	15,405	162	251
Vermont	138	3,432	1,533	380	**5,483**	5,148	37	151
Virginia	1,853	23,032	13,981	4,068	**42,934**	46,590	623	1,669
Washington	918	19,576	7,966	2,171	**30,631**	43,106	460	900
West Virginia	339	6,432	3,704	794	**11,269**	11,636	102	250
Wisconsin	2,568	28,816	10,002	5,113	**46,499**	40,833	468	1,991
Wyoming	47	2,657	480	90	**3,274**	4,185	47	92
District of Columbia	74	443	567	100	**1,184**	998	29	109
Federal Government	15	7,529	1,635	67	**9,246**	4,988	5	22
TOTAL	**69,626**	**1,110,486**	**542,274**	**142,864**	**1,865,250**	**2,324,830**	**39,287**	**92,609**

Note: Toyota includes Lexus, Nissan includes Infiniti. *PACCAR is Kenworth and Peterbilt.
Source: The Polk Co. Further use prohibited without written permission from The Polk Company.

New Truck Registrations by Manufacturer and State

NEW TRUCK REGISTRATIONS BY MANUFACTURER AND STATE, 1999 — continued

State	Total Ford	Cadillac	Chevrolet	GMC	Olds	Pontiac	Total GM	Toyota
Alabama	37,155	421	29,046	9,902	719	597	40,685	8,822
Alaska	6,670	27	4,308	1,631	178	87	6,231	1,113
Arizona	43,984	544	31,671	13,682	925	642	47,464	12,949
Arkansas	23,395	331	21,539	8,864	392	423	31,549	3,991
California	254,956	2,549	139,975	44,936	2,921	3,811	194,192	122,053
Colorado	57,200	562	27,191	10,791	761	930	40,235	12,849
Connecticut	18,715	129	14,858	3,339	608	380	19,314	7,009
Delaware	7,514	41	5,387	1,662	265	235	7,590	1,313
Florida	150,688	1,445	92,478	25,619	4,825	4,614	128,981	43,791
Georgia	105,042	780	54,241	18,177	1,410	1,865	76,473	18,095
Hawaii	6,966	26	3,708	803	270	460	5,267	4,514
Idaho	11,565	69	7,266	3,936	137	128	11,536	2,145
Illinois	89,006	751	67,840	17,683	4,633	3,853	94,760	16,117
Indiana	49,218	495	44,931	16,569	3,702	2,807	68,504	5,548
Iowa	22,871	170	21,046	4,524	1,154	842	27,736	2,258
Kansas	24,382	158	16,663	5,296	744	545	23,406	3,635
Kentucky	26,171	214	21,511	4,362	707	607	27,401	7,342
Louisiana	40,839	289	33,081	13,535	548	623	48,076	9,157
Maine	8,895	25	6,174	5,285	185	140	11,809	1,823
Maryland	44,190	328	29,826	7,080	1,149	925	39,308	12,661
Massachusetts	41,187	267	21,848	8,832	893	824	32,664	16,067
Michigan	163,399	2,842	109,489	50,100	8,860	9,919	181,210	8,318
Minnesota	50,841	263	43,770	10,117	1,566	1,670	57,386	4,276
Mississippi	23,075	230	16,008	6,352	338	252	23,180	4,512
Missouri	50,387	324	35,969	10,665	1,539	1,489	49,986	5,721
Montana	8,073	61	5,745	2,785	125	128	8,844	1,136
Nebraska	15,292	169	12,079	3,011	713	445	16,417	1,510
Nevada	18,093	325	10,317	4,717	353	298	16,010	5,451
New Hampshire	13,484	63	8,435	2,553	258	174	11,483	4,441
New Jersey	66,654	542	31,964	13,080	1,554	1,706	48,846	17,066
New Mexico	15,554	151	10,029	4,378	302	258	15,118	3,541
New York	92,873	802	65,547	20,908	3,471	3,157	93,885	26,123
North Carolina	73,990	592	51,912	11,557	1,613	1,306	66,980	16,779
North Dakota	5,811	39	5,937	1,538	208	168	7,890	387
Ohio	113,412	858	85,359	25,549	5,642	4,226	121,634	21,682
Oklahoma	27,532	213	26,945	8,532	442	610	36,742	3,372
Oregon	33,505	213	15,145	4,838	358	576	21,130	10,246
Pennsylvania	89,715	605	62,895	18,978	3,429	2,643	88,550	19,418
Rhode Island	5,204	27	2,077	1,094	72	111	3,381	1,401
South Carolina	34,445	282	27,181	6,747	832	819	35,861	7,257
South Dakota	7,389	45	5,957	1,729	197	196	8,124	621
Tennessee	44,444	586	31,024	11,943	1,078	830	45,461	10,127
Texas	252,688	1,953	178,290	44,625	2,724	2,360	229,952	40,713
Utah	15,818	188	10,929	3,896	219	212	15,444	4,267
Vermont	5,336	18	4,579	1,392	140	113	6,242	1,999
Virginia	48,882	342	29,889	8,979	1,415	1,975	42,600	16,423
Washington	44,466	283	23,756	6,536	565	856	31,996	12,849
West Virginia	11,988	62	12,206	2,906	419	318	15,911	4,289
Wisconsin	43,292	321	42,951	12,023	2,331	2,218	59,844	6,633
Wyoming	4,324	52	3,041	1,966	93	81	5,233	671
District of Columbia	1,136	21	511	100	21	13	666	499
Federal Government	5,015	2	2,370	735	4	6	3,117	70
TOTAL	2,456,726	22,095	1,666,894	530,837	68,007	64,471	2,352,304	575,050

Note: Toyota includes Lexus, Nissan includes Infiniti. *PACCAR is Kenworth and Peterbilt.
Source: The Polk Co. Further use prohibited without written permission from The Polk Company.

New Truck Registrations by Manufacturer and State

NEW TRUCK REGISTRATIONS BY MANUFACTURER AND STATE, 1999 — continued

State	Nissan	Freightliner	Mack	Navistar	PACCAR*	Volvo	Other	Total
Alabama	4,772	1,784	958	2,349	1,192	587	9,997	129,370
Alaska	326	119	12	208	161	14	2,198	20,990
Arizona	10,732	2,938	210	968	659	503	13,217	164,976
Arkansas	2,277	2,632	292	2,947	716	102	3,614	92,711
California	37,024	6,115	668	5,519	4,073	1,165	88,296	867,184
Colorado	4,281	1,209	370	3,717	1,093	203	15,663	173,248
Connecticut	4,486	319	182	882	165	63	10,084	86,810
Delaware	763	1,783	133	1,080	176	267	2,446	31,428
Florida	21,676	3,475	2,176	4,331	1,713	1,017	62,538	524,497
Georgia	10,921	2,736	1,740	3,868	1,341	731	22,074	297,492
Hawaii	2,664	48	14	108	39	33	4,884	30,263
Idaho	421	336	183	301	541	142	2,385	36,932
Illinois	7,050	10,289	1,948	6,131	2,745	1,417	26,923	348,020
Indiana	1,971	3,963	1,124	3,443	1,283	988	9,489	184,866
Iowa	953	2,944	509	1,497	1,146	1,061	3,537	83,384
Kansas	1,129	622	89	969	1,024	87	4,507	78,153
Kentucky	2,623	863	350	1,455	444	230	5,572	92,459
Louisiana	5,454	1,132	392	1,428	577	247	8,577	141,903
Maine	661	246	133	404	152	117	2,647	34,764
Maryland	4,817	1,775	662	2,601	665	211	17,293	168,020
Massachusetts	5,593	1,206	853	1,947	486	158	21,415	167,052
Michigan	2,329	2,211	542	2,788	1,365	826	13,265	499,635
Minnesota	1,236	2,565	680	2,796	1,786	674	10,607	171,905
Mississippi	3,060	1,250	308	1,064	396	102	3,822	72,590
Missouri	2,857	2,738	244	2,398	2,651	629	8,802	161,691
Montana	342	461	18	168	486	185	1,765	27,646
Nebraska	812	2,767	243	723	1,675	92	2,957	53,275
Nevada	2,576	446	35	696	390	122	6,409	62,992
New Hampshire	1,607	424	284	566	174	22	4,791	50,101
New Jersey	10,784	4,923	1,247	3,048	1,005	633	27,250	239,375
New Mexico	1,455	479	76	509	302	111	3,464	50,570
New York	19,855	2,558	1,720	5,135	1,145	601	40,317	396,155
North Carolina	10,348	4,693	1,073	3,282	1,686	2,045	21,476	255,499
North Dakota	87	169	53	159	303	105	572	19,300
Ohio	7,411	4,991	1,577	6,194	1,991	1,556	27,736	400,328
Oklahoma	2,942	7,193	647	2,986	3,994	1,170	6,203	112,929
Oregon	2,780	2,042	88	600	659	191	10,112	104,919
Pennsylvania	8,005	5,413	1,922	5,346	2,107	622	27,192	341,037
Rhode Island	726	350	152	376	64	89	2,387	19,206
South Carolina	3,658	1,000	726	1,289	763	253	8,820	117,634
South Dakota	152	268	20	266	260	87	1,137	22,977
Tennessee	8,930	6,033	894	2,556	2,067	2,144	12,193	165,333
Texas	22,800	6,178	2,484	6,436	4,457	1,158	52,685	754,221
Utah	1,258	1,769	56	587	925	369	5,284	60,529
Vermont	627	162	71	335	86	48	2,180	22,569
Virginia	7,640	1,222	666	3,274	650	399	21,189	185,879
Washington	3,987	1,770	167	1,036	1,854	247	14,938	143,941
West Virginia	1,156	237	125	506	275	89	3,034	48,879
Wisconsin	1,548	3,224	737	2,329	1,727	531	9,612	175,976
Wyoming	160	153	8	108	219	25	578	14,753
District of Columbia	194	11	8	36	0	1	864	4,599
Federal Government	26	449	299	66	5	7	297	18,597
TOTAL	261,942	114,683	30,168	103,811	55,858	24,476	689,294	8,529,562

Note: Toyota includes Lexus, Nissan includes Infiniti. *PACCAR is Kenworth and Peterbilt.
Source: The Polk Co. Further use prohibited without written permission from The Polk Company.

Car, Truck and Bus Registrations by State

TOTAL MOTOR VEHICLE REGISTRATIONS BY STATE, 1997-1998

State	Passenger Cars		Trucks and Buses		Total	
	1997	1998	1997	1998	1997	1998
Alabama	1,905,811	2,062,734	1,763,628	1,796,194	3,669,439	3,858,928
Alaska	224,770	232,170	317,628	313,695	542,398	545,865
Arizona	1,852,690	1,728,185	1,290,453	1,215,831	3,143,143	2,944,016
Arkansas	857,314	928,958	776,516	825,257	1,633,830	1,754,215
California	15,705,806	16,174,220	9,239,170	9,426,030	24,944,976	25,600,250
Colorado	1,919,850	1,843,385	1,602,740	1,622,709	3,522,590	3,466,094
Connecticut	1,963,185	1,998,457	696,333	702,176	2,659,518	2,700,633
Delaware	403,797	416,709	209,904	199,783	613,701	616,492
District of Columbia	196,077	192,097	37,593	36,619	233,670	228,716
Florida	7,374,840	7,437,597	3,499,191	3,838,792	10,874,031	11,276,389
Georgia	3,688,005	4,032,998	2,554,202	2,860,321	6,242,207	6,893,319
Hawaii	442,889	449,731	249,915	254,105	692,804	703,836
Idaho	494,486	501,509	586,566	617,384	1,081,052	1,118,893
Illinois	5,853,560	6,425,276	2,589,262	2,881,434	8,442,822	9,306,710
Indiana	3,247,725	3,273,026	2,098,051	2,098,627	5,345,776	5,371,653
Iowa	1,636,347	1,737,582	1,215,036	1,315,553	2,851,383	3,053,135
Kansas	1,137,271	1,127,367	1,014,836	994,043	2,152,107	2,121,410
Kentucky	1,633,671	1,715,524	1,147,135	1,129,088	2,780,806	2,844,612
Louisiana	1,930,142	1,966,954	1,480,881	1,463,763	3,411,023	3,430,717
Maine	637,418	565,338	421,181	364,267	1,058,599	929,605
Maryland	2,628,171	2,621,923	1,157,883	1,128,352	3,786,054	3,750,275
Massachusetts	3,832,386	3,782,940	1,238,046	1,376,228	5,070,432	5,159,168
Michigan	5,110,851	5,104,781	2,912,880	3,023,369	8,023,731	8,128,150
Minnesota	2,317,021	2,412,412	1,610,228	1,765,429	3,927,249	4,177,841
Mississippi	1,262,969	1,250,200	970,828	1,005,544	2,233,797	2,255,744
Missouri	2,549,791	2,600,722	1,800,753	1,776,798	4,350,544	4,377,520
Montana	455,140	458,116	524,560	530,161	979,700	988,277
Nebraska	811,678	834,188	695,318	691,810	1,506,996	1,525,998
Nevada	659,079	665,940	486,577	554,337	1,145,656	1,220,277
New Hampshire	739,132	687,770	388,255	350,695	1,127,387	1,038,465
New Jersey	4,268,888	4,215,195	1,547,692	1,565,141	5,816,580	5,780,336
New Mexico	779,596	821,031	734,903	773,761	1,514,499	1,594,792
New York	8,063,496	7,664,320	2,809,752	2,757,713	10,873,248	10,422,033
North Carolina	3,479,993	3,530,711	2,305,540	2,331,119	5,785,533	5,861,830
North Dakota	336,610	330,275	358,496	341,883	695,106	672,158
Ohio	6,700,396	6,664,356	3,407,255	3,375,132	10,107,651	10,039,488
Oklahoma	1,528,947	1,548,949	1,354,772	1,370,237	2,883,719	2,919,186
Oregon	1,578,081	1,588,313	1,312,871	1,391,751	2,890,952	2,980,064
Pennsylvania	6,050,365	6,131,725	2,774,582	2,847,089	8,824,947	8,978,814
Rhode Island	515,446	522,292	194,234	192,725	709,680	715,017
South Carolina	1,765,458	1,822,640	1,084,903	1,070,421	2,850,361	2,893,061
South Dakota	377,737	381,752	340,666	386,755	718,403	768,507
Tennessee	2,755,950	2,695,539	1,778,892	1,773,526	4,534,842	4,469,065
Texas	7,085,404	7,455,714	5,837,849	5,868,453	12,923,253	13,324,167
Utah	850,812	850,487	678,697	681,766	1,529,509	1,532,253
Vermont	290,593	295,664	205,123	200,489	495,716	496,153
Virginia	3,630,241	3,774,372	2,078,750	2,043,922	5,708,991	5,818,294
Washington	2,690,616	2,776,482	2,011,536	2,047,505	4,702,152	4,823,987
West Virginia	754,685	776,583	600,307	601,252	1,354,992	1,377,835
Wisconsin	2,551,207	2,544,109	1,681,524	1,659,210	4,232,731	4,203,319
Wyoming	222,311	219,220	331,063	339,771	553,374	558,991
Total	129,748,704	131,838,538	78,004,956	79,778,015	207,753,660	211,616,553

NOTE: Registrations include both privately and publicly owned motor vehicles, except those owned by the military.
SOURCE: U.S. Department of Transportation, Federal Highway Administration.

Total Motor Truck Registrations by State

TOTAL MOTOR TRUCK REGISTRATIONS BY STATE, 1995-1998

State	Privately Owned[1]				Privately and Publicly Owned[2]			
	1995	1996	1997	1998	1995	1996	1997	1998
Alabama	1,676,791	1,528,218	1,729,251	1,761,393	1,702,290	1,553,872	1,755,052	1,787,553
Alaska	227,586	292,426	307,569	303,406	235,635	300,506	315,550	311,499
Arizona	970,260	1,194,588	1,268,172	1,193,078	987,824	1,212,276	1,285,967	1,211,377
Arkansas	789,404	754,320	759,701	808,095	800,305	765,273	770,702	819,262
California	7,298,902	9,526,351	8,946,151	9,125,074	7,539,043	9,771,261	9,194,701	9,380,604
Colorado	1,076,750	1,501,899	1,572,048	1,591,459	1,101,377	1,526,688	1,597,019	1,616,989
Connecticut	509,344	633,231	661,320	666,394	534,220	658,434	686,847	692,437
Delaware	182,583	190,231	205,146	195,013	185,003	192,760	207,859	197,772
Dist. of Columbia	27,681	28,793	28,712	27,587	33,867	35,021	34,971	34,037
Florida	2,600,378	3,425,551	3,318,329	3,653,773	2,734,253	3,561,872	3,457,115	3,795,715
Georgia	1,823,576	2,369,057	2,479,223	2,782,908	1,879,066	2,426,027	2,537,703	2,843,253
Hawaii	257,929	269,965	239,863	243,178	264,616	276,329	245,956	249,998
Idaho	433,174	553,008	565,420	595,881	453,147	572,857	582,923	613,780
Illinois	2,327,400	2,490,532	2,556,208	2,847,783	2,344,913	2,507,383	2,572,445	2,863,926
Indiana	1,640,237	1,986,007	2,034,018	2,033,144	1,677,375	2,023,886	2,072,643	2,072,722
Iowa	949,620	1,179,936	1,181,547	1,281,006	975,880	1,206,182	1,207,001	1,307,450
Kansas	977,595	930,161	993,048	972,283	995,080	947,909	1,011,023	990,239
Kentucky	983,234	1,070,144	1,127,853	1,109,302	989,989	1,077,620	1,135,323	1,117,054
Louisiana	1,286,388	1,373,494	1,438,931	1,420,838	1,306,922	1,394,443	1,460,296	1,442,837
Maine	329,248	367,020	407,405	350,265	339,998	377,873	418,357	361,368
Maryland	916,197	1,031,321	1,124,273	1,094,112	937,894	1,053,197	1,146,316	1,116,616
Massachusetts	950,769	1,113,269	1,191,773	1,328,611	984,018	1,147,344	1,226,683	1,364,674
Michigan	2,262,430	2,821,785	2,814,169	2,923,241	2,335,026	2,895,058	2,888,109	2,998,227
Minnesota	1,288,507	1,549,661	1,575,102	1,727,750	1,314,173	1,572,845	1,596,411	1,750,710
Mississippi	708,357	886,616	942,680	973,509	725,637	904,335	960,747	995,359
Missouri	1,479,887	1,745,728	1,771,282	1,746,695	1,496,160	1,762,022	1,788,008	1,763,632
Montana	410,393	517,814	505,023	510,327	427,024	533,205	521,740	527,363
Nebraska	596,464	648,881	672,574	668,681	612,083	665,057	689,821	686,251
Nevada	438,490	460,782	470,873	538,350	452,328	474,686	484,829	552,631
New Hampshire	378,795	363,123	375,641	338,082	388,802	373,530	386,466	348,960
New Jersey	1,104,146	1,307,948	1,429,763	1,443,844	1,197,598	1,403,947	1,528,365	1,545,560
New Mexico	628,012	748,474	710,562	748,747	648,217	768,981	731,361	770,129
New York	2,211,130	2,506,142	2,662,545	2,609,294	2,310,928	2,606,026	2,763,560	2,709,077
North Carolina	1,905,780	2,160,114	2,229,780	2,252,915	1,961,771	2,215,933	2,275,679	2,300,380
North Dakota	311,935	329,680	347,640	330,960	320,841	338,648	356,213	339,584
Ohio	2,518,775	3,060,630	3,304,262	3,269,087	2,584,252	3,127,633	3,372,811	3,339,602
Oklahoma	1,170,037	1,338,044	1,295,728	1,309,696	1,211,802	1,380,673	1,339,234	1,354,302
Oregon	1,117,276	1,281,116	1,271,533	1,348,984	1,114,356	1,310,438	1,300,275	1,378,996
Pennsylvania	2,374,777	2,610,941	2,680,277	2,750,082	2,433,003	2,669,913	2,740,670	2,811,780
Rhode Island	146,791	177,610	186,913	185,961	152,306	183,211	192,489	190,894
South Carolina	930,070	988,205	1,045,542	1,030,258	953,078	1,011,972	1,069,700	1,055,022
South Dakota	314,286	365,910	324,952	370,925	326,462	378,151	337,967	384,059
Tennessee	1,393,457	1,761,726	1,706,190	1,699,764	1,447,790	1,816,551	1,761,492	1,755,950
Texas	4,774,945	5,595,062	5,516,791	5,535,162	5,005,001	5,831,593	5,759,985	5,788,362
Utah	631,871	618,369	663,148	665,811	645,781	632,491	677,474	680,534
Vermont	166,812	193,713	196,667	191,907	173,136	200,281	203,207	198,558
Virginia	1,586,004	1,886,139	2,026,468	1,990,599	1,620,307	1,920,994	2,061,273	2,026,139
Washington	1,498,099	1,920,843	1,964,849	1,999,193	1,535,293	1,958,448	2,003,060	2,038,417
West Virginia	531,687	567,909	564,789	566,256	565,136	600,736	597,001	597,953
Wisconsin	1,515,962	1,444,412	1,626,452	1,602,748	1,556,647	1,485,803	1,668,552	1,645,772
Wyoming	219,894	316,872	317,065	325,356	230,819	328,032	328,457	337,110
Total	62,850,115	73,983,771	75,335,221	77,038,767	64,748,472	75,940,206	77,307,408	79,062,475

(1) Excludes farm trucks registered in certain states and restricted for use in vicinity of owner's farm.
(2) Includes federal, state, county and municipal vehicles; excludes vehicles owned by military.
SOURCE: U.S. Department of Transportation, Federal Highway Administration.

Truck Registrations by State and Type

TOTAL MOTOR TRUCK REGISTRATIONS BY STATE AND TYPE, 1998

State	Truck Tractors	Farm Trucks	Pickups	Vans	Sport Utilities	Other Light	Total
Alabama	52,496	21,169	904,272	245,255	170,177	348,695	1,742,064
Alaska	2,784	467	161,517	86,381	44,778	3,566	299,493
Arizona	14,068	0	664,139	284,997	202,838	9,211	1,175,253
Arkansas	17,619	20,234	540,823	139,216	111,357	4,654	833,903
California	109,136	0	3,815,243	2,030,596	1,951,561	52,376	7,958,912
Colorado	7,636	86,878	722,163	516,387	255,645	10,898	1,599,607
Connecticut [1]	2,571	0	252,207	234,150	169,393	5,639	663,960
Delaware	4,056	3,342	81,404	54,510	49,674	1,338	194,324
District of Columbia	184	0	5,740	10,680	10,195	672	27,471
Florida	68,699	0	1,425,339	834,923	915,619	24,734	3,269,314
Georgia [2]	69,243	0	1,425,637	599,374	512,977	20,684	2,627,915
Hawaii	798	0	119,288	56,951	61,815	2,102	240,954
Idaho	6,172	0	349,795	123,764	69,849	3,990	553,570
Illinois	63,350	39,928	1,124,823	631,301	825,890	21,638	2,706,930
Indiana	53,819	47,804	1,025,244	345,238	480,340	12,551	1,964,996
Iowa	55,621	24,150	650,356	193,128	249,776	8,567	1,181,598
Kansas	20,405	83,811	512,548	155,343	176,393	6,265	954,765
Kentucky	22,476	83,736	657,384	185,489	185,419	6,856	1,141,360
Louisiana	29,923	91,921	893,823	233,101	224,898	8,692	1,482,358
Maine	4,733	5,804	196,849	72,571	60,804	2,223	342,984
Maryland	15,890	11,039	435,292	307,130	311,205	8,037	1,088,593
Massachusetts	12,888	8,087	470,778	451,324	364,175	11,219	1,325,371
Michigan	66,472	50,841	1,215,576	657,215	807,461	13,385	2,810,950
Minnesota	30,267	50,543	750,687	357,743	377,850	11,743	1,578,833
Mississippi [2]	10,340	0	653,266	152,076	129,448	7,463	952,593
Missouri	48,721	176,732	943,717	317,014	352,846	12,732	1,851,762
Montana	15,497	108,050	300,888	92,514	54,112	3,332	574,393
Nebraska	30,597	150,023	339,670	116,221	115,401	5,024	756,936
Nevada	3,176	0	246,988	142,388	76,488	3,569	472,609
New Hampshire [1]	5,523	1,986	156,341	88,873	75,418	2,376	330,517
New Jersey [1]	11,202	13,050	403,555	550,949	461,441	13,615	1,453,812
New Mexico	13,041	18,993	290,804	104,917	66,497	3,438	497,690
New York [1]	15,589	52,100	637,094	613,993	623,318	20,885	1,962,979
North Carolina	55,686	88,539	1,168,132	452,891	425,858	16,581	2,207,687
North Dakota	10,298	39,201	175,147	51,654	45,105	1,747	323,152
Ohio	77,569	35,323	1,465,362	652,793	935,093	20,950	3,187,090
Oklahoma	11,400	165,628	768,689	188,426	181,647	8,508	1,324,298
Oregon	19,493	18,470	701,306	291,398	238,801	10,389	1,279,857
Pennsylvania [1]	66,373	540	1,010,419	757,684	659,310	19,846	2,514,172
Rhode Island [1]	2,578	0	75,357	50,401	47,816	1,324	177,476
South Carolina	17,176	25,898	571,167	216,299	194,435	7,936	1,032,911
South Dakota	15,796	0	172,120	59,139	48,885	2,003	297,943
Tennessee	44,526	43,869	981,485	337,586	291,043	9,718	1,708,227
Texas	149,296	200,305	3,120,226	1,259,717	893,400	32,438	5,655,382
Utah	32,000	12,500	324,611	189,586	100,547	5,027	664,271
Vermont	2,785	2,919	100,123	46,840	35,806	1,345	189,818
Virginia	32,906	25,232	952,714	504,982	445,383	14,176	1,975,393
Washington	24,166	21,056	1,000,703	455,023	398,926	16,473	1,916,347
West Virginia	9,839	3,099	329,287	117,588	81,675	3,135	544,623
Wisconsin	40,302	91,783	712,465	330,373	400,832	8,875	1,584,630
Wyoming	3,365	5,142	194,807	74,278	32,904	2,213	312,709
Total	**1,500,546**	**1,931,092**	**36,203,370**	**17,022,370**	**16,002,524**	**854,853**	**73,514,755**

NOTE: The registrations given in this table are as reported by the States in most instances, but have been supplemented in some cases by estimates based on data from other sources. In this partial classification a vehicle may be included more than once; for instance, a truck-tractor in farm use could appear in both columns.

(1) Except for Georgia and Mississippi (Footnote 2), farm registrations are shown for all States that have a special "Farm" classification. The numbers of vehicles shown do not necessarily represent the total number or registered vehicles used on the farm. The following farm trucks, registered at a nominal fee and restricted to use in the vicinity of the owner's farm, are not included in this table: Connecticut, 5,546; New Hampshire, 5,163; New Jersey, 6,730; New York, 30,509; Pennsylvania, 22,852; and Rhode Island, 1,137.

(2) Although Georgia and Mississippi have a special "Farm" classification, their registration reports do not show a complete segregation of farm trucks from private carriers.

SOURCE: U.S. Department of Transportation, Federal Highway Administration.

Private, Commercial and Publicly Owner Trailer Registrations by State

TRAILER REGISTRATIONS BY STATE, 1998

| State | Private and Commercial Trailers[1] | | | | Publicly Owned Trailers | | | Grand Total |
	Commercial Trailers[2]	Car and Light Farm Trailers[3]	House Trailers[4]	Total	Federal Government	State, County and Municipal	Total	
Alabama	61,543	61,027	20,541	143,111	14	1,062	1,076	144,187
Alaska	17,941	84,995	0	102,936	125	1,379	1,504	104,440
Arizona	22,120	76,977	34,963	134,060	92	3,793	3,885	137,945
Arkansas	39,638	352,469	16,592	408,699	5	271	276	408,975
California	652,551	1,418,407	517,195	2,588,153	354	47,868	48,222	2,636,375
Colorado	87,930	215,574	90,769	394,273	77	2,099	2,176	396,449
Connecticut	43,196	131,387	0	174,583	12	2,697	2,709	177,292
Delaware	18,270	31,576	0	49,846	7	802	809	50,655
District of Columbia	79	845	0	924	144	336	480	1,404
Florida	118,927	1,080,786	0	1,199,713	174	28,138	28,312	1,228,025
Georgia	131,483	438,231	30,929	600,643	123	3,824	3,947	604,590
Hawaii	3,276	14,309	0	17,585	5	791	796	18,381
Idaho	13,023	47,912	53,427	114,362	57	2,714	2,771	117,133
Illinois	104,705	471,508	111,069	687,282	222	460	682	687,964
Indiana	59,990	324,605	87,017	471,612	37	2,115	2,152	473,764
Iowa	112,641	281,145	68,150	461,936	19	4,861	4,880	466,816
Kansas	82,275	23,765	18,695	124,735	22	856	878	125,613
Kentucky	26,103	30,503	35,250	91,856	58	115	173	92,029
Louisiana	198,959	278,300	11,371	488,630	25	2,664	2,689	491,319
Maine	639,885	105,427	0	745,312	7	2,226	2,233	747,545
Maryland	19,307	225,936	0	245,243	98	397	495	245,738
Massachusetts	25,776	240,353	0	266,129	70	180	250	266,379
Michigan	110,948	810,901	131,938	1,053,787	81	4,432	4,513	1,058,300
Minnesota	165,193	621,137	89,539	875,869	78	2,880	2,958	878,827
Mississippi	30,388	71,894	10,598	112,880	30	1,674	1,704	114,584
Missouri	99,975	281,492	0	381,467	119	480	599	382,066
Montana	22,487	117,222	52,223	191,932	50	2,548	2,598	194,530
Nebraska	86,983	173,763	0	260,746	12	980	992	261,738
Nevada	5,504	77,361	34,401	117,266	45	1,148	1,193	118,459
New Hampshire	10,750	109,724	0	120,474	3	1,093	1,096	121,570
New Jersey	21,468	309,644	0	331,112	153	100	253	331,365
New Mexico	44,329	36,477	47,136	127,942	133	3,092	3,225	131,167
New York	20,422	477,914	0	498,336	338	6,308	6,646	504,982
North Carolina	85,200	519,342	1,337	605,879	43	7,777	7,820	613,699
North Dakota	22,505	27,782	16,988	67,275	9	895	904	68,179
Ohio	121,603	458,336	105,434	685,373	119	8,310	8,429	693,802
Oklahoma	95,788	63,739	14,291	173,818	33	1,924	1,957	175,775
Oregon	48,980	131,110	124,267	304,357	94	10,289	10,383	314,740
Pennsylvania	136,030	417,024	209,779	762,833	195	4,043	4,238	767,071
Rhode Island	6,351	37,152	0	43,503	7	886	893	44,396
South Carolina	37,786	29,341	124	67,251	31	1,126	1,157	68,408
South Dakota	44,104	65,147	34,064	143,315	29	1,175	1,204	144,519
Tennessee	55,658	37,447	176	93,281	67	334	401	93,682
Texas	232,902	1,201,123	0	1,434,025	172	54,897	55,069	1,489,094
Utah	36,057	55,713	53,230	145,000	72	440	512	145,512
Vermont	4,423	64,763	0	69,186	3	978	981	70,167
Virginia	83,585	171,233	73,215	328,033	58	2,710	2,768	330,801
Washington	60,192	443,711	83,654	587,557	151	1,972	2,123	589,680
West Virginia	44,364	59,412	29,744	133,520	9	3,839	3,848	137,368
Wisconsin	176,540	16,131	39,263	231,934	27	1,601	1,628	233,562
Wyoming	15,089	201,297	25,205	241,591	85	1,016	1,101	242,692
Total	4,405,222	13,023,369	2,272,574	19,701,165	3,993	238,595	242,588	19,943,753

(1) The completeness of data on trailer registrations varies greatly. Data are reported to the extent available and in some cases are supplemented by estimates of the Federal Highway Administration.
(2) This column includes all commercial type vehicles and semitrailers that are in private or for-hire use.
(3) Several States do not require the registration of light farm or automobile trailers.
(4) Mobile homes and house trailers are shown in this column for States which require them to be registered and are able to segregate them from other trailers. In States where this classification is not available, house trailers are included with light car trailers.
SOURCE: U.S. Department of Transportation, Federal Highway Administration.

Bus Registrations by State

TOTAL MOTOR BUS REGISTRATIONS BY STATE, 1998

State	Private and Commercial		Publicly Owned		Total Privately and Publicly Owned		
	Commercial Buses[1]	School and Other[2]	Federal	School[3]	Commercial and Federal	School	Total Buses
Alabama	2,103	204	39	6,295	2,142	6,499	8,641
Alaska	1,515	486	75	120	1,590	606	2,196
Arizona	1,033	206	379	2,836	1,412	3,042	4,454
Arkansas	44	1,261	29	4,661	73	5,922	5,995
California	20,990	8,216	470	15,750	21,460	23,966	45,426
Colorado	670	985	43	4,022	713	5,007	5,720
Connecticut	2,938	5,978	12	811	2,950	6,789	9,739
Delaware	406	1,023	7	575	413	1,598	2,011
District of Columbia	2,053	146	276	107	2,329	253	2,582
Florida	4,352	1,250	208	37,267	4,560	38,517	43,077
Georgia	1,382	2,559	106	13,021	1,488	15,580	17,068
Hawaii	2,497	660	28	922	2,525	1,582	4,107
Idaho	770	501	150	2,183	920	2,684	3,604
Illinois	6,305	10,235	86	882	6,391	11,117	17,508
Indiana	4,020	4,708	55	17,122	4,075	21,830	25,905
Iowa	1,202	279	14	6,608	1,216	6,887	8,103
Kansas	388	1,123	12	2,281	400	3,404	3,804
Kentucky	1,005	751	159	10,119	1,164	10,870	12,034
Louisiana	1,022	14,360	25	5,519	1,047	19,879	20,926
Maine	174	452	12	2,261	186	2,713	2,899
Maryland	2,957	3,976	152	4,651	3,109	8,627	11,736
Massachusetts	3,875	7,163	83	433	3,958	7,596	11,554
Michigan	3,109	7,002	78	14,953	3,187	21,955	25,142
Minnesota	2,357	4,699	8	7,655	2,365	12,354	14,719
Mississippi	924	2,630	79	6,552	1,003	9,182	10,185
Missouri	1,137	3,932	36	8,061	1,173	11,993	13,166
Montana	442	670	19	1,667	461	2,337	2,798
Nebraska	542	662	10	4,345	552	5,007	5,559
Nevada	1,266	176	142	122	1,408	298	1,706
New Hampshire	364	1,048	2	321	366	1,369	1,735
New Jersey	4,521	12,303	57	2,700	4,578	15,003	19,581
New Mexico	547	2,090	310	685	857	2,775	3,632
New York	13,652	7,986	222	26,776	13,874	34,762	48,636
North Carolina	2,028	7,292	54	21,365	2,082	28,657	30,739
North Dakota	138	524	66	1,571	204	2,095	2,299
Ohio	10,919	2,718	84	21,809	11,003	24,527	35,530
Oklahoma	386	1,912	137	13,500	523	15,412	15,935
Oregon	1,463	2,300	70	8,922	1,533	11,222	12,755
Pennsylvania	9,364	18,411	124	7,410	9,488	25,821	35,309
Rhode Island	357	1,463	6	5	363	1,468	1,831
South Carolina	854	3,476	33	11,036	887	14,512	15,399
South Dakota	335	406	119	1,836	454	2,242	2,696
Tennessee	2,033	1,434	80	14,029	2,113	15,463	17,576
Texas	2,895	13,568	252	63,376	3,147	76,944	80,091
Utah	343	94	38	757	381	851	1,232
Vermont	92	544	5	1,290	97	1,834	1,931
Virginia	2,309	243	245	14,986	2,554	15,229	17,783
Washington	859	2,377	198	5,654	1,057	8,031	9,088
West Virginia	842	63	45	2,349	887	2,412	3,299
Wisconsin	1,464	7,457	24	4,493	1,488	11,950	13,438
Wyoming	852	119	11	1,679	863	1,798	2,661
Total	**128,095**	**174,121**	**4,974**	**408,350**	**133,069**	**582,471**	**715,540**

(1) Includes municipally owned transit buses.
(2) In some instances church, industrial and other private buses are included here; and in other instances privately-owned school buses could not be segregated from commercial buses, and are included with the latter.
(3) This column consists primarily of publicly owned school buses but includes a few privately owned school, institutional, and industrial buses registered free or at a reduced rate.
SOURCE: U.S. Department of Transportation, Federal Highway Administration.

School Bus Ownership and Usage by State

SCHOOL BUS OWNERSHIP AND USAGE BY STATE, 1997-1998 SCHOOL YEAR

	Pupils Transported at Public Expense	Bus Ownership			Total Miles of Service	Transportation Expenditures Including Capital Outlays
		Publicly Owned	Contractor	Total		
Alabama	397,032	6,471	277	6,748	66,990,240	159,613,301
Alaska	47,011	128	704	832	11,227,267	37,904,321
Arizona	283,817	N.A.	N.A.	6,500	63,802,000	N.A.
Arkansas	N.A.	5,800	250	6,050	45,000,000	85,000,000
California	962,272	15,035	8,118	23,153	246,734,583	1,004,658,122
Colorado	293,301	N.A.	N.A.	N.A.	48,418,275	N.A.
Connecticut	394,120	520	4,712	5,232	N.A.	212,582,024
Delaware	96,162	467	1,048	1,515	21,463,010	44,821,769
District of Columbia	4,000	180	280	460	N.A.	N.A.
Florida	969,000	16,525	1,540	18,065	255,566,130	594,823,894
Georgia	1,016,598	14,430	88	14,518	136,830,060	329,600,161
Hawaii	33,370	7	782	789	6,174,000	19,287,500
Idaho	108,955	1,884	630	2,514	22,419,050	51,890,083
Illinois	1,161,344	8,500	8,500	17,000	196,251,549	434,566,217
Indiana	720,381	9,075	2,790	11,865	75,882,402	310,843,039
Iowa	263,427	N.A.	N.A.	5,886	46,561,474	78,411,943
Kansas	206,599	5,028	1,446	6,474	47,287,068	126,706,718
Kentucky	414,083	9,026	229	9,255	101,463,251	184,166,552
Louisiana	560,737	4,397	3,328	7,725	30,898,080	227,676,450
Maine	182,288	2,017	592	2,609	N.A.	59,919,872
Maryland	606,855	3,388	2,968	6,356	76,912,907	298,883,209
Massachusetts	N.A.	1,681	5,319	7,000	N.A.	N.A.
Michigan	838,522	14,369	1,416	15,785	183,885,757	531,219,202
Minnesota	816,106	4,190	6,161	10,351	133,957,720	331,245,153
Mississippi	404,047	5,177	69	5,246	45,989,319	108,528,916
Missouri	440,051	6,777	5,267	12,044	103,343,349	284,860,353
Montana	68,510	1,208	931	2,139	18,858,672	39,889,853
Nebraska	85,877	1,966	540	2,506	29,202,161	57,112,407
Nevada	N.A.	1,496	0	1,496	26,222,140	N.A.
New Hampshire	150,000	414	1,710	2,124	N.A.	51,700,051
New Jersey	732,000	6,500	12,900	19,400	N.A.	N.A.
New Mexico	167,617	N.A.	N.A.	2,309	N.A.	N.A.
New York	1,989,528	20,000	25,000	45,000	N.A.	1,447,763,744
North Carolina	688,012	12,957	0	12,957	141,300,000	221,700,000
North Dakota	48,445	1,097	356	1,453	24,025,594	28,371,324
Ohio	1,326,677	18,421	2,300	20,721	177,532,660	413924061
Oklahoma	328,922	N.A.	N.A.	7,212	53,576,130	113,165,066
Oregon	249,767	3,845	2,043	5,888	49,224,580	140,013,327
Pennsylvania	1,500,625	5,820	19,203	25,023	676,000,000	N.A.
Rhode Island	106,408	N.A.	N.A.	1,400	15,185,921	51,633,235
South Carolina	492,000	5,588	0	5,588	72,751,023	106,937,584
South Dakota	N.A.	1,100	500	1,600	12,935,537	26,963,682
Tennessee	458,331	N.A.	N.A.	7,557	84,049,200	168,019,021
Texas	1,345,143	N.A.	N.A.	32,060	306,682,000	675,590,000
Utah	164,030	2,075	81	2,156	14,031,740	54,490,678
Vermont	79,016	483	863	1,346	N.A.	24,767,233
Virginia	868,499	13,582	0	13,582	107,734,441	349,481,082
Washington	493,723	7,196	1,145	8,341	59,761,000	231,668,000
West Virginia	225,486	3,691	0	3,691	41,743,210	129,464,816
Wisconsin	612,900	1,980	8,300	10,280	N.A.	N.A.
Wyoming	35,814	1,592	9	1,601	12,820,717	29,605,588
	23,437,408	246,083	132,395	441,402	3,214,694,217	10,555,469,551

N.A. Not available.
SOURCE: Bobit Publishing Company, *School Bus Fleet Fact Book*.

Government Ownership of Motor Vehicles by State

GOVERNMENT OWNERSHIP OF MOTOR VEHICLES BY STATE, 1998

State	Federal[1]				State, County and Municipal[2]				Total Publicly Owned Vehicles
	Passenger Cars	Trucks	Buses	Total	Passenger Cars	Trucks	Buses	Total	
Alabama	1,818	5,093	39	6,950	13,505	21,067	6,295	40,867	47,817
Alaska	550	3,281	75	3,906	1,317	4,812	120	6,249	10,155
Arizona	2,432	9,551	379	12,362	14,108	8,748	2,836	25,692	38,054
Arkansas	1,013	2,850	29	3,892	8,506	8,317	4,661	21,484	25,376
California	13,825	46,255	470	60,550	166,663	209,275	15,750	391,688	452,238
Colorado	1,901	9,086	43	11,030	8,063	16,444	4,022	28,529	39,559
Connecticut	963	4,532	12	5,507	10,371	21,511	811	32,693	38,200
Delaware	297	800	7	1,104	7,520	1,959	575	10,054	11,158
District of Columbia	2,771	3,878	276	6,925	1,590	2,572	107	4,269	11,194
Florida	5,155	15,486	208	20,849	91,803	126,456	37,267	255,526	276,375
Georgia	2,712	7,537	106	10,355	21,267	52,808	13,021	87,096	97,451
Hawaii	559	1,786	28	2,373	5,391	5,034	922	11,347	13,720
Idaho	722	5,086	150	5,958	5,065	12,813	2,183	20,061	26,019
Illinois	3,821	10,996	86	14,903	58,665	5,147	882	64,694	79,597
Indiana	1,503	4,589	55	6,147	20,607	34,989	17,122	72,718	78,865
Iowa	751	3,402	14	4,167	11,858	23,042	6,608	41,508	45,675
Kansas	867	3,276	12	4,155	6,542	14,680	2,281	23,503	27,658
Kentucky	1,723	4,515	159	6,397	19,727	3,237	10,119	33,083	39,480
Louisiana	1,766	4,999	25	6,790	34,123	17,000	5,519	56,642	63,432
Maine	466	1,250	12	1,728	4,512	9,853	2,261	16,626	18,354
Maryland	2,798	7,089	152	10,039	10,495	15,415	4,651	30,561	40,600
Massachusetts	2,890	7,076	83	10,049	13,845	28,987	433	43,265	53,314
Michigan	2,840	9,030	78	11,948	43,526	65,956	14,953	124,435	136,383
Minnesota	1,630	5,646	8	7,284	8,347	17,314	7,655	33,316	40,600
Mississippi	1,448	3,594	79	5,121	9,148	18,256	6,552	33,956	39,077
Missouri	3,306	4,869	36	8,211	4,313	12,068	8,061	24,442	32,653
Montana	954	5,098	19	6,071	4,251	11,938	1,667	17,856	23,927
Nebraska	1,164	2,825	10	3,999	10,267	14,745	4,345	29,357	33,356
Nevada	1,240	6,562	142	7,944	8,548	7,719	122	16,389	24,333
New Hampshire	641	1,124	2	1,767	3,255	9,754	321	13,330	15,097
New Jersey	2,381	10,466	57	12,904	44,236	91,250	2,700	138,186	151,090
New Mexico	1,467	6,904	310	8,681	12,061	14,478	685	27,224	35,905
New York	9,048	18,513	222	27,783	61,134	81,270	26,776	169,180	196,963
North Carolina	1,956	5,480	55	7,491	27,272	41,985	21,365	90,622	98,113
North Dakota	644	1,953	66	2,663	3,237	6,671	1,571	11,479	14,142
Ohio	3,340	9,172	84	12,596	40,140	61,343	21,809	123,292	135,888
Oklahoma	1,625	4,947	137	6,709	9,627	39,659	13,500	62,786	69,495
Oregon	1,478	9,173	70	10,721	24,225	20,839	8,922	53,986	64,707
Pennsylvania	5,448	12,907	124	18,479	38,663	48,791	7,410	94,864	113,343
Rhode Island	257	1,127	6	1,390	2,849	3,806	5	6,660	8,050
South Carolina	1,703	4,977	33	6,713	8,402	19,787	11,036	39,225	45,938
South Dakota	604	2,694	119	3,417	3,750	10,440	1,836	16,026	19,443
Tennessee	3,609	9,703	80	13,392	18,812	46,483	14,029	79,324	92,716
Texas	6,773	23,523	252	30,548	209,594	229,677	63,376	502,647	533,195
Utah	998	4,508	38	5,544	9,019	10,215	757	19,991	25,535
Vermont	357	488	5	850	2,875	6,163	1,290	10,328	11,178
Virginia	2,732	8,969	245	11,946	32,129	26,571	14,986	73,686	85,632
Washington	3,010	12,738	198	15,946	15,539	26,486	5,654	47,679	63,625
West Virginia	944	2,030	45	3,019	15,306	29,667	2,349	47,322	50,341
Wisconsin	1,188	4,834	24	6,046	13,691	38,190	4,493	56,374	62,420
Wyoming	416	2,943	11	3,370	4,315	8,811	1,679	14,805	18,175
Total	114,504	359,210	4,975	478,689	1,224,074	1,664,498	408,350	3,296,922	3,775,611

(1) Vehicles of the civilian branches of the Federal government are given in this table. Vehicles of the military services are not included. Distribution by State is estimated by the Federal Highway Administration.
(2) This information, compiled chiefly from reports of State authorities, is incomplete in many cases. Some States give State-owned vehicles only; others excludes from registration certain classes, such as fire apparatus and police vehicles. For the states not reporting state, county and municipal vehicles separately from private and commercial vehicles and those reporting unsegregated totals only, classification by vehicle type has been approximately on the basis of other available data.
SOURCE: U.S. Department of Transportation, Federal Highway Administration.

Passenger Cars in Operation by Model Year and Average Age of Cars in Use

CARS IN OPERATION BY MODEL YEAR, 1986-1999 (as of July 1 of each year)

Units in Thousands

Model Year	1986	1987	1988	1989	1990	1991	1992	1993	1994	1995	1996	1997	1998	1999
2000	—	—	—	—	—	—	—	—	—	—	—	—	—	102
1999	—	—	—	—	—	—	—	—	—	—	—	—	65	6,117
1998	—	—	—	—	—	—	—	—	—	—	—	76	5,554	7,714
1997	—	—	—	—	—	—	—	—	—	—	143	5,546	8,049	7,971
1996	—	—	—	—	—	—	—	—	—	8	6,011	7,696	7,564	7,488
1995	—	—	—	—	—	—	—	—	96	6,030	9,179	8,968	8,926	8,811
1994	—	—	—	—	—	—	—	11	5,540	8,150	7,973	7,938	7,878	7,771
1993	—	—	—	—	—	—	29	5,259	8,201	8,218	8,040	8,013	7,953	7,826
1992	—	—	—	—	—	60	5,227	7,739	7,718	7,651	7,474	7,430	7,320	7,204
1991	—	—	—	—	103	5,703	8,100	8,176	7,995	7,941	7,753	7,665	7,536	7,354
1990	—	—	—	—	5,958	8,696	8,372	8,362	8,225	8,151	7,932	7,821	7,620	7,387
1989	—	—	—	6,467	9,729	9,713	9,309	9,253	9,126	8,957	8,692	8,479	8,187	7,797
1988	—	—	6,830	10,304	10,245	10,124	9,761	9,686	9,410	9,146	8,803	8,463	8,008	7,475
1987	—	7,019	10,380	10,304	10,140	10,049	9,640	9,471	9,205	8,839	8,431	7,944	7,439	6,780
1986	7,072	10,694	10,635	10,489	10,366	10,214	9,752	9,501	9,134	8,665	8,134	7,504	6,870	6,089
1985	10,532	10,430	10,276	10,162	9,989	9,732	9,214	8,863	8,419	7,822	7,191	6,469	5,774	4,987
1984	10,298	10,131	10,036	9,870	9,549	9,208	8,567	8,068	7,510	6,843	6,106	5,342	4,636	—
1983	7,584	7,504	7,394	7,178	6,884	6,543	5,998	5,543	5,082	4,527	3,945	3,365	—	—
1982	7,214	7,083	6,864	6,592	6,188	5,721	5,077	4,507	3,988	3,429	2,871	—	—	—
1981	7,882	7,632	7,317	6,901	6,323	5,673	4,887	4,192	3,613	3,024	—	—	—	—
1980	8,208	7,886	7,423	6,843	6,111	5,326	4,448	3,709	3,138	—	—	—	—	—
1979	9,283	8,848	8,251	7,508	6,624	5,743	4,808	4,020	—	—	—	—	—	—
1978	9,040	8,432	7,673	6,761	5,791	4,891	4,024	—	—	—	—	—	—	—
1977	8,125	7,382	6,479	5,492	4,569	3,759	—	—	—	—	—	—	—	—
1976	6,413	5,555	4,620	3,733	2,981	—	—	—	—	—	—	—	—	—
1975	4,136	3,450	2,782	2,193	—	—	—	—	—	—	—	—	—	—
1974	4,258	3,440	2,722	2,120	—	—	—	—	—	—	—	—	—	—
1973	3,929	3,161	2,500	—	—	—	—	—	—	—	—	—	—	—
1972	2,992	2,431	—	—	—	—	—	—	—	—	—	—	—	—
1971	2,030	—	—	—	—	—	—	—	—	—	—	—	—	—
1970	—	—	—	—	—	—	—	—	—	—	—	—	—	—
1969	—	—	—	—	—	—	—	—	—	—	—	—	—	—
Prior Years	8,263	8,764	9,331	9,835	11,720	12,167	13,073	14,636	15,572	15,805	15,935	15,954	16,587	17,996
Year Not Given	9	7	7	6	6	6	61	59	25	36	*	*	*	*
Total	117,268	119,849	121,520	122,758	123,276	123,328	120,347	121,055	121,997	123,242	124,613	124,673	125,966	126,869

AVERAGE AGE OF PASSENGER CARS IN USE IN THE U.S., 1941-1999 (Age in Years)

Year	Mean[1]	Median[2]	Year	Mean[1]	Median[2]
1999	8.9	8.3	1976	6.2	5.5
1998	8.8	8.3	1974	5.7	5.2
1997	8.6	8.1	1972	5.7	5.1
1996	8.5	7.9	1970	5.6	4.9
1995	8.4	7.7	1968	5.6	4.7
1994	8.3	7.5	1966	5.7	4.8
1993	8.1	7.3	1964	6.0	5.3
1992	7.9	7.0	1962	6.0	5.7
1991	7.8	6.7	1960	5.9	5.4
1990	7.6	6.5	1958	5.6	5.1
1989	7.6	6.5	1956	5.6	5.1
1988	7.6	6.8	1954	6.2	4.8
1986	7.6	7.0	1952	6.8	4.5
1984	7.5	6.7	1950	7.8	6.2
1982	7.2	6.2	1948	8.8	8.0
1980	6.6	6.0	1946	9.0	8.8
1978	6.3	5.7	1941	5.5	4.9

*Includes all earlier models.
(1) Mean-The sum of the products of units multiplied by age, divided by the total units.
(2) Median-A value in an ordered set of values below and above which there are an equal number of values.
SOURCE: The Polk Company. Permission for further use must be obtained from The Polk Company.

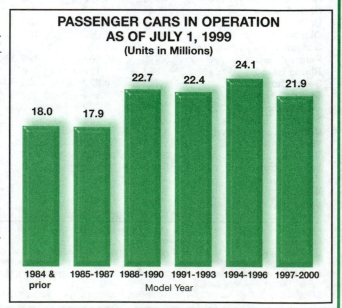

PASSENGER CARS IN OPERATION AS OF JULY 1, 1999
(Units in Millions)

Model Year	Units
1984 & prior	18.0
1985-1987	17.9
1988-1990	22.7
1991-1993	22.4
1994-1996	24.1
1997-2000	21.9

Trucks in Operation by Model Year and Average Age of Trucks in Use

TRUCKS IN OPERATION BY MODEL YEAR, 1986-1999 (as of July 1 of each year)

Units in Thousands

Model Year	1986	1987	1988	1989	1990	1991	1992	1993	1994	1995	1996	1997	1998	1999
2000	—	—	—	—	—	—	—	—	—	—	—	—	—	56
1999	—	—	—	—	—	—	—	—	—	—	—	—	206	5,897
1998	—	—	—	—	—	—	—	—	—	—	—	92	4,824	6,750
1997	—	—	—	—	—	—	—	—	—	—	234	4,532	6,550	6,507
1996	—	—	—	—	—	—	—	—	—	26	4,264	5,828	5,545	5,492
1995	—	—	—	—	—	—	—	—	29	4,068	6,448	6,362	6,165	6,063
1994	—	—	—	—	—	—	—	22	3,896	6,096	5,847	5,733	5,593	5,437
1993	—	—	—	—	—	—	23	3,371	5,181	5,176	4,976	4,838	4,711	4,539
1992	—	—	—	—	—	8	2,797	4,380	4,323	4,228	4,097	4,015	3,870	3,739
1991	—	—	—	—	153	2,911	4,254	4,305	4,223	4,136	4,020	3,912	3,800	3,626
1990	—	—	—	—	2,858	4,187	4,222	4,232	4,109	4,033	3,906	3,802	3,647	3,494
1989	—	—	—	3,133	4,872	4,913	4,864	4,859	4,753	4,620	4,498	4,340	4,171	3,940
1988	—	—	3,265	4,882	4,913	4,922	4,848	4,829	4,682	4,523	4,385	4,203	3,979	3,738
1987	—	2,954	4,450	4,441	4,435	4,414	4,333	4,298	4,160	3,972	3,844	3,633	3,418	3,145
1986	3,063	4,739	4,741	4,731	4,704	4,670	4,558	4,496	4,346	4,134	3,969	3,741	3,448	3,142
1985	4,218	4,179	4,166	4,139	4,097	4,041	3,915	3,858	3,712	3,509	3,360	3,111	2,855	2,560
1984	3,796	3,764	3,739	3,705	3,641	3,572	3,449	3,369	3,207	3,030	2,847	2,624	2,367	—
1983	2,471	2,439	2,419	2,388	2,332	2,279	2,173	2,111	1,996	1,873	1,748	1,596	—	—
1982	2,143	2,118	2,080	2,045	1,978	1,917	1,816	1,752	1,532	1,528	1,414	—	—	—
1981	2,028	1,979	1,939	1,891	1,813	1,708	1,650	1,580	1,447	1,344	—	—	—	—
1980	2,026	1,962	1,906	1,847	1,722	1,625	1,564	1,478	1,327	—	—	—	—	—
1979	3,580	3,452	3,332	3,178	3,020	2,854	2,726	2,569	—	—	—	—	—	—
1978	3,291	3,150	2,972	2,841	2,675	2,508	2,374	—	—	—	—	—	—	—
1977	2,902	2,708	2,559	2,425	2,255	2,094	—	—	—	—	—	—	—	—
1976	2,258	2,108	1,963	1,832	1,687	—	—	—	—	—	—	—	—	—
1975	1,557	1,436	1,320	1,223	—	—	—	—	—	—	—	—	—	—
1974	1,876	1,701	1,547	1,398	—	—	—	—	—	—	—	—	—	—
1973	1,774	1,610	1,456	—	—	—	—	—	—	—	—	—	—	—
1972	1,459	1,319	—	—	—	—	—	—	—	—	—	—	—	—
1971	996	—	—	—	—	—	—	—	—	—	—	—	—	—
1970	—	—	—	—	—	—	—	—	—	—	—	—	—	—
1969	—	—	—	—	—	—	—	—	—	—	—	—	—	—
Prior Years	5,377	5,721	6,362	7,098	8,862	9,552	11,555	13,662	13,751	13,884	13,824	14,036	13,928	14,515
Year Not Given*	10	5	6	5	4	3	51	89	43	19	—	—	—	—
Total	44,825	47,344	50,222	53,202	56,021	58,178	61,172	65,260	66,717	70,199	73,681	76,398	79,077	82,640

AVERAGE AGE OF TRUCKS IN USE IN THE U.S., 1941-1999 (Age in Years)

Year	Mean(1)	Median(2)	Year	Mean(1)	Median(2)
1999	8.2	7.2	1976	7.0	5.8
1998	8.3	7.5	1974	7.0	5.6
1997	8.3	7.8	1972	7.2	6.0
1996	8.3	7.7	1970	7.3	5.9
1995	8.4	7.6	1968	7.6	6.2
1994	8.4	7.5	1966	7.8	6.8
1993	8.6	7.5	1964	8.1	7.7
1992	8.4	7.2	1962	8.0	7.6
1991	8.1	6.8	1960	7.7	7.4
1990	8.0	6.5	1958	7.2	6.7
1989	7.9	6.7	1956	6.8	6.1
1988	7.9	7.1	1954	6.6	5.7
1986	8.0	7.7	1952	6.6	4.8
1984	8.2	7.4	1950	7.0	4.7
1982	7.8	6.8	1948	7.8	7.8
1980	7.1	6.3	1946	8.6	8.3
1978	6.9	5.8	1941	5.6	4.8

*Includes all earlier models.
(1) Mean-The sum of the products of units multiplied by age, divided by the total units.
(2) Median-A value in an ordered set of values below and above which there are an equal number of values.
SOURCE: The Polk Company. Permission for further use must be obtained from The Polk Company.

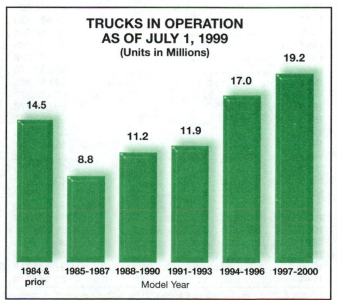

TRUCKS IN OPERATION AS OF JULY 1, 1999 (Units in Millions)

Model Year	Units in Millions
1984 & prior	14.5
1985-1987	8.8
1988-1990	11.2
1991-1993	11.9
1994-1996	17.0
1997-2000	19.2

Motor Vehicles in Operation by Year

MOTOR VEHICLES IN OPERATION, 1948-1999 (as of July 1 of each year)

Year	Passenger Cars	Trucks	Total	% Change	Truck % of Total
1999	126,868,744	82,640,417	209,509,161	2.2	39.4
1998	125,965,709	79,076,930	205,042,639	2.0	38.6
1997	124,672,920	76,397,477	201,070,397	1.4	38.0
1996	124,612,787	73,680,672	198,293,459	2.5	37.2
1995	123,241,881	70,198,512	193,440,393	2.5	36.3
1994	121,996,580	66,717,417	188,713,997	1.3	35.4
1993	121,055,398	65,260,066	186,315,464	2.6	35.0
1992	120,346,746	61,172,404	181,519,150	0.0	33.7
1991	123,327,046	58,178,883	181,505,929	1.2	32.1
1990	123,276,268	56,022,934	179,299,202	1.9	31.2
1989	122,758,378	53,201,657	175,960,035	2.5	30.2
1988	121,519,074	50,221,502	171,740,576	2.7	29.2
1987	119,848,769	47,344,319	167,193,088	3.1	28.3
1986	117,268,071	44,825,523	162,093,594	3.2	27.7
1985	114,662,333	42,386,882	157,049,215	3.2	27.0
1984	112,018,640	40,142,872	152,161,512	3.4	26.4
1983	108,961,215	38,143,304	147,104,519	2.3	25.9
1982	106,867,108	36,986,537	143,853,645	1.4	25.7
1981	105,838,582	36,069,197	141,907,779	1.5	25.4
1980	104,563,781	35,267,535	139,831,316	1.9	25.2
1979	104,676,507	32,582,991	137,259,498	2.8	23.7
1978	102,956,713	30,564,701	133,521,414	4.2	22.9
1977	99,903,594	28,221,661	128,125,255	3.0	22.0
1976	97,818,221	26,560,296	124,378,517	3.6	21.4
1975	95,240,602	24,812,843	120,053,445	3.6	20.7
1974	92,607,551	23,312,245	115,919,796	4.2	20.1
1973	89,805,159	21,411,931	111,217,090	4.7	19.3
1972	86,438,957	19,772,938	106,211,895	4.5	18.6
1971	83,137,324	18,462,287	101,599,611	3.5	18.2
1970	80,448,463	17,687,505	98,135,968	3.2	18.0
1969	78,494,938	16,586,368	95,081,306	4.4	17.4
1968	75,358,034	15,684,917	91,042,951	3.5	17.2
1967	72,967,686	14,988,491	87,956,177	2.7	17.0
1966	71,263,738	14,356,591	85,620,329	4.3	16.8
1965	68,939,770	13,126,579	82,066,349	4.5	16.0
1964	66,051,415	12,444,964	78,496,379	4.1	15.9
1963	63,493,277	11,902,039	75,395,316	4.2	15.8
1962	60,919,579	11,463,381	72,382,960	3.6	15.8
1961	58,854,380	11,042,770	69,897,150	2.9	15.8
1960	57,102,676	10,802,959	67,905,635	3.5	15.9
1959	55,086,761	10,532,145	65,618,906	4.9	16.1
1958	52,492,509	10,056,567	62,549,076	2.2	16.1
1957	51,432,460	9,775,950	61,208,410	3.1	16.0
1956	49,803,977	9,544,082	59,348,059	5.0	16.1
1955	47,377,970	9,162,444	56,540,414	6.3	16.2
1954	44,387,113	8,800,408	53,187,521	4.5	16.5
1953	42,202,349	8,692,574	50,894,923	5.6	17.1
1952	39,769,741	8,419,855	48,189,596	3.5	17.5
1951	38,515,538	8,064,883	46,580,421	7.1	17.3
1950	35,923,583	7,577,037	43,500,620	9.2	17.4
1949	32,730,718	7,087,128	39,817,846	8.9	17.8
1948	29,967,719	6,605,290	36,573,009	9.3	18.1

SOURCE: The Polk Company. Permission for further use must be obtained from the Polk Company.

Lease Penetration Rates and Used Vehicle Sales

LEASE PENETRATION RATES BY VEHICLE SEGMENT*

Segment	1985	1990	1995	1996	1997	1998	2000	2002
PASSENGER CARS								
Budget	2.2%	5.5%	12.1%	13.6%	13.4%	12.1%	10.5%	10.0%
Small	1.8	5.3	18.9	18.5	15.4	14.8	14.3	12.2
Lower Middle	8.2	12.8	26.9	27.3	28.1	27.3	25.5	23.1
Core Middle	11.5	16.2	30.4	31.8	31.1	28.6	27.4	26.4
Upper Middle	11.5	14.7	26.2	27.3	28.1	29.1	30.3	33.7
Near Luxury	16.6	25.2	50.5	52.6	57.3	58.3	61.1	63.8
Luxury	39.6	52.6	62.0	64.2	65.9	65.2	64.3	63.2
Specialty	11.1	24.6	59.7	61.3	58.5	57.5	62.9	64.7
Sport	16.2	18.8	26.2	30.4	34.4	39.3	42.8	43.7
LIGHT TRUCKS								
Compact Pickup	1.3	4.4	14.6	15.2	16.3	15.7	16.2	16.5
Compact Sport Utility	5.2	9.6	34.3	36.7	38.4	39.7	42.5	45.2
Full Size Pickup	4.6	8.2	18.3	19.4	22.7	25.3	27.7	28.8
Full Size Sport Utility	4.2	9.3	36.9	38.2	42.1	42.7	46.9	48.5
Full Size Van	7.1	12.1	20.0	21.3	22.7	22.4	21.6	20.9
Minivan	4.2	8.4	25.8	28.1	32.8	33.5	37.2	38.4
Total	3.5	7.3	24.2	27.2	29.3	31.5	32.2	34.1

USED VEHICLE SALES (In Thousands)

	Franchised Dealers	Independent Dealers	Casual	Total
1999	16,340	14,270	10,280	40,890
1998	15,910	13,650	10,660	40,220
1997	15,890	13,530	10,850	40,270
1996	15,710	13,247	11,871	40,828
1995	15,680	14,120	11,958	41,758
1994	15,050	14,550	10,541	40,141
1993	14,790	14,010	9,257	38,057
1992	14,620	11,680	10,650	36,950
1991	14,570	10,630	12,090	37,290
1990	14,220	10,680	12,630	37,530

AVERAGE USED VEHICLE TRANSACTION PRICES

	Franchised Dealers	Independent Dealers	Casual	Total
1999	$12,630	$7,590	$4,505	$8,828
1998	12,165	7,172	4,190	8,341
1997	12,350	7,155	4,164	8,399
1996	12,256	7,076	4,283	8,257
1995	11,585	7,413	4,316	8,093
1994	11,150	7,209	3,762	7,781
1993	9,871	7,157	3,554	7,335
1992	8,895	6,934	3,405	6,693
1991	7,830	7,260	3,172	6,157
1990	7,410	7,125	2,956	5,830

*Figures shown are estimates representing lease transactions as a percent of new vehicle retail transactions. The total of all segments combined is based on a weighted average.
SOURCE: CNW Marketing/Research

Passenger Car Fleet Registrations and Fleets by State

FLEETS AND VEHICLES BY STATE, 1999

	Fleets (10+Vehicles)	Automobiles	Trucks Class 1-2	Trucks Class 3-5	Trucks Class 6-8	Total Vehicles
Alabama	2,085	69,444	55,265	27,331	54,432	206,472
Alaska	397	8,978	7,430	7,463	7,120	30,991
Arizona	1,523	55,228	44,806	41,847	31,713	173,594
Arkansas	1,385	26,160	32,577	16,680	36,089	111,506
California	12,005	474,627	443,869	205,883	321,332	1,445,711
Colorado	2,068	58,043	52,587	36,963	45,210	192,803
Connecticut	2,349	65,794	57,905	28,365	59,073	211,137
Delaware	462	11,366	12,453	7,991	17,299	49,109
District of Columbia	267	14,135	12,663	5,348	12,087	44,233
Florida	5,986	233,209	208,919	88,230	199,408	729,766
Georgia	3,524	104,932	92,191	31,597	105,199	333,919
Hawaii	492	11,205	12,159	8,883	9,129	41,376
Idaho	844	17,326	18,802	13,737	14,117	63,982
Illinois	5,653	178,939	149,886	76,441	179,770	585,036
Indiana	2,968	83,745	69,457	23,615	93,565	270,382
Iowa	2,173	48,558	45,948	31,955	53,525	179,786
Kansas	1,849	32,925	39,217	17,666	41,999	131,807
Kentucky	1,915	54,451	53,820	24,528	42,521	175,320
Louisiana	2,217	56,263	56,322	27,425	61,167	201,177
Maine	916	19,625	17,664	15,223	16,710	69,222
Maryland	2,720	80,899	81,163	34,735	74,225	271,022
Massachusetts	3,294	80,942	81,643	41,344	82,222	286,151
Michigan	3,945	149,536	103,684	53,670	104,373	411,263
Minnesota	2,698	64,876	60,209	33,554	78,812	237,451
Mississippi	1,253	37,801	32,887	18,281	25,553	114,522
Missouri	2,751	69,035	66,236	36,164	84,360	255,795
Montana	698	12,294	15,337	12,928	11,641	52,200
Nebraska	1,302	24,727	27,199	16,823	37,824	106,573
Nevada	685	18,006	20,236	14,438	11,433	64,113
New Hampshire	849	18,778	15,484	13,079	11,195	58,536
New Jersey	3,919	139,327	121,717	35,172	119,839	416,055
New Mexico	802	25,864	23,830	8,348	18,187	76,229
New York	6,706	227,144	191,415	78,215	182,015	678,789
North Carolina	3,821	102,047	109,667	38,342	142,354	392,410
North Dakota	691	10,144	11,915	11,073	11,819	44,951
Ohio	5,418	177,830	130,846	60,350	163,627	532,653
Oklahoma	1,728	44,528	44,480	11,798	53,681	154,487
Oregon	1,780	51,856	42,639	29,964	45,074	169,533
Pennsylvania	5,973	166,880	148,086	52,840	179,086	546,892
Rhode Island	548	13,800	13,206	5,000	13,359	45,365
South Carolina	1,772	48,934	49,119	19,241	59,580	176,874
South Dakota	433	11,056	13,156	5,340	11,396	40,948
Tennessee	2,510	93,915	72,339	26,757	84,598	277,609
Texas	8,851	260,885	262,270	107,599	247,960	878,714
Utah	818	22,461	24,419	14,995	24,259	86,134
Vermont	446	8,507	9,295	7,469	7,349	32,620
Virginia	3,025	108,230	90,087	32,083	99,310	329,710
Washington	2,496	79,272	61,298	30,208	59,724	230,502
West Virginia	912	24,476	26,847	18,492	16,594	86,409
Wisconsin	3,261	64,291	73,938	54,762	80,964	273,955
Wyoming	408	5,907	7,624	4,345	6,611	24,487
Total	**127,591**	**3,869,201**	**3,516,211**	**1,664,580**	**3,550,489**	**12,600,281**

SOURCE: Bobit Publishing Company, Automotive Fleet Magazine.

Total Motor Vehicle Registrations by Country

MOTOR VEHICLE REGISTRATIONS BY COUNTRY, 1997-1998

Country	1997 Passenger Cars	1997 Commercial Vehicles	1997 Total	1998 Passenger Cars	1998 Commercial Vehicles	1998 Total	Population (000)	Persons Per Car
AFRICA								
Algeria	320,061	432,538	752,599	320,100	432,500	752,600	30,774	96.1
Angola	26,200	26,200	52,400	28,200	30,600	58,800	12,479	442.5
Benin	7,300	6,000	13,300	7,300	6,200	13,500	5,937	813.3
Botswana	66,000	74,900	140,900	83,800	77,700	161,500	1,597	19.1
Burkina Faso	35,500	19,500	55,000	35,500	19,500	55,000	11,616	327.2
Burundi	8,200	11,800	20,000	8,200	11,800	20,000	6,565	800.6
Cameroon	50,418	47,378	97,796	50,400	47,700	98,100	14,693	291.5
Central African Republic	400	300	700	400	400	800	3,550	8,875.0
Congo	29,000	16,600	45,600	29,000	16,600	45,600	2,864	98.8
Ethipoia	55,200	41,300	96,500	55,644	43,797	99,441	61,095	1,098.0
Ghana	31,900	38,400	70,300	32,600	38,400	71,000	19,678	603.6
Ivory Coast	76,215	35,302	111,517	78,100	36,300	114,400	14,526	186.0
Kenya	43,200	52,300	95,500	46,988	60,239	107,227	29,549	628.9
Liberia	17,400	10,700	28,100	17,400	10,700	28,100	2,930	168.4
Libya	296,900	180,900	477,800	305,900	180,900	486,800	5,471	17.9
Madagascar	11,300	15,500	26,800	11,500	17,000	28,500	15,497	1,347.6
Malawi	9,000	12,000	21,000	9,000	12,300	21,300	10,640	1,182.2
Mali	6,300	7,600	13,900	6,300	7,600	13,900	10,960	1,739.7
Mauritania	5,300	6,300	11,600	5,400	6,600	12,000	2,598	481.1
Mauritius	77,600	27,900	105,500	80,578	30,197	110,775	1,150	14.3
Morocco	164,614	113,500	278,114	178,043	132,907	310,950	27,867	156.5
Mozambique	27,200	14,500	41,700	27,200	14,500	41,700	19,286	709.0
Niger	7,100	7,400	14,500	7,100	7,400	14,500	10,400	1,464.8
Nigeria	589,600	363,900	953,500	589,600	363,900	953,500	108,945	184.8
Reunion	179,981	31,365	211,346	180,400	33,000	213,400	691	3.8
Senegambia	28,200	22,700	50,900	28,200	24,300	52,500	10,508	372.6
Sierra Leone	32,400	11,900	44,300	32,400	11,900	44,300	4,717	145.6
South Africa	3,664,000	1,868,000	5,532,000	3,952,201	1,868,000	5,820,201	39,900	10.1
Sudan	11,400	28,200	39,600	11,600	28,600	40,200	28,883	2,489.9
Tanzania	13,800	42,500	56,300	13,800	42,500	56,300	32,793	2,376.3
Togo	74,700	34,600	109,300	74,700	34,600	109,300	4,512	60.4
Tunisia	122,300	96,400	218,700	137,876	107,620	245,496	9,460	68.6
Uganda	7,900	15,900	23,800	7,900	19,100	27,000	21,143	2,676.3
Zaire	32,900	28,700	61,600	32,900	28,700	61,600	50,335	1,529.9
Zambia	24,900	26,200	51,100	24,900	26,200	51,100	8,976	360.5
Zimbabwe	78,300	71,700	150,000	80,600	77,500	158,100	11,529	143.0
Total	**6,232,689**	**3,840,883**	**10,073,572**	**6,591,730**	**3,907,760**	**10,499,490**	**654,114**	**110.9**
AMERICA, Caribbean								
Bahamas	66,054	16,209	82,263	67,400	16,800	84,200	301	4.5

Total Motor Vehicle Registrations by Country

MOTOR VEHICLE REGISTRATIONS BY COUNTRY, 1997-1998 — Continued

Country	1997 Passenger Cars	1997 Commercial Vehicles	1997 Total	1998 Passenger Cars	1998 Commercial Vehicles	1998 Total	Population (000)	Persons Per Car
Barbados	53,800	4,800	58,600	56,868	6,361	63,229	269	4.7
Bermuda	19,342	3,953	23,295	19,900	4,300	24,200	62	3.1
Cuba	8,500	9,700	18,200	10,600	11,100	21,700	11,160	1,052.8
Dominican Republic	113,835	131,700	245,535	120,000	140,000	260,000	8,364	69.7
Guadeloupe	107,600	34,100	141,700	108,700	35,600	144,300	450	4.1
Haiti	19,900	21,600	41,500	20,200	23,100	43,300	8,087	400.3
Jamaica	97,265	43,010	140,275	97,300	44,000	141,300	2,560	26.3
Netherlands Antilles	67,900	24,600	92,500	72,563	26,722	99,285	215	3.0
Puerto Rico	669,900	207,100	877,000	746,608	247,847	994,455	3,839	5.1
Trinidad and Tobago	57,550	18,136	75,686	61,900	20,500	82,400	1,289	20.8
Virgin Islands (U.S.)	20,488	10,283	30,771	20,500	11,000	31,500	120	5.9
Total	**1,302,134**	**525,191**	**1,827,325**	**1,402,539**	**587,330**	**1,989,869**	**36,716**	**25.2**
AMERICA, Central & South								
Argentina	3,137,500	522,800	3,660,300	3,468,082	647,119	4,115,201	36,577	10.5
Belize	2,000	2,800	4,800	2,805	3,011	5,816	235	83.8
Bolivia	35,400	76,500	111,900	37,000	82,000	119,000	8,142	220.1
Brazil	9,385,800	2,087,500	11,473,300	10,828,765	2,429,511	13,258,276	167,988	15.5
Chile	980,704	641,547	1,622,251	1,020,516	679,897	1,700,413	15,019	14.7
Colombia	584,100	339,100	923,200	725,384	420,898	1,146,282	41,564	57.3
Costa Rica	90,200	122,000	212,200	92,800	126,400	219,200	3,933	42.4
Ecuador	159,800	183,900	343,700	186,050	220,000	406,050	12,411	66.7
El Salvador	46,003	52,016	98,019	49,016	56,738	105,754	6,154	125.6
French Guiana	28,200	9,400	37,600	28,200	9,900	38,100	168	6.0
Guatemala	84,300	90,200	174,500	90,203	97,163	187,366	11,090	122.9
Guyana	9,500	3,100	12,600	9,500	3,200	12,700	855	90.0
Honduras	16,520	49,127	65,647	17,242	53,947	71,189	6,316	366.3
Nicaragua	29,500	47,400	76,900	31,176	50,459	81,635	4,938	158.4
Panama	150,200	94,200	244,400	169,217	104,037	273,254	2,812	16.6
Paraguay	68,400	67,100	135,500	75,746	75,750	151,496	5,358	70.7
Peru	292,700	220,200	512,900	323,981	220,232	544,213	25,230	77.9
Suriname	20,447	31,813	52,260	20,400	31,800	52,200	415	20.3
Uruguay	294,199	87,526	381,725	308,500	99,100	407,600	3,313	10.7
Venezuela	1,313,900	352,100	1,666,000	1,444,000	434,000	1,878,000	23,706	16.4
Total	**16,729,373**	**5,080,329**	**21,809,702**	**18,928,583**	**5,845,162**	**24,773,745**	**376,224**	**18.2**
AMERICA, Central & South								
Canada	13,300,000	3,010,400	16,310,400	13,887,270	3,694,077	17,581,347	30,857	2.2
Mexico	4,900,000	2,750,000	7,650,000	4,950,000	2,800,000	7,750,000	97,365	19.7
United States	125,965,709	79,076,930	205,042,639	131,838,538	79,062,475	210,901,013	276,218	2.1
Total	**144,165,709**	**84,837,330**	**229,003,039**	**150,675,808**	**85,556,552**	**236,232,360**	**404,440**	**2.8**

Total Motor Vehicle Registrations by Country

MOTOR VEHICLE REGISTRATIONS BY COUNTRY, 1997-1998 — Continued

Country	1997 Passenger Cars	1997 Commercial Vehicles	1997 Total	1998 Passenger Cars	1998 Commercial Vehicles	1998 Total	Population (000)	Persons Per Car
ASIA, Far East								
Afghanistan	1,600	600	2,200	9,100	600	9,700	21,923	2,409.1
Bangladesh	57,100	73,300	130,400	57,068	75,599	132,667	126,947	2,224.5
Brunei	84,800	11,200	96,000	94,136	14,766	108,902	322	3.4
Burma	4,800	11,000	15,800	5,100	11,500	16,600	45,059	8,835.1
Hong Kong	652,865	255,350	908,215	715,377	262,037	977,414	6,801	9.5
India	4,446,500	2,220,200	6,666,700	4,820,000	2,610,000	7,430,000	998,056	207.1
Indonesia	409,800	1,743,700	2,153,500	491,457	2,097,674	2,589,131	209,255	425.8
Japan	45,861,700	18,622,800	64,484,500	50,353,749	20,855,831	71,209,580	126,505	2.5
South Korea	6,694,100	2,523,500	9,217,600	7,850,926	2,888,673	10,739,599	46,480	5.9
Malaysia	2,102,400	322,800	2,425,200	2,373,200	445,824	2,819,024	21,830	9.2
Pakistan	306,300	227,200	533,500	322,513	227,198	549,711	152,331	472.3
Peoples Republic of China ..	2,493,700	7,163,500	9,657,200	2,940,243	8,313,493	11,253,736	1,266,838	430.9
Philippines	671,007	486,104	1,157,111	749,204	579,244	1,328,448	74,454	99.4
Singapore	365,900	130,600	496,500	393,103	142,615	535,718	3,522	9.0
Sri Lanka	210,300	319,700	530,000	210,600	319,700	530,300	18,639	88.5
Taiwan	4,201,000	701,800	4,902,800	4,536,605	834,158	5,370,763	22,113	4.9
Thailand	1,509,900	3,094,700	4,604,600	1,712,900	3,442,500	5,155,400	60,856	35.5
Vietnam	70,200	94,600	164,800	76,500	103,385	179,885	78,705	1,028.8
Total	**70,143,972**	**38,002,654**	**108,146,626**	**77,711,781**	**43,224,797**	**120,936,578**	**3,280,636**	**40.9**
ASIA, Middle East								
Bahrain	73,600	25,700	99,300	81,074	29,272	110,346	606	7.5
Cyprus	194,000	82,400	276,400	193,980	88,953	282,933	778	4.0
Egypt	558,700	466,600	1,025,300	628,017	508,080	1,136,097	67,226	107.0
Iran	572,925	346,401	919,326	684,500	355,100	1,039,600	66,796	97.6
Iraq	154,700	137,200	291,900	154,700	137,200	291,900	22,450	145.1
Israel	965,200	246,700	1,211,900	1,073,570	288,211	1,361,781	6,101	5.7
Jordan	64,800	70,000	134,800	74,217	77,552	151,769	6,482	87.3
Kuwait	346,900	165,700	512,600	372,967	185,501	558,468	1,897	5.1
Lebanon	386,000	164,400	550,400	385,961	171,005	556,966	3,236	8.4
Oman	183,600	163,800	347,400	205,577	190,367	395,944	2,460	12.0
Qatar	57,500	56,800	114,300	66,100	67,638	133,738	589	8.9
Saudi Arabia	971,700	906,500	1,878,200	1,032,071	1,005,006	2,037,077	20,899	20.2
Syria	81,900	152,500	234,400	81,867	174,550	256,417	15,725	192.1
Turkey	3,482,500	1,133,300	4,615,800	3,838,631	1,317,349	5,155,980	65,546	17.1
United Arab Emirates	695,700	385,700	1,081,400	742,874	419,650	1,162,524	2,398	3.2
Yemen	264,000	319,000	583,000	264,000	321,700	585,700	17,488	66.2
Total	**9,053,725**	**4,822,701**	**13,876,426**	**9,880,106**	**5,337,134**	**15,217,240**	**300,677**	**31.2**
EUROPE, East								
Bulgaria	1,809,400	283,800	2,093,200	1,809,350	283,755	2,093,105	8,279	4.6

Total Motor Vehicle Registrations by Country

MOTOR VEHICLE REGISTRATIONS BY COUNTRY, 1997-1998 — Continued

Country	1997			1998			Population (000)	Persons Per Car
	Passenger Cars	Commercial Vehicles	Total	Passenger Cars	Commercial Vehicles	Total		
Czechoslovakia (former) ...	4,778,400	600,400	5,378,800	4,895,247	600,409	5,495,656	15,644	3.2
Hungary	2,225,100	349,900	2,575,000	2,365,000	370,686	2,735,686	10,076	4.3
Poland	5,603,400	939,600	6,543,000	5,603,398	939,608	6,543,006	38,740	6.9
Romania	2,391,900	513,300	2,905,200	2,391,900	513,300	2,905,200	22,402	9.4
Soviet Union (former)	14,240,200	9,856,000	24,096,200	14,689,100	9,856,000	24,545,100	326,078	22.2
Yugoslavia (former)	1,153,500	331,000	1,484,500	1,312,000	343,800	1,655,800	22,953	17.5
Total	**32,201,900**	**12,874,000**	**45,075,900**	**33,065,995**	**12,907,558**	**45,973,553**	**444,172**	**12.1**
EUROPE, West								
Austria	3,885,000	743,000	4,628,000	3,887,174	752,135	4,639,309	8,177	2.1
Belgium and Luxembourg ..	4,682,000	553,000	5,235,000	4,702,139	569,934	5,272,073	10,578	2.2
Denmark	1,840,961	301,895	2,142,856	1,877,117	311,442	2,188,559	5,282	2.8
Finland	2,021,100	289,700	2,310,800	2,021,116	289,650	2,310,766	5,165	2.6
France	26,300,000	5,375,000	31,675,000	26,800,000	5,500,000	32,300,000	58,886	2.2
Germany	41,371,992	4,299,737	45,671,729	41,673,781	4,356,511	46,030,292	82,178	2.0
Gibraltar	20,500	12,300	32,800	21,900	12,400	34,300	29	1.3
Greece	2,437,497	977,407	3,414,904	2,675,676	1,013,677	3,689,353	10,626	4.0
Iceland	132,468	17,510	149,978	140,372	18,094	158,466	279	2.0
Ireland	1,060,300	164,200	1,224,500	1,196,901	188,219	1,385,120	3,705	3.1
Italy	24,613,600	2,790,300	27,403,900	27,000,001	3,000,000	30,000,001	57,343	2.1
Malta	169,819	42,589	212,408	175,020	43,957	218,977	386	2.2
Netherlands	5,466,900	600,100	6,067,000	5,931,000	709,000	6,640,000	15,735	2.7
Norway	1,686,595	400,259	2,086,854	1,786,404	427,047	2,213,451	4,442	2.5
Portugal	3,080,412	1,005,100	4,085,512	3,150,000	1,085,200	4,235,200	9,873	3.1
Spain	14,753,810	3,009,309	17,763,119	16,050,057	3,561,556	19,611,613	39,634	2.5
Sweden	3,702,778	336,593	4,039,371	3,792,056	353,215	4,145,271	8,892	2.3
Switzerland	3,323,421	219,400	3,542,821	3,383,273	282,841	3,666,114	7,344	2.2
United Kingdom	21,881,000	3,096,000	24,977,000	22,115,000	3,168,900	25,283,900	58,744	2.7
Total	**162,430,153**	**24,233,399**	**186,663,552**	**168,378,987**	**25,643,778**	**194,022,765**	**387,298**	**2.2**
PACIFIC								
Australia	7,785,800	2,069,200	9,855,000	8,400,102	2,266,098	10,666,200	18,705	2.2
Fiji	16,200	18,900	35,100	16,300	19,700	36,000	806	49.4
French Pacific Ocean	37,105	20,703	57,808	38,700	22,700	61,400	231	6.0
Guam	125,100	43,500	168,600	125,100	43,500	168,600	164	1.3
New Caledonia	57,900	23,000	80,900	60,600	25,100	85,700	210	3.5
New Zealand	1,789,700	456,900	2,246,600	1,789,669	456,906	2,246,575	3,828	2.1
Papua New Guinea	21,700	85,500	107,200	21,700	89,700	111,400	4,702	216.7
Samoa (American)	5,400	5,500	10,900	5,400	5,500	10,900	177	32.8
Vanuatu	2,700	3,500	6,200	2,700	3,800	6,500	186	68.9
Total	**9,841,605**	**2,726,703**	**12,568,308**	**10,460,271**	**2,933,004**	**13,393,275**	**29,009**	**2.7**
WORLD TOTAL	**452,101,260**	**176,943,190**	**629,044,450**	**477,095,800**	**185,943,075**	**663,038,875**	**5,913,286**	**12.3**

SOURCE: Auto Strategies International

U.S. Motor Vehicle Exports by Country of Destination and Vehicle Type

U.S. EXPORTS BY COUNTRY OF DESTINATION AND VEHICLE TYPE, 1999

COUNTRY	Passenger Cars Units	Passenger Cars Value ($000)	Trucks Units	Trucks Value ($000)	Buses Units	Buses Value ($000)	Total Units	Total Value ($000)
Albania	4	101	4	132	0	0	8	233
Algeria	2	107	3	116	2	39	7	262
Andorra	31	1,058	18	71	0	0	49	1,129
Angola	74	2,202	36	1,588	1	56	111	3,846
Anguilla	12	234	7	394	1	10	20	638
Antigua	99	2,035	44	1,326	1	20	144	3,381
Argentina	1,977	26,175	210	5,136	3	72	2,190	31,383
Aruba	261	3,158	47	1,211	10	94	318	4,463
Australia	9,209	164,369	3,620	81,134	11	91	12,840	245,594
Austria	360	8,911	193	720	0	0	553	9,631
Azerbaijan	7	147	4	117	0	0	11	264
Bahamas	1,200	16,639	1,196	13,356	14	235	2,410	30,230
Bahrain	289	5,057	102	2,500	0	0	391	7,557
Barbados	39	710	17	408	0	0	56	1,118
Belgium	17,359	267,519	18,960	287,995	21	234	36,340	555,748
Belize	78	1,027	164	2,124	50	410	292	3,561
Benin	26	556	5	45	0	0	31	601
Bermuda	10	272	35	1,354	1	18	46	1,644
Bolivia	87	2,039	36	871	0	0	123	2,910
Bosnia-Hercegovina	5	175	0	0	0	0	5	175
Brazil	1,482	15,837	101	4,915	57	727	1,640	21,479
British Virgin Islands	41	801	15	156	0	0	56	957
Brunei	7	239	0	0	0	0	7	239
Bulgaria	29	558	0	0	0	0	29	558
Cambodia	38	300	0	0	156	347	194	647
Cameroon	6	201	14	163	0	0	20	364
Canada	583,999	8,625,821	230,062	5,329,313	3,466	194,848	817,527	14,149,982
Cayman Islands	804	13,054	68	1,766	6	164	878	14,984
Chile	1,881	24,782	1,188	18,656	13	228	3,082	43,666
China	1,585	4,247	353	16,759	4	28	1,942	21,034
Colombia	194	3,365	867	19,206	13	225	1,074	22,796
Congo (DROC)	1	26	0	0	0	0	1	26
Congo (ROC)	0	0	3	20	3	11	6	31
Costa Rica	945	13,886	748	10,192	82	1,101	1,775	25,179
Cote d'Ivoire	45	1,212	234	5,031	0	0	279	6,243
Croatia	56	1,579	4	373	0	0	60	1,952
Cyprus	88	1,888	18	1,005	0	0	106	2,893
Czech Republic	74	1,792	14	275	0	0	88	2,067
Denmark	278	5,650	8	104	4	7	290	5,761
Djibouti	8	85	0	0	0	0	8	85
Dominica	199	2,699	6	129	1	3	206	2,831
Dominican Republic	1,631	31,475	641	20,625	92	1,035	2,364	53,135
Ecuador	1,373	2,376	283	8,794	23	816	1,679	11,986

U.S. Motor Vehicle Exports by Country of Destination and Vehicle Type

U.S. EXPORTS BY COUNTRY OF DESTINATION AND VEHICLE TYPE, 1999 — continued

COUNTRY	Passenger Cars Units	Passenger Cars Value ($000)	Trucks Units	Trucks Value ($000)	Buses Units	Buses Value ($000)	Total Units	Total Value ($000)
Egypt	672	11,703	512	19,007	0	0	1,184	30,710
El Salvador	42	656	782	5,929	185	911	1,009	7,496
Equatorial Guinea	11	299	42	3,806	0	0	53	4,105
Estonia	42	1,050	0	0	1	5	43	1,055
Ethiopia	4	59	0	0	0	0	4	59
Fed. States of Micronesia	1	3	6	1,044	5	92	12	1,139
Finland	169	3,195	86	1,964	2	43	257	5,202
France	2,782	59,873	98	3,037	427	3,404	3,307	66,314
French Polynesia	18	382	26	502	4	141	48	1,025
Gabon	5	175	5	131	0	0	10	306
Gambia	3	48	1	5	0	0	4	53
Georgia	20	562	12	62	0	0	32	624
Germany	42,415	963,490	693	18,684	102	3,456	43,210	985,630
Ghana	60	624	50	1,189	10	163	120	1,976
Greece	808	8,428	20	572	0	0	828	9,000
Grenada	8	149	9	1,251	1	106	18	1,506
Guadeloupe	71	1,090	5	113	0	0	76	1,203
Guatemala	704	11,561	1,972	19,089	271	1,521	2,947	32,171
Guinea	12	226	7	148	10	185	29	559
Guyana	15	194	8	689	0	0	23	883
Haiti	44	776	664	9,651	33	401	741	10,828
Honduras	387	6,397	848	6,578	250	1,721	1,485	14,696
Hong Kong	964	13,375	37	601	0	0	1,001	13,976
Hungary	24	547	76	1,113	159	1,356	259	3,016
Iceland	31	726	10	396	2	25	43	1,147
India	8	282	8	39	3	20	19	341
Indonesia	191	2,823	56	6,441	0	0	247	9,264
Ireland	270	5,695	22	416	0	0	292	6,111
Israel	2,401	30,345	1,157	25,408	24	490	3,582	56,243
Italy	2,033	42,413	51	1,039	18	187	2,102	43,639
Jamaica	261	4,743	271	7,211	6	154	538	12,108
Japan	36,602	622,448	3,923	73,937	145	1,299	40,670	697,684
Jordan	88	1,545	38	943	0	0	126	2,488
Kazakhstan	3	107	5	1,100	0	0	8	1,207
Kenya	4	47	1	25	0	0	5	72
Korea	664	12,074	111	11,403	4	90	779	23,567
Kuwait	1,650	29,188	1,137	23,290	2	21	2,789	52,499
Kyrgystan	10	352	0	0	0	0	10	352
Latvia	24	1,085	1	28	1	5	26	1,118
Lebanon	489	9,036	54	2,053	6	97	549	11,186
Liberia	5	69	13	258	2	10	20	337
Lithuania	16	462	0	0	0	0	16	462
Luxembourg	97	3,299	0	0	0	0	97	3,299

U.S. Motor Vehicle Exports by Country of Destination and Vehicle Type

U.S. EXPORTS BY COUNTRY OF DESTINATION AND VEHICLE TYPE, 1999 — continued

COUNTRY	Passenger Cars Units	Passenger Cars Value ($000)	Trucks Units	Trucks Value ($000)	Buses Units	Buses Value ($000)	Total Units	Total Value ($000)
Macao	25	457	1	112	0	0	26	569
Macedonia	53	931	3	146	0	0	56	1,077
Madagascar	6	192	0	0	0	0	6	192
Malaysia	106	3,581	39	1,081	0	0	145	4,662
Mali	2	27	38	587	0	0	40	614
Malta & Gozo	6	210	4	192	0	0	10	402
Marshall Islands	10	175	12	150	5	27	27	352
Martinique	5	148	0	0	0	0	5	148
Mauritius	9	258	7	51	0	0	16	309
Mexico	117,018	1,807,335	22,216	356,455	883	9,060	140,117	2,172,850
Moldova	1	21	0	0	0	0	1	21
Monaco	1	35	0	0	0	0	1	35
Mongolia	8	280	0	0	0	0	8	280
Morocco	85	1,545	67	2,217	0	0	152	3,762
Mozambique	6	91	0	0	0	0	6	91
Namibia	6	277	53	1,572	0	0	59	1,849
Netherlands	1,137	20,439	404	11,887	15	247	1,556	32,573
Netherlands Antilles	245	4,465	121	3,372	6	192	372	8,029
New Caledonia	6	192	18	386	0	0	24	578
New Zealand	1,267	12,111	170	8,564	2	47	1,439	20,722
Nicaragua	66	1,116	175	2,036	131	745	372	3,897
Nigeria	794	6,458	136	2,726	20	356	950	9,540
Norway	988	13,779	240	2,230	1	19	1,229	16,028
Oman	531	9,290	102	3,166	0	0	633	12,456
Pakistan	1	35	0	0	0	0	1	35
Panama	917	13,427	665	14,041	138	987	1,720	28,455
Paraguay	16	412	10	194	15	169	41	775
Peru	146	3,151	248	6,497	10	356	404	10,004
Philippines	2,036	26,321	163	4,936	10	38	2,209	31,295
Poland	110	2,056	26	1,785	1	30	137	3,871
Portugal	298	5,292	18	3,852	0	0	316	9,144
Qatar	230	4,184	179	7,642	8	40	417	11,866
Romania	60	1,806	7	264	0	0	67	2,070
Russia	91	2,557	17	1,065	14	1,635	122	5,257
Saudi Arabia	5,076	87,997	4,370	140,398	202	1,687	9,648	230,082
Senegal	12	220	5	78	0	0	17	298
Singapore	304	4,857	158	8,088	4	32	466	12,977
Slovakia	53	1,811	10	75	0	0	63	1,886
Slovenia	48	1,573	0	0	0	0	48	1,573
South Africa	337	4,301	572	34,117	1	11	910	38,429
Spain	9,749	120,408	65	1,660	16	265	9,830	122,333
Sri Lanka	10	139	0	0	0	0	10	139
St Kitts-Nevis	10	305	8	118	0	0	18	423

U.S. Motor Vehicle Exports by Country of Destination and Vehicle Type

U.S. EXPORTS BY COUNTRY OF DESTINATION AND VEHICLE TYPE, 1999 — continued

COUNTRY	Passenger Cars Units	Passenger Cars Value ($000)	Trucks Units	Trucks Value ($000)	Buses Units	Buses Value ($000)	Total Units	Total Value ($000)
St Lucia	12	243	6	96	1	5	19	344
St Vincent & Grenadines	4	95	1	38	1	18	6	151
Suriname	50	947	15	324	4	43	69	1,314
Sweden	1,583	30,101	105	1,934	3	50	1,691	32,085
Switzerland	1,589	42,602	339	1,434	4	446	1,932	44,482
Syria	24	361	5	381	0	0	29	742
Taiwan	8,054	93,960	297	28,844	47	1,254	8,398	124,058
Tanzania	10	189	0	0	0	0	10	189
Thailand	85	1,246	24	5,403	6	95	115	6,744
Trin & Tobago	129	2,164	85	1,956	0	0	214	4,120
Tunisia	13	320	58	3,290	0	0	71	3,610
Turkey	248	6,206	33	4,649	14	35	295	10,890
Turkmenistan	18	485	0	0	0	0	18	485
Turks & Caicos Islands	163	2,177	30	482	3	72	196	2,731
Uganda	3	78	36	1,627	0	0	39	1,705
Ukraine	64	1,727	23	788	2	12	89	2,527
United Arab Emirates	1,180	21,514	706	23,004	25	633	1,911	45,151
United Kingdom	28,349	432,437	989	22,775	51	1,670	29,389	456,882
Uruguay	130	1,332	9	682	5	220	144	2,234
Uzbekistan	24	1,015	4	313	0	0	28	1,328
Venezuela	1,466	26,820	947	45,505	54	1,147	2,467	73,472
Vietnam	3	48	14	935	4	47	21	1,030
Yemen	18	361	1	96	0	0	19	457
Yugoslavia	194	13,337	0	0	0	194	13,337	
Zambia	7	199	0	0	0	0	7	199
Zimbabwe	10	345	116	1,950	0	0	126	2,295
Others	74	1,572	29	1,589	9	45	112	3,206
Total	**905,410**	**13,952,111**	**306,344**	**6,857,067**	**7,423**	**238,457**	**1,219,177**	**21,047,635**

U.S. EXPORTS OF PASSENGER CARS BY COUNTRY OF DESTINATION, 1987-1999

Year	Canada	France	Germany	Japan	Kuwait	Mexico	Saudi Arabia	Taiwan	Other Countries	Total Exports
1999	583,999	2,782	42,415	36,602	1,650	117,018	5,076	8,054	107,814	905,410
1998	566,481	2,675	44,611	43,580	2,519	70,130	11,956	9,604	147,080	898,636
1997	626,629	2,514	57,426	71,789	2,565	62,911	10,146	24,697	216,626	1,075,303
1996	502,652	3,802	59,462	109,917	7,708	46,562	18,253	35,141	190,137	973,634
1995	492,107	2,538	26,690	130,524	6,661	18,649	12,523	61,002	238,673	989,367
1994	559,513	6,083	39,568	100,400	9,246	36,569	18,587	72,491	176,801	1,019,258
1993	480,909	2,942	44,038	56,741	7,923	4,036	32,827	71,332	163,490	864,238
1992	459,910	8,704	56,615	40,598	15,208	4,261	35,502	90,231	140,045	851,074
1991	495,373	5,563	38,285	28,160	16,312	10,592	28,270	44,934	87,461	754,950
1990	505,352	10,475	34,485	39,188	2,919	12,827	23,288	66,609	98,614	793,757
1989	569,039	13,215	19,732	21,966	13,179	1,080	16,995	58,362	64,805	778,373
1988	618,647	5,713	19,110	21,725	10,522	692	19,670	46,622	38,470	781,171
1987	562,078	8,306	6,532	4,738	7,443	472	14,422	10,214	19,045	633,250

Source: Compiled from official statistics of the U.S. Department of Commerce.

U.S. Motor Vehicle Imports by Country of Origin and Vehicle Type

U.S. IMPORTS BY COUNTRY OF ORIGIN AND VEHICLE TYPE, 1999

Country of Origin	Passenger Cars Units	Passenger Cars Value ($000)	Trucks Units	Trucks Value ($000)	Buses Units	Buses Value ($000)	Total Units	Total Value ($000)
Australia	7,129	138,255	2	774	24	74	7,155	139,103
Austria	62	2,271	17	102	3	15	82	2,388
Belgium	58,628	1,293,245	15	479	614	174,736	59,257	1,468,460
Brazil	46	1,456	32	607	0	0	78	2,063
Canada	2,125,876	33,537,900	494,467	11,447,466	23,226	917,333	2,643,569	45,902,699
Finland	11,463	404,444	27	2,970	0	0	11,490	407,414
France	98	2,951	1,797	52,117	0	0	1,895	55,068
Germany	456,246	13,394,417	2,267	39,333	84	15,711	458,597	13,449,461
Hungary	2,039	47,961	0	0	491	26,716	2,530	74,677
Italy	1,379	136,333	41	1,042	1	200	1,421	137,575
Japan	1,560,857	28,674,901	33,661	646,249	2	83	1,594,520	29,321,233
Korea	369,264	2,868,475	1,665	37,860	11	48	370,940	2,906,383
Malaysia	0	5	314	0	0.0	5		123,738
Mexico	637,486	10,027,813	269,076	5,229,384	2,467	123,424	909,029	15,283,925
Netherlands	18,644	343,050	10	619	139	26,728	18,793	370,397
South Africa	5	39	1	250	0	0	6	289
Spain	4	87	0	0	8	1,889	12	1,976
Sweden	82,808	2,086,365	7	350	0	0	82,815	2,086,715
Switzerland	2	15	33	959	25	84	60	1,058
Taiwan	64	484	365	2,091	0	0	429	2,575
United Kingdom	67,689	2,329,965	112	2,924	40	2,010	67,841	2,334,899
Other	27	530	103	2,658	1	11	131	3,199
Total	5,399,816	95,290,957	803,703	17,468,548	27,136	1,289,062	6,230,655	114,048,567

U.S. IMPORTS OF NEW ASSEMBLED PASSENGER CARS BY COUNTRY OF ORIGIN, 1965-1999*

Year	Canada	Germany	Japan	South Korea	Mexico	Sweden	United Kingdom	Other	Total Imports
1999	2,125,876	456,246	1,560,857	369,264	637,486	82,808	67,689	99,590	5,399,816
1998	1,817,836	372,632	1,317,702	207,165	586,973	84,404	49,037	65,690	4,501,439
1997	1,722,199	298,032	1,383,519	222,535	539,384	79,725	43,726	68,100	4,357,220
1996	1,688,123	234,480	1,190,581	225,613	550,622	86,595	43,616	44,817	4,064,447
1995	1,678,276	206,892	1,387,193	216,618	463,305	82,634	42,176	36,823	4,113,917
1994	1,591,326	187,999	1,593,169	217,962	360,370	63,867	28,239	54,082	4,097,014
1993	1,468,272	184,356	1,597,391	126,576	299,634	58,742	20,048	53,441	3,808,460
1992	1,200,358	206,124	1,637,066	133,244	266,149	76,832	11,007	43,942	3,574,722
1991	1,195,987	172,446	1,789,138	191,449	249,499	62,905	14,874	60,164	3,736,462
1990	1,220,221	245,286	1,867,794	201,475	215,986	93,084	27,271	73,485	3,944,602
1985	1,144,805	473,110	2,527,467	N.A.	13,647	142,640	24,474	71,536	4,397,679
1980	594,770	338,711	1,991,502	N.A.	1	61,496	32,517	97,451	3,116,448
1975	733,766	370,012	695,573	N.A.	0	51,993	67,106	156,203	2,074,653
1970	692,783	674,945	381,338	N.A.	N.A.	57,844	76,257	130,253	2,013,420
1965	33,378	376,950	25,538	N.A.	N.A.	26,010	66,565	35,232	563,673

N.A.-Not available.
*Data include imports into Puerto Rico; data do not include automobiles assembled in U.S. foreign trade zones.
Source: Compiled from official statistics of the U.S. Department of Commerce.

World Trade in Motor Vehicles

EXPORTS AND IMPORTS OF MOTOR VEHICLES FOR SELECTED COUNTRIES, 1998

Country	Exports Passenger Cars	Commercial Vehicles	Passenger Total	Imports Passenger Cars	Commercial Vehicles	Total
Argentina*	173,824	63,633	237,457	160,425	24,354	184,779
Austria	88,122	10,998	99,120	328,206	35,659	363,865
Belgium	918,836	107,495	1,026,331	346,706	61,183	407,889
Brazil	279,388	105,285	384,673	341,586	3,450	345,036
Canada*	1,847,761	372,755	2,220,516	732,759	201,782	934,541
China	1,421	10,117	11,538	18,604	21,111	39,715
Czech Republic	286,502	29,394	315,896	191,609	7,569	199,178
Finland	33,700	34	33,734	141,357	21,684	163,041
France	2,761,502	361,289	3,122,791	1,416,273	164,206	1,578,900
Germany	3,269,367	241,538	3,510,905	1,671,496	177,504	1,849,000
Italy	609,012	203,378	812,390	1,666,576	96,997	1,763,573
Japan	3,684,150	844,725	4,528,875	267,529	3,524	271,053
Korea, South	1,228,144	134,020	1,362,164	763	2,222	2,985
Mexico*	590,648	386,325	976,973	45,443	92,589	138,032
The Netherlands*	183,760	11,821	195,581	564,069	5,422	569,491
Norway*	0	0	0	151,338	29,934	181,272
Portugal*	173,707	67,311	241,018	201,493	43,655	245,148
Spain	1,742,234	494,270	2,236,504	747,551	175,352	922,903
Sweden	315,209	110,733	425,942	25,428	2,669	28,097
Switzerland	0	0	0	310,947	21,261	332,208
Turkey	24,669	7,168	31,837	109,901	66,223	176,124
United Kingdom	1,020,727	102,841	1,123,568	1,591,983	114,322	1,706,305
United States	898,636	349,178	1,247,814	4,501,439	647,708	5,149,147
Total	20,131,319	4,014,308	24,145,627	15,533,481	2,020,380	17,552,282

*Imports reflect 1997 data.

WORLD MOTOR VEHICLE EXPORTS, 1970 - 1998

Motor Vehicle Exports by Country of Origin (In Thousands)

Year	World Total[1]	Belgium	Canada	France	Germany	Italy	Japan	Sweden	United Kingdom	United States
1998	24,145.6	1,026.3	2,220.5	3,122.8	3,510.9	812.4	4,528.9	425.9	1,123.6	1,247.8
1997	23,620.8	1,050.8	2,220.5	2,822.5	3,035.6	739.3	4,553.2	416.6	1,065.3	1,591.0
1996	21,691.1	1,192.7	2,134.8	2,272.0	2,841.8	799.2	3,711.7	194.5	1,073.3	1,289.6
1995	20,142.7	1,218.8	1,908.6	2,261.2	2,639.5	806.5	3,790.8	206.3	837.0	1,243.6
1994	19,795.6	1,215.7	1,852.0	2,428.5	2,410.3	669.6	4,460.3	192.8	718.2	1,293.2
1993	19,095.9	1,097.8	2,023.8	2,263.0	2,176.1	504.0	5,017.8	194.4	632.0	1,045.3
1992	20,250.5	1,130.6	1,765.4	2,295.8	2,729.9	697.6	5,667.7	210.8	708.4	1,012.5
1991	19,598.6	1,127.8	1,639.1	2,420.6	2,346.7	806.2	5,753.4	203.4	701.0	962.9
1990	18,315.8	1,225.9	1,699.4	2,315.9	2,765.6	900.9	5,831.2	205.2	510.3	953.1
1989	19,498.8	1,203.0	1,664.2	2,379.1	2,897.7	846.6	5,883.9	205.4	431.3	975.8
1988	19,322.6	1,188.7	1,643.3	2,279.2	2,676.9	827.3	6,104.2	214.6	331.9	1,016.7
1987	18,653.3	1,166.8	1,364.8	2,103.0	2,607.3	766.0	6,304.9	273.4	299.6	861.0
1985	17,810.5	979.8	1,612.1	1,892.8	2,745.9	565.7	6,730.5	260.1	291.8	890.6
1980	15,161.7	883.8	938.5	2,218.9	2,084.3	591.6	5,967.0	192.9	481.0	807.2
1975	10,807.2	792.1	1,005.6	1,938.3	1,653.5	710.5	2,677.6	195.3	695.9	864.1
1970	8,660.5	733.5	928.8	1,525.4	2,103.9	671.0	1,086.8	209.5	862.7	379.1

Percent of World Motor Vehicle Exports

Year		Belgium	Canada	France	Germany	Italy	Japan	Sweden	United Kingdom	United States
1998	100.0	4.3	12.9	14.5	3.4	18.8	1.8	4.7	5.2	
1997	100.0	4.4	9.4	11.9	12.9	3.1	19.3	1.8	4.5	6.7
1996	100.0	5.5	9.8	10.5	13.1	3.7	17.1	0.9	4.9	5.9
1995	100.0	6.1	9.5	11.2	13.1	4.0	18.8	1.0	4.2	6.2
1994	100.0	6.1	9.4	12.3	12.2	3.4	22.5	0.0	3.6	6.5
1993	100.0	5.7	10.6	11.9	11.4	2.6	26.3	1.0	3.3	5.5
1992	100.0	5.6	8.7	11.3	13.5	3.4	27.0	1.0	3.5	4.0
1991	100.0	5.8	8.4	12.4	11.0	4.1	29.4	1.0	3.6	4.9
1990	100.0	6.7	9.3	12.6	15.1	4.9	31.8	1.1	2.8	5.2
1989	100.0	6.2	8.5	12.2	14.9	4.3	30.2	1.1	2.2	5.0
1988	100.0	6.2	8.5	11.8	13.9	4.3	31.6	1.1	1.7	5.3
1987	100.0	6.3	7.3	11.3	13.0	4.1	33.8	1.5	1.6	4.6
1985	100.0	5.5	9.1	10.6	15.4	3.2	37.8	1.5	1.6	5.0
1980	100.0	5.8	6.2	14.6	13.7	3.9	39.4	1.3	3.2	5.3
1975	100.0	7.3	9.3	17.9	15.3	6.6	24.8	1.8	6.4	7.0
1970	100.0	8.5	10.7	17.6	24.3	7.7	12.5	2.4	9.0	4.4

(1) World total includes countries with vehicle exports not shown separately.
SOURCE: Compiled by Ward's Communications from various sources.

Material Usage by the Automotive Industry

AUTOMOTIVE CONSUMPTION OF MATERIALS BY TYPE, 1995-1999

Material	U.S. Total Consumption	Automotive Consumption	Automotive Percentage	Material/Year	U.S. Total Consumption	Automotive Consumption	Automotive Percentage
ALUMINUM (Thousands of Pounds)				**PLASTIC (Thousands of Pounds)**			
1999	24,616,000	7,938,000	32.2	1999	87,390,487	3,557,320	4.1
1998	20,405,000	6,305,000	30.9	1998	85,530,994	3,350,942	3.9
1997	19,580,000	5,626,000	28.7	1997	82,714,959	3,199,348	3.9
1996	18,354,000	5,188,000	28.3	1996	78,747,672	3,091,535	3.9
1995	18,206,000	4,939,000	27.1	1995	71,194,809	3,054,670	4.3
COPPER AND COPPER ALLOY (Thousands of Pounds)				**NATURAL RUBBER (Metric Tons)**			
1999	9,300,000	1,100,000	11.8	1999	N.A.	N.A.	N.A.
1998	8,636,000	1,122,000	13.0	1998	1,309,000	1,001,000	76.5
1997	8,300,000	1,060,000	12.8	1997	1,056,000	803,000	76.0
1996	7,591,000	919,000	12.1	1996	1,001,726	775,661	77.4
1995	7,651,000	834,000	10.9	1995	1,003,495	792,350	79.0
GRAY IRON (Tons)				**SYNTHETIC RUBBER (Metric Tons)**			
1999	5,769,000	1,752,000	30.4	1999	N.A.	N.A.	N.A.
1998	5,950,000	1,870,000	31.4	1998	2,203,000	1,256,000	57.0
1997	6,039,000	2,115,000	35.6	1997	2,305,000	1,269,000	55.1
1996	5,747,000	2,117,000	36.8	1996	2,186,602	1,232,202	56.4
1995	6,239,000	2,146,000	34.4	1995	2,172,321	1,237,652	57.0
DUCTILE IRON (Tons)				**ALLOY STEEL (Tons)**			
1999	3,964,000	1,257,000	31.7	1999	5,420,669	552,908	10.2
1998	3,837,000	1,174,000	30.6	1998	5,768,641	577,048	10.0
1997	3,986,000	1,165,000	29.2	1997	6,449,181	594,735	9.2
1996	3,746,000	1,131,000	30.2	1996	5,561,920	605,442	10.9
1995	4,003,000	1,204,000	30.1	1995	5,114,841	543,227	10.6
MALLEABLE IRON (Tons)				**STAINLESS STEEL (Tons)**			
1999	177,000	92,000	52.0	1999	2,086,495	465,288	22.3
1998	194,000	101,000	52.1	1998	2,026,483	431,132	21.3
1997	201,000	115,000	57.2	1997	2,057,002	428,848	20.8
1996	232,000	157,000	67.7	1996	1,942,776	448,822	23.1
1995	238,000	165,000	69.3	1995	1,894,326	382,163	20.2
TOTAL IRON (Tons)				**TOTAL STEEL (Tons)**			
1999	9,910,000	3,101,000	31.3	1999	106,201,045	16,771,000	15.8
1998	9,981,000	3,145,000	31.5	1998	102,420,000	15,842,000	15.5
1997	10,226,000	3,395,000	33.2	1997	105,858,000	14,253,667	13.5
1996	9,725,000	3,405,000	35.0	1996	100,877,829	14,664,738	14.5
1995	10,480,000	3,515,000	33.5	1995	97,493,710	14,623,389	15.0
LEAD (Metric Tons)				**ZINC (Tons)**			
1999	1,660,000	1,258,400	75.8	1999	1,340,000	308,200	23.0
1998	1,630,000	1,260,100	77.3	1998	1,290,000	296,700	23.0
1997	1,620,000	1,225,050	75.6	1997	1,260,000	289,800	23.0
1996	1,610,000	1,132,800	70.4	1996	1,212,000	278,760	23.0
1995	1,598,890	1,088,078	68.1	1995	1,243,000	285,890	23.0

NOTE: For most materials listed, automotive consumption includes materials used for cars, trucks, buses and replacement parts.
SOURCE: Ward's Communications from various sources.

Material Usage, Vehicles Retired From Use and Vehicle Recycling

POUNDS OF MATERIAL IN A TYPICAL FAMILY VEHICLE, 1978 - 2000

Material	1978 Pounds	1978 Percent	1985 Pounds	1985 Percent	1990 Pounds	1990 Percent	2000 Pounds	2000 Percent
Regular Steel, Sheet, Strip, Bar and Rod	1,915.0	53.6	1,481.5	46.5	1,405.0	44.7	1,373.0	41.8
High and Medium Strength Steel	133.0	3.7	217.5	6.8	238.0	7.6	339.0	10.3
Stainless Steel	26.0	0.7	29.0	0.9	34.0	1.1	53.0	1.6
Other Steels	55.0	1.5	54.5	1.7	39.5	1.3	22.5	0.7
Iron	512.0	14.3	468.0	14.7	454.0	14.5	352.5	10.7
Plastics and Plastic Composites	180.0	5.0	211.5	6.6	229.0	7.3	248.5	7.6
Aluminum	112.5	3.2	138.0	4.3	158.5	5.0	245.5	7.5
Copper and Brass	37.0	1.0	44.0	1.4	48.5	1.5	46.0	1.4
Powder Metal Parts	15.5	0.4	19.0	0.6	24.0	0.8	36.0	1.1
Zinc Die Castings	31.0	0.9	18.0	0.6	18.5	0.6	11.5	0.3
Magnesium Castings	1.0	0.0	2.5	0.0	3.0	0.0	8.0	0.2
Fluids and Lubricants	198.0	5.5	184.0	5.8	182.0	5.8	198.0	6.0
Rubber	146.5	4.1	136.0	4.3	136.5	4.3	144.0	4.4
Glass	86.5	2.4	85.0	2.7	86.5	2.8	98.5	2.0
Other Materials	120.5	3.4	99.0	3.1	83.5	2.7	110.0	3.3
Total	**3,569.5**	**100.0**	**3,187.5**	**100.0**	**3,140.5**	**100.0**	**3,286.0**	**100.0**

SOURCE: American Metal Market from Industry Reports. Copywrite 2000, Cahners Business Information.

MOTOR VEHICLES RETIRED FROM USE, 1957 - 1999 (In Thousands)

Year Ending June 30	Passenger Cars	Trucks & Buses	Total
1999	7,216	4,447	11,664
1998	6,819	4,846	11,665
1997	8,244	4,265	12,509
1996	7,527	3,284	10,811
1995	7,414	2,918	10,332
1994	7,824	4,545	12,369
1993	7,366	1,048	8,413
1992	11,194	1,587	12,781
1991	8,565	2,284	10,850
1990	8,897	2,177	11,073
1989	8,981	2,189	11,170
1988	8,754	2,251	11,005
1987	8,103	2,364	10,467
1986	8,442	2,309	10,752
1985	7,729	2,100	9,829
1983	6,243	1,491	7,734
1981	7,542	1,519	9,061
1979	9,312	1,916	11,228
1977	8,234	1,668	9,902
1975	5,669	908	6,576
1973	7,987	1,208	9,195
1971	6,021	1,044	7,065
1969	6,348	966	7,314
1967	6,984	947	7,931
1965	5,704	736	6,440
1963	4,741	720	5,461
1961	4,294	647	4,941
1959	2,982	372	3,354
1957	4,309	630	4,939

NOTE: Figures represent vehicles which are not re-registered.
SOURCE: The Polk Company. Permission for further use must be obtained from The Polk Company.

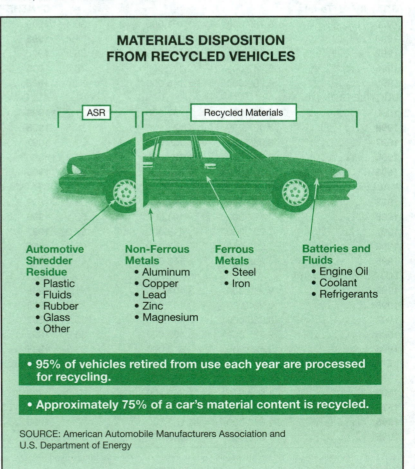

MATERIALS DISPOSITION FROM RECYCLED VEHICLES

| ASR | Recycled Materials |

Automotive Shredder Residue
- Plastic
- Fluids
- Rubber
- Glass
- Other

Non-Ferrous Metals
- Aluminum
- Copper
- Lead
- Zinc
- Magnesium

Ferrous Metals
- Steel
- Iron

Batteries and Fluids
- Engine Oil
- Coolant
- Refrigerants

- 95% of vehicles retired from use each year are processed for recycling.

- Approximately 75% of a car's material content is recycled.

SOURCE: American Automobile Manufacturers Association and U.S. Department of Energy

Licensed Drivers by Age Group, Sex and State

LICENSED DRIVERS BY STATE,1998

State	Male (000)	Female (000)	Total (000)
Alabama	1,713	1,721	3,434
Alaska	246	211	457
Arizona	1,623	1,576	3,199
Arkansas	961	957	1,918
California	10,682	9,817	20,499
Colorado	1,481	1,465	2,946
Connecticut ...	1,172	1,177	2,349
Delaware	269	277	546
Dist. of Columbia	180	169	349
Florida	6,025	6,002	12,027
Georgia	2,613	2,703	5,316
Hawaii	395	352	747
Idaho	425	437	862
Illinois	3,848	3,853	7,701
Indiana	2,033	1,944	3,977
Iowa	962	988	1,950
Kansas	919	932	1,851
Kentucky	1,315	1,325	2,640
Louisiana	1,337	1,399	2,736
Maine	453	459	912
Maryland	1,491	1,687	3,178
Massachusetts	2,206	2,188	4,394
Michigan	3,380	3,422	6,802
Minnesota	1,457	1,411	2,868
Mississippi	858	900	1,758
Missouri	1,881	1,917	3,798
Montana	328	319	647
Nebraska	595	590	1,185
Nevada	651	595	1,246
New Hampshire	457	450	907
New Jersey ...	2,765	2,798	5,563
New Mexico ...	601	603	1,204
New York	5,546	5,008	10,554
North Carolina .	2,747	2,787	5,534
North Dakota ..	229	226	455
Ohio	3,905	4,037	7,942
Oklahoma	1,123	1,182	2,305
Oregon	1,216	1,201	2,417
Pennsylvania ..	4,252	4,153	8,405
Rhode Island ..	337	345	682
South Carolina	1,295	1,385	2,680
South Dakota ..	268	267	535
Tennessee	2,000	2,073	4,073
Texas	6,773	6,550	13,323
Utah	699	694	1,393
Vermont	257	240	497
Virginia	2,361	2,426	4,787
Washington ...	2,073	2,006	4,079
West Virginia ..	648	633	1,281
Wisconsin	1,865	1,845	3,710
Wyoming	183	176	359
Total	93,105	91,875	184,980

SOURCE: U.S. Department of Transportation, Federal Highway Administration

DRIVERS BY AGE GROUP AND SEX, 1998

Age(In Years)	Male (000)	Female (000)	Total (000)
Under 16	18	16	34
16	862	808	1,670
17	1,215	1,137	2,352
18	1,424	1,323	2,747
19	1,538	1,443	2,981
20	1,567	1,482	3,049
21	1,525	1,456	2,981
22	1,525	1,456	2,981
23	1,584	15,813	17,397
24	1,666	1,592	3,258
25-29	9,198	8,830	18,028
30-34	9,742	9,438	19,180
35-39	10,632	10,505	21,137
40-44	10,256	10,207	20,463
45-49	9,101	9,063	18,164
50-54	7,701	7,624	15,325
55-59	5,959	5,880	11,839
60-64	4,755	4,692	9,447
65-69	4,166	4,171	8,337
70-74	3,637	3,794	7,431
75-79	2,676	2,869	5,545
80-84	1,520	1,658	3,178
85 AND OVER	839	918	1,757
Total	93,105	91,875	184,980

DRIVERS BY SEX, 1967-1998

Year	Male (000)	Percent Male	Female (000)	Percent Female	Total (000)
1998	93,105	50.33	91,875	49.67	184,980
1997	91,905	50.30	90,804	49.70	182,709
1996	90,519	50.42	89,021	49.58	179,539
1995	89,214	50.51	87,414	49.49	176,628
1994	89,194	50.85	86,209	49.15	175,403
1993	87,993	50.82	85,156	49.18	173,149
1992	88,387	51.05	84,738	48.95	173,125
1991	86,665	51.28	82,330	48.72	168,995
1990	85,792	51.37	81,223	48.63	167,015
1989	85,378	51.57	80,177	48.43	165,555
1988	85,230	51.91	78,967	48.09	164,197
1987	84,084	51.91	77,891	48.09	161,975
1986	82,494	52.02	76,100	47.98	158,594
1985	81,592	52.01	75,276	47.99	156,868
1984	80,977	52.10	74,447	47.90	155,424
1983	80,894	52.40	73,495	47.60	154,389
1982	78,553	52.29	71,681	47.71	150,234
1981	77,888	52.96	69,187	47.04	147,075
1980	77,187	53.12	68,108	46.88	145,295
1979	76,531	53.41	66,753	46.59	143,284
1978	75,594	53.67	65,249	46.33	140,844
1977	74,467	53.91	63,654	46.09	138,121
1976	72,523	54.11	61,513	45.89	134,036
1975	70,505	54.32	59,286	45.68	129,791
1974	68,574	54.67	56,853	45.33	125,427
1973	67,115	55.22	54,431	44.78	121,546
1972	66,027	55.76	52,387	44.24	118,414
1971	64,291	56.19	50,135	43.81	114,426
1970	63,302	56.75	48,241	43.25	111,543
1969	62,346	57.56	45,960	42.44	108,306
1968	61,204	58.06	44,206	41.94	105,410
1967	60,379	58.52	42,793	41.48	103,172

Demographics of New Car Buyers and Initial Vehicle Quality

DEMOGRAPHICS OF NEW VEHICLE BUYERS AND INITIAL VEHICLE QUALITY, 2000 MODEL YEAR

Characteristic	NEW PASSENGER CAR BUYERS				Characteristic	NEW LIGHT TRUCK BUYERS			
	Domestic[1]	European[2]	Asian[2]	Total		Domestic[1]	European[2]	Asian[2]	Total
Gender					Gender				
Male	51.0%	54.0%	47.6%	50.0%	Male	70.9%	62.7%	58.2%	67.7%
Female	43.3	40.1	47.3	44.5	Female	24.6	34.5	36.8	27.7
No Answer	5.7	5.9	5.1	5.5	No Answer	4.5	2.8	5.0	4.6
Total	**100.0**	**100.0**	**100.0**	**100.0**	**Total**	**100.0**	**100.0**	**100.0**	**100.0**
Age of Principal Purchaser (In Years)					**Age of Principal Purchaser (In Years)**				
Under 25	5.2%	3.5%	5.7%	5.1%	Under 25	2.9%	0.4%	2.1%	2.7%
25-29	5.7	7.0	7.2	6.5	25-29	5.4	3.5	6.4	5.6
30-34	5.1	9.1	7.4	6.7	30-34	8.1	8.0	10.4	8.6
35-39	6.0	9.4	8.4	7.5	35-39	10.7	10.3	13.4	11.3
40-44	7.6	11.4	9.4	8.9	40-44	11.4	17.1	12.5	11.7
45-49	9.3	12.1	11.1	10.5	45-49	11.1	13.6	12.1	11.3
50-54	10.4	13.3	12.6	11.7	50-54	12.0	14.9	10.8	11.7
55-59	7.9	8.6	8.2	8.2	55-59	10.2	9.6	7.9	9.6
60-64	7.6	6.0	6.4	6.9	60-64	7.4	6.7	6.3	7.1
65 and over	25.0	9.8	13.7	18.0	65 and over	12.5	6.5	8.9	11.6
No Answer	10.4	9.9	9.9	10.1	No Answer	8.5	9.4	9.2	8.7
Total	**100.0**	**100.0**	**100.0**	**100.0**	**Total**	**100.0**	**100.0**	**100.0**	**100.0**
Highest Education Level					**Highest Education Level**				
8th Grade or Less	1.0%	0.1%	0.5%	0.7%	8th Grade or Less	1.4%	0.0%	0.4%	1.2%
Some High School	3.0	1.0	2.0	2.3	Some High School	2.7	0.4	1.2	2.3
High School Graduate	22.6	6.6	14.0	16.6	High School Graduate	21.7	4.3	11.4	19.0
Technical/Trade School	7.7	2.4	5.0	5.8	Trade/Technical School	8.9	3.4	6.1	8.2
Some College	29.1	19.9	28.5	27.5	Some College	29.3	15.5	26.9	28.5
College Graduate	17.6	28.7	22.2	21.2	College Graduate	18.3	33.3	23.1	19.6
Post Graduate	6.8	10.3	8.2	7.9	Post Graduate	6.4	9.6	8.1	6.8
Advanced Degree	12.0	31.0	19.6	18.0	Advanced Degree	11.3	33.5	22.7	14.3
Total	**100.0**	**100.0**	**100.0**	**$100**	**Total**	**100.0**	**100.0**	**100.0**	**100.0**
Census Region					**Census Region**				
Northeast	25.5%	28.3%	26.3%	26.3%	Northeast	19.1%	27.2%	21.6%	19.8%
North Central	25.9	11.0	16.0	19.6	North Central	29.6	8.6	14.3	25.6
South	31.5	28.5	32.4	31.4	South	32.0	26.9	34.6	32.5
West	17.0	32.2	25.3	22.7	West	19.3	37.3	29.5	22.0
Total	**100.0**	**100**	**100**	**100**	**Total**	**100.0**	**100.0**	**100.0**	**100.0**
Median Household					**Median Household**				
Income	$55,885	$116,888	$64,685	$65,220	Income	$68,916	$159,901	$76,030	$71,083
Initial Quality					**Initial Quality**				
Study 2 Results	**151.2**	**150.6**	**129.3**	**141.8**	**Study 2 Results**	**171.6**	**198.7**	**152.5**	**167.2**
(Problems per 100 passenger cars)					(Problems per 100 passenger cars)				

NOTE: Study conducted among personal use buyers of 2000 model year vehicles.
(1) Domestic figures include captive import buyers.
(2) Import figures include North American assembled vehicle buyers.
SOURCE: J.D. Power and Associates, 1999 Vehicle Quality Survey

Passenger Car Operating Costs

PASSENGER CAR OPERATING COSTS, 1950-2000 MODEL YEARS

Model Year	Variable Cost in Cents Per Mile				Cost Per 10,000 Miles			
	Gas & Oil	Maintenance	Tires	Total	Variable Cost	Fixed Cost	Total Cost	Total Cost Per Mile
2000	7.30¢	3.60¢	1.70¢	12.60¢	$1,260	$4,523	$5,783	57.83¢
1999	5.70	3.40	1.60	10.70	1,070	4,456	5,526	55.26
1998	6.30	3.10	1.40	10.80	1,080	4,403	5,483	54.83
1997	6.60	2.80	1.40	10.80	1,080	4,228	5,308	53.08
1996	5.90	2.80	1.40	10.10	1,010	4,133	5,143	51.43
1995	6.00	2.60	1.40	10.00	1,000	3,891	4,891	48.91
1994	5.60	2.50	1.10	9.20	920	3,745	4,665	46.65
1993	6.00	2.40	0.90	9.30	930	3,584	4,514	45.14
1991	6.70	2.20	0.90	9.80	980	3,384	4,364	43.64
1989	5.20	1.90	0.80	7.90	790	3,030	3,820	38.20
1987	4.80	1.60	0.80	7.20	720	2,544	3,264	32.64
1985	6.16	1.23	0.65	8.04	804	1,916	2,720	27.20
1983	6.64	1.04	0.68	8.36	836	2,506	3,342	33.42
1981	6.27	1.18	0.72	8.17	817	2,375	3,192	31.92
1979	4.11	1.10	0.65	5.86	586	1,811	2,397	23.97
1977	4.11	1.03	0.66	5.80	580	1,439	2,019	20.19
1975	4.82	0.97	0.66	6.45	645	1,186	1,831	18.31
1973	3.35	0.78	0.62	4.75	475	1,172	1,647	16.47
1971	2.96	0.73	0.56	4.25	425	1,125	1,550	15.50
1969	2.76	0.68	0.51	3.95	395	1,053	1,448	14.48
1967	2.65	0.68	0.47	3.80	380	982	1,362	13.62
1965	2.58	0.68	0.44	3.70	370	807	1,177	11.77
1960	2.62	0.79	0.49	3.90	390	808	1,198	11.98
1950	2.14	0.68	0.46	3.28	328	533	861	8.61

ANNUAL FIXED COST OF OPERATING A PASSENGER CAR, 1950-2000 MODEL YEARS

Model Year	Insurance		Property Damage & Liability[3]	License, Registration & Taxes	Depreciation	Finance Charge	Total	Average Fixed Cost Per Day
	Fire & Theft[1]	Collision[2]						
2000	$124	$280	$481	$218	$3,408	$827	$5,338	$14.62
1999	123	278	484	223	3,355	812	5,275	14.45
1998	115	262	479	223	3,294	802	5,175	14.18
1997	106	302	401	220	3,268	793	5,090	13.95
1996	109	247	426	229	3,208	778	4,997	13.69
1995	95	211	410	211	3,099	729	4,755	13.03
1994	91	206	400	204	2,988	695	4,584	12.56
1993	107	232	385	183	2,883	696	4,486	12.29
1991	115	258	353	169	2,543	779	4,217	11.55
1989	109	245	309	151	2,094	626	3,534	9.68
1987	87	196	252	140	1,506	601	2,782	7.62
1985	92	198	213	115	1,253	570	2,441	6.69
1983	80	201	222	102	1,343	558	2,506	6.87
1981	76	180	254	88	1,287	490	2,375	6.51
1979	74	168	241	90	942	296	1,811	4.96
1977	80	188	250	74	847	—	1,439	3.94
1975	53	141	189	30	773	—	1,186	3.25
1973	45	143	179	28	777	—	1,172	3.21
1971	62	125	175	25	738	—	1,125	3.08
1969	44	102	154	24	729	—	1,053	2.88
1967	39	85	148	26	684	—	982	2.69
1965	31	—	126	24	626	—	807	2.21
1960	30	—	110	22	646	—	808	2.21
1950	16	—	60	15	442	—	533	1.46

(1) No deductible prior to 1973; $50 deductible 1973-1977; $100 deductible 1978-1992; $250 deductible 1993-2000.
(2) $100 deductible 1967-1977; $250 deductible 1978-1992; $500 deductible 1993-2000.
(3) Coverage: 1949 to 1955-$15,000/$30,000; 1957 to 1965-$25,000/$50,000; 1967 to 2000-$100,000/$300,000
NOTE: Beginning in 1985 ownership costs are based on a six year /60,000 mile retention cycle rather than four year/60,000 miles.
SOURCE: American Automobile Association.

Automobile Financing

NEW AND USED CAR FINANCING WITH FINANCE COMPANIES, 1980-1999

Year	Average Interest Rate	Average Maturity (Months)	Average Amount Financed	Average Monthly Payment
NEW CARS				
1999	6.7%	52.7	$19,880	$436.49
1998	6.3	52.1	19,083	419.60
1997	7.1	54.1	18,077	391.45
1996	9.8	51.6	16,987	404.75
1995	11.2	54.1	16,210	382.98
1994	9.8	54.0	15,375	353.25
1993	9.5	54.5	14,332	324.79
1992	9.8	54.0	13,607	313.01
1991	12.4	55.1	12,494	298.14
1990	12.6	54.6	12,071	291.31
1988	12.6	56.2	11,663	275.95
1986	9.4	50.0	10,665	258.74
1984	14.6	48.3	9,337	256.90
1982	15.9	46.0	8,178	238.16
1980	14.8	45.0	6,322	183.91
USED CARS				
1999	12.6%	55.9	$13,642	$324.15
1998	12.6	53.5	12,691	311.51
1997	13.3	51.0	12,281	316.54
1996	13.5	51.4	12,182	313.39
1995	14.5	52.2	11,590	300.66
1994	13.5	50.2	10,709	280.37
1993	12.8	48.8	9,875	260.63
1992	13.7	47.9	9,211	250.70
1990	16.0	46.1	8,289	249.35
1988	15.1	46.7	7,824	222.68
1986	16.0	42.6	6,555	202.52
1984	17.9	39.7	5,691	190.92
1982	20.8	37.0	4,746	174.84
1980	19.1	34.8	3,810	143.44

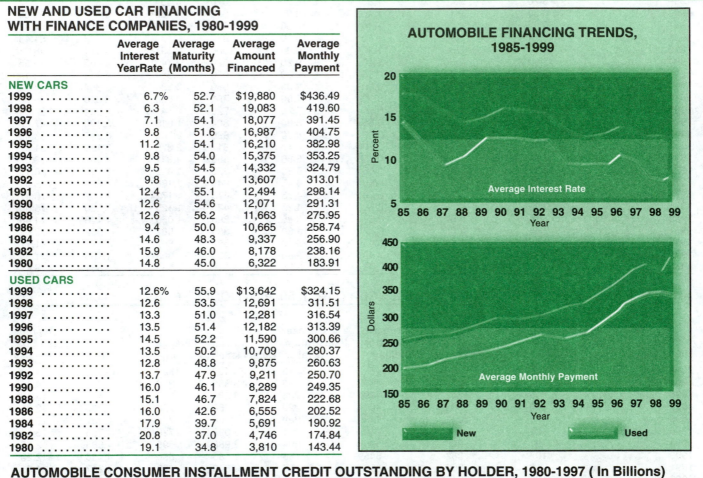

AUTOMOBILE FINANCING TRENDS, 1985-1999

AUTOMOBILE CONSUMER INSTALLMENT CREDIT OUTSTANDING BY HOLDER, 1980-1997 (In Billions)

	Commercial Banks		Finance Companies		Others		
	Amount	Percent of Total	Amount	Percent of Total	Amount	Percent of Total	Total
1997	$155.3	37.2%	$87.0	20.8%	$175.9	42.1%	$418.2
1996	151.9	40.0	86.4	22.7	141.9	37.3	380.2
1995	144.8	42.0	75.4	21.9	124.5	36.1	344.7
1994	132.6	43.0	67.3	21.8	108.6	35.2	308.5
1993	115.8	42.2	60.6	22.1	98.1	35.7	274.5
1992	110.7	42.2	63.3	24.1	88.4	33.7	262.4
1991	117.5	43.5	69.1	25.6	83.6	30.9	270.2
1990	126.6	43.9	80.1	27.8	81.7	28.3	288.4
1988	123.4	43.4	97.2	34.2	63.7	22.4	284.3
1986	101.5	41.0	92.5	37.4	53.4	21.6	247.4
1984	83.9	48.3	51.9	29.9	37.8	21.8	173.6
1982	59.6	47.3	44.1	35.0	22.2	17.6	125.9
1980	61.5	55.0	29.4	26.2	21.0	18.8	111.9

SOURCE: Board of Governors of the Federal Reserve System and Ward's Communications.

Personal Consumption Expenditures for Transportation

AVERAGE EXPENDITURE PER NEW CAR, 1967-1999

Year	Average Expenditure Per New Car[1]			Estimated Average New Car Price for a 1967 "Comparable Car"		Annual Median Family Earnings[4]	Weeks of Median Family Earnings to Equal		
				With Added Safety & Emissions Equipment[2]	Without Added Safety & Emissions Equipment[3]			Cost of "Comparable Car"	
	Domestic*	Import	Average				Average New Car Expenditure[5]	With Added Safety & Emissions Equipment[6]	Without Added Safety & Emissions Equipment[7]
1999	18,724	30,347	21,020	13,163	9,157	50,784	21.5	13.5	9.4
1998	18,579	31,986	20,849	13,205	9,233	48,000	22.6	14.3	10.0
1997	17,838	28,193	19,551	13,240	9,297	45,326	22.4	15.2	10.7
1996	17,468	26,205	18,777	13,184	9,281	42,789	22.8	16.0	11.3
1995	16,864	23,202	17,959	12,857	9,115	40,572	23.0	16.5	11.7
1994	16,930	21,989	17,903	12,429	8,925	38,178	24.4	16.9	12.2
1993	15,976	20,261	16,871	11,808	8,631	36,764	23.9	16.7	12.2
1992	15,644	18,593	16,636	11,488	8,424	35,672	24.3	16.7	12.3
1991	15,192	16,327	15,475	11,187	8,224	34,775	23.1	16.7	12.3
1989	13,936	15,510	14,371	10,282	7,825	32,448	23.0	16.5	12.5
1987	12,922	14,470	13,386	9,775	7,518	29,744	23.4	17.1	13.1
1985	11,589	12,853	11,838	9,014	6,958	27,144	22.7	17.3	13.3
1983	10,516	10,868	10,606	8,415	6,544	24,580	22.4	17.8	13.8
1981	8,912	8,896	8,910	7,726	6,115	22,388	20.7	17.9	14.2
1979	6,889	6,704	6,847	6,198	5,337	19,661	18.1	16.4	14.1
1977	5,985	5,072	5,814	5,292	4,593	16,009	18.9	17.2	14.9
1975	5,084	4,384	4,950	4,689	4,103	13,719	18.8	17.8	15.6
1973	4,181	3,344	4,052	3,903	3,572	12,051	17.5	16.8	15.4
1971	3,919	2,769	3,742	3,777	3,601	10,285	18.9	19.1	18.2
1969	3,697	2,496	3,557	3,464	3,357	9,433	19.6	19.1	18.5
1967	3,313	2,276	3,216	3,196	3,185	7,933	21.1	20.9	20.9

*Includes transplants
(1) U.S. Departments of Commerce, Bureau of Economic Analysis (BEA) , "Average Transaction Price Per New Car." Includes purchases by business, government, and consumers.
(2) 1967 "Average Transaction Price" plus the value of added safety and emissions equipment as determined by the U.S. Bureau of Labor Statistics (BLS), all inflated to current dollars using the BLS, "New Car Consumer Price Index - All Urban Consumers." For example, 1969 is equal to the 1968 value plus the BLS stated value of added safety and emissions equipment for the 1969 model year multiplied by 1968-1969 monthly changes in the New Car Consumer Price Index. The cost to improve fuel economy, which prior to 1980 was included with "Other Quality Adjustments", has since been included by the BLS with the cost of emissions improvements.
(3) 1967 "Average Transaction Price" inflated to current dollars.
(4) BLS, "Median Family Earnings."
(5) "Average Expenditure," as reported by the BEA, divided by "Annual Median Family Earnings", multiplied by 52 weeks. This index is not a good reflection car prices because it includes upgrading - the purchase of more expensive types of vehicles with more options - and downgrading.
(6) "Estimated Average New Car Price of Comparable Cars With New Safety and Emissions Equipment Added", divided by "Annual Median Family Earnings", multiplied by 52 weeks. This index is a good reflection of price as seen by car purchasers who would not otherwise buy safety / emissions equipment.
(7) "Estimated Average New Car Price of Comparable Cars Without New Safety and Emissions Equipment" divided by "Annual Median Family Earnings", multiplied by 52 weeks. This index is a good reflection of price as seen by purchasers who place full value on new safety / emissions equipment.

INDICES OF CONSUMER COSTS, 1980-1999

Year	Consumer Price Index - All Urban Consumers (1982-4 = 100)							Calculated New Car Index With Added Safety & Emissions*
	All Items	Housing	Medical Care	Public Transportation	Gasoline	Used Cars	New Cars	
1999	166.6	163.9	250.6	197.7	100.1	152.0	139.6	156.5
1998	163.0	160.4	242.1	190.3	91.6	150.6	140.7	157.0
1997	160.5	156.8	234.6	186.7	105.8	151.1	141.7	157.4
1996	156.9	152.8	228.2	181.9	105.9	157.1	141.5	156.7
1995	152.4	148.5	220.5	175.9	99.8	156.5	139.0	152.9
1994	148.2	144.8	211.0	172.0	98.2	141.7	136.0	147.8
1993	144.5	141.2	201.4	167.0	97.7	133.9	131.5	140.4
1992	140.3	137.5	190.1	151.4	99.0	123.2	128.4	136.6
1991	136.2	133.6	177.0	148.9	99.2	118.1	125.3	133.0
1990	130.7	128.5	162.8	142.6	101.0	117.6	121.0	126.2
1986	109.6	110.9	122.0	117.0	77.0	108.8	110.6	112.1
1984	103.9	103.6	106.8	105.7	97.8	112.5	102.8	103.6
1982	96.5	96.9	92.5	94.9	102.8	88.8	97.4	96.4
1980	82.4	81.1	74.9	69.0	97.5	62.3	88.4	81.9

*Calculated by Ward's Communications.
SOURCE: U.S. Department of Labor, Bureau of Labor Statistics.

Personal Consumption Expenditures for Transportation

PERSONAL CONSUMPTION EXPENDITURES FOR TRANSPORTATION, 1988-1999 (In Millions)

	1988	1990	1992	1994	1996	1997	1998	1999
User-Operated Transportation								
New Autos	$101,041	$96,692	$78,016	$86,478	$81,872	$82,462	$87,771	$97,349
Net Purchases of Used Autos	30,532	33,663	31,176	43,001	51,436	53,070	55,313	58,738
Other Motor Vehicles*	45,577	49,586	60,523	77,682	84,349	88,982	104,048	119,859
Tires, Tubes, Accessories and Parts	20,685	22,483	30,523	35,165	38,654	39,636	41,709	44,779
Repair, Greasing, Washing, Parking, Storage and Rental	73,531	82,538	90,293	109,980	134,175	146,287	153,119	162,115
Gasoline and Oil	86,899	108,471	104,880	108,955	124,160	128,123	115,238	128,336
Bridge, Tunnel, Ferry and Road Tolls	1,774	2,024	2,839	3,255	3,726	3,985	4,176	4,351
Insurance Premiums, Less Claims Paid	16,842	18,066	25,728	27,767	31,781	36,335	38,002	39,066
Total User-Operated Transportation	**$376,881**	**$413,523**	**$423,978**	**$492,283**	**$550,153**	**$578,880**	**$599,376**	**$654,593**
Purchased Local Transportation								
Transit Systems	$5,377	$5,707	$6,463	$7,091	$7,691	7,829	8,010	8,239
Taxicabs	2,935	3,209	2,586	2,953	3,530	3,746	4,053	4,025
Total Purchased Local Transportation	**$8,312**	**$8,916**	**$9,049**	**$10,044**	**$11,221**	**$11,575**	**$12,063**	**$12,264**
Purchased Intercity Transportation								
Railway Excluding Commutation	$588	$708	$647	$603	$642	684	712	747
Bus	2,181	1,396	1,595	1,518	1,769	1,845	2,087	2,174
Airline	22,993	26,467	21,281	23,665	26,183	28,977	29,511	30,717
Other	2,229	2,644	3,592	4,025	4,677	4,710	4,858	5,053
Total Purchased Intercity Transportation	**$27,991**	**$31,215**	**$27,115**	**$29,811**	**$33,271**	**$36,216**	**$37,168**	**$38,691**
Total Transportation Expenditures	**$413,184**	**$453,654**	**$460,142**	**$532,138**	**$594,645**	**$626,671**	**$648,607**	**$705,548**
Total Personal Consumption Expenditures	**$3,296,126**	**$3,748,417**	**$4,209,653**	**$4,716,394**	**$5,237,499**	**$5,529,283**	**$5,850,863**	**$6,268,650**

*New and used trucks, recreation vehicles, etc.
SOURCE: U.S. Department of Commerce, Bureau of Economic Analysis.

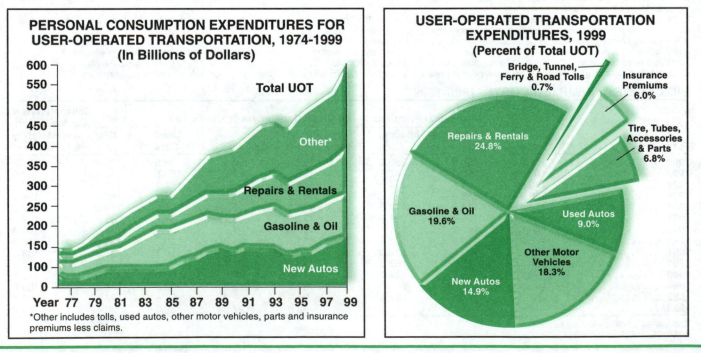

PERSONAL CONSUMPTION EXPENDITURES FOR USER-OPERATED TRANSPORTATION, 1974-1999 (In Billions of Dollars)

Total UOT
Other*
Repairs & Rentals
Gasoline & Oil
New Autos

*Other includes tolls, used autos, other motor vehicles, parts and insurance premiums less claims.

USER-OPERATED TRANSPORTATION EXPENDITURES, 1999 (Percent of Total UOT)

Bridge, Tunnel, Ferry & Road Tolls 0.7%
Insurance Premiums 6.0%
Tire, Tubes, Accessories & Parts 6.8%
Repairs & Rentals 24.8%
Gasoline & Oil 19.6%
Used Autos 9.0%
Other Motor Vehicles 18.3%
New Autos 14.9%

U.S. Motor Vehicle Thefts by State, Area and Year

MOTOR VEHICLE THEFTS BY STATE, 1997-1998

State	1997	1998	Percent Change	State	1997	1998	Percent Change
Alabama	15,407	14,871	-3.5	Montana	2,179	2,014	-7.6
Alaska	2,784	2,607	-6.4	Nebraska	5,541	5,788	4.5
Arizona	44,201	40,391	-8.6	Nevada	13,220	13,766	4.1
Arkansas	7,938	7,187	-9.5	New Hampshire	1,593	1,474	-7.5
California	228,722	195,517	-14.5	New Jersey	41,165	35,185	-14.5
Colorado	16,107	16,087	-0.1	New Mexico	12,407	10,767	-13.2
Connecticut	14,541	12,705	-12.6	New York	79,697	68,171	-14.5
Delaware	3,718	3,186	-14.3	North Carolina	24,442	24,616	0.7
Dist. of Columbia	7,569	6,501	-14.1	North Dakota	1,154	1,127	-2.3
Florida	107,195	104,250	-2.7	Ohio	45,419	43,021	-5.3
Georgia	44,572	42,538	-4.6	Oklahoma	14,644	13,565	-7.4
Hawaii	6,468	5,594	-13.5	Oregon	19,280	17,262	-10.5
Idaho	2,429	2,282	-6.1	Pennsylvania	44,213	42,008	-3.5
Illinois	55,423	52,932	-4.5	Rhode Island	4,195	3,829	-8.7
Indiana	25,099	21,187	-15.6	South Carolina	15,755	15,948	1.2
Iowa	6,682	5,974	-10.6	South Dakota	858	763	-11.1
Kansas	6,491	5,988	-7.7	Tennessee	33,742	28,099	-16.7
Kentucky	9,694	8,573	-11.6	Texas	101,721	96,646	-4.0
Louisiana	26,374	23,661	-10.3	Utah	9,144	7,700	-15.8
Maine	1,642	1,509	-8.1	Vermont	800	874	9.2
Maryland	30,668	28,212	-8.0	Virginia	18,892	18,355	-2.8
Massachusetts	29,452	26,403	-10.4	Washington	31,855	35,200	10.5
Michigan	65,327	58,338	-10.7	West Virginia	3,287	3,390	3.1
Minnesota	17,869	15,366	-14.0	Wisconsin	15,640	14,210	-9.1
Mississippi	9,328	9,322	-0.1	Wyoming	647	669	3.4
Missouri	26,517	24,466	-7.7	Total	1,353,707	1,317,324	-2.7

SOURCE: Federal Bureau of Investigation.

MOTOR VEHICLE THEFTS, 1970-1998

Year	Thefts*	Motor Vehicle Registrations	Ratio of Vehicles Stolen/Registered	Year	Thefts*	Motor Vehicle Registrations	Ratio of Vehicles Stolen/Registered
1998	1,317,324	205,042,639	1 in 156	1980	1,114,651	139,831,316	1 in 125
1997	1,353,707	201,070,397	1 in 149	1975	1,000,500	120,053,445	1 in 120
1996	1,394,238	198,293,459	1 in 142	1970	921,400	98,135,968	1 in 107
1995	1,472,441	193,440,393	1 in 131				
1994	1,539,287	188,713,997	1 in 123				
1993	1,563,060	186,315,464	1 in 119				
1992	1,610,834	181,519,150	1 in 113				
1991	1,661,738	181,505,929	1 in 109				
1990	1,635,907	179,299,202	1 in 109				
1989	1,564,800	175,960,035	1 in 112				
1988	1,432,916	171,740,576	1 in 120				
1987	1,288,674	167,193,088	1 in 130				
1986	1,224,137	162,093,594	1 in 132				
1985	1,102,862	157,049,215	1 in 142				
1984	1,032,165	152,161,512	1 in 147				
1983	1,007,933	147,104,519	1 in 146				

* Includes cars, motorcycles, trucks and buses.

TOP TEN AUTO THEFT AREAS, 1998

1. New York, New York
2. Chicago, Illinois
3. Los Angeles, California
4. Houston, Texas
5. Phoenix, Arizona
6. Dallas, Texas
7. Las Vegas, Nevada
8. San Diego, California
9. Memphis, Tennessee
10. New Orleans, Louisiana

SOURCE: National Insurance Crime Bureau

Vehicle Miles of Travel and Fuel Consumption

VEHICLE MILES OF TRAVEL AND FUEL CONSUMPTION, 1960-1998

| | Passenger Vehicles | | | | Trucks | | | |
	Passenger Cars	Light Trucks	Buses	Total	Single Unit Trucks	Combination Trucks	Total	All Motor Vehicles
VEHICLE MILES OF TRAVEL (In Millions)								
1998	1,545,830	866,228	6,996	2,419,054	67,894	128,159	196,053	2,615,107
1997	1,502,556	850,739	6,842	2,360,137	66,893	124,584	191,477	2,551,614
1996	1,469,854	816,540	6,563	2,292,957	64,072	118,899	182,971	2,475,928
1994	1,416,329	764,634	6,409	2,187,372	61,284	108,932	170,216	2,357,588
1992	1,381,126	706,863	5,778	2,093,767	53,874	99,510	153,384	2,247,151
1990	1,417,823	574,571	5,726	1,998,120	51,901	94,341	146,242	2,144,362
1985	1,255,884	390,961	4,478	1,651,323	45,441	78,063	123,504	1,774,827
1980	1,121,810	290,935	6,059	1,418,804	39,813	68,678	108,491	1,527,295
1970	919,679	123,286	4,544	1,047,509	27,081	35,134	62,215	1,109,724
1960	587,012	N.A.	4,346	N.A.	N.A.	28,854	28,854	718,762
AVERAGE ANNUAL MILES TRAVELED PER VEHICLE								
1998	11,725	12,061	9,777	11,844	12,542	70,009	27,064	12,183
1997	11,581	12,115	9,809	11,768	12,637	69,601	27,032	12,107
1996	11,330	11,811	9,446	11,497	12,167	68,075	26,092	11,813
1994	10,759	12,156	9,560	11,205	12,491	64,783	25,838	11,683
1992	10,571	12,381	8,962	11,114	12,329	59,396	25,373	11,558
1990	10,277	11,902	9,133	10,693	11,567	55,206	23,603	11,107
1985	9,419	10,506	7,545	9,649	9,893	55,629	20,597	10,020
1980	8,813	10,437	11,458	9,112	9,103	48,472	18,736	9,458
1970	9,989	8,676	12,035	9,821	7,356	38,819	13,565	9,976
1960	9,518	N.A.	15,970	N.A.	N.A.	N.A.	10,693	9,732
FUEL CONSUMED (Millions of Gallons)								
1998	72,209	50,579	1,049	122,788	9,740	21,100	30,841	154,884
1997	69,892	49,388	1,027	119,280	9,576	20,302	29,878	150,386
1996	69,221	47,354	990	116,575	9,408	20,193	29,601	147,365
1994	68,079	44,112	964	113,155	9,032	18,653	27,685	140,839
1992	65,627	40,929	878	107,434	8,237	17,216	25,453	132,888
1990	69,759	35,611	895	106,266	8,357	16,133	24,490	130,755
1985	71,700	27,363	834	99,897	7,399	14,005	21,404	121,301
1980	70,186	23,796	1,018	95,000	6,923	13,037	19,960	114,960
1970	67,879	12,313	820	81,013	3,968	7,348	11,316	92,329
1960	41,171	N.A.	827	N.A.	N.A.	N.A.	15,882	57,880
AVERAGE ANNUAL FUEL CONSUMPTION PER VEHICLE (Gallons)								
1998	548	704	1,466	603	1,799	11,526	4,257	719
1997	539	703	1,472	596	1,809	11,342	4,218	711
1996	534	685	1,425	586	1,787	11,561	4,221	700
1994	517	701	1,438	580	1,841	11,093	4,202	698
1992	502	717	1,362	570	1,885	10,276	4,210	683
1990	506	738	1,428	569	1,862	9,441	3,953	677
1985	538	735	1,405	584	1,611	9,980	3,570	685
1980	551	854	1,926	610	1,583	9,201	3,447	712
1970	737	866	2,172	760	1,078	8,119	2,467	830
1960	668	N.A.	3,039	N.A.	N.A.	N.A.	1,333	784

*Passenger cars include motorcycles through 1994.
N.A.-Not available.
SOURCE: U.S. Department of Transportation, Federal Highway Administration.

Annual Motor Vehicle Miles of Travel

VEHICLE MILES OF TRAVEL, 1998 (In Millions)

	Rural Interstate	Total Rural	Urban Interstate	Total Urban	Total
Alabama	5,777	28,022	5,615	27,183	55,205
Alaska	811	2,347	549	2,167	4,514
Arizona	6,414	16,145	4,383	29,341	45,486
Arkansas	3,624	18,396	2,442	9,950	28,346
California	14,516	55,714	58,652	230,728	286,442
Colorado	4,868	15,942	4,779	23,341	39,283
Connecticut	1,658	7,360	7,665	21,962	29,322
Delaware	0	3,266	1,350	4,938	8,204
Dist. of Columbia	0	0	449	3,307	3,307
Florida	11,159	35,644	16,528	101,851	137,495
Georgia	10,125	40,618	16,050	56,412	97,030
Hawaii	80	2,233	1,662	5,754	7,987
Idaho	2,008	8,658	1,013	4,775	13,433
Illinois	9,921	30,679	18,409	70,594	101,273
Indiana	7,984	34,949	7,136	33,916	68,865
Iowa	4,301	18,592	1,992	10,320	28,912
Kansas	3,185	14,234	2,953	12,861	27,095
Kentucky	5,933	26,405	5,615	20,172	46,577
Louisiana	5,338	22,489	4,838	17,837	40,326
Maine	2,015	9,968	547	3,572	13,540
Maryland	3,737	15,097	10,670	33,246	48,343
Massachusetts	2,450	8,676	12,436	43,153	51,829
Michigan	6,979	36,301	13,846	57,615	93,916
Minnesota	4,096	24,289	7,046	25,339	49,628
Mississippi	3,959	23,728	1,870	10,482	34,210
Missouri	6,669	29,171	10,538	35,363	64,534
Montana	2,182	7,408	247	2,181	9,589
Nebraska	2,572	10,929	877	6,629	17,558
Nevada	1,838	5,945	2,115	11,350	17,295
New Hampshire	1,597	6,785	885	4,788	11,573
New Jersey	2,526	12,590	9,999	51,920	64,510
New Mexico	4,397	13,844	1,769	8,349	22,193
New York	6,424	34,041	16,192	89,335	123,376
North Carolina	7,867	42,268	8,208	43,015	85,283
North Dakota	1,235	5,541	247	1,792	7,333
Ohio	9,781	40,780	19,389	64,144	104,924
Oklahoma	4,682	21,189	3,985	20,843	42,032
Oregon	4,103	17,301	3,761	16,073	33,374
Pennsylvania	10,535	43,987	11,034	55,921	99,908
Rhode Island	358	1,071	1,665	6,912	7,983
South Carolina	7,780	26,899	3,217	15,922	42,821
South Dakota	1,852	6,248	332	1,849	8,097
Tennessee	8,643	28,099	8,506	34,463	62,562
Texas	15,185	68,060	31,527	137,963	206,023
Utah	3,156	8,066	3,977	13,204	21,270
Vermont	1,169	4,701	349	1,895	6,596
Virginia	9,258	31,579	11,890	39,107	70,686
Washington	4,424	16,738	9,934	35,189	51,927
West Virginia	3,627	13,560	1,408	5,106	18,666
Wisconsin	6,082	30,897	3,549	25,758	56,655
Wyoming	2,182	5,861	312	2,170	8,031
U.S. Total	**251,062**	**1,033,310**	**374,407**	**1,592,057**	**2,625,367**

NOTE: Includes travel by motorcycle.
SOURCE: U.S. Department of Transportation, Federal Highway Administration.

TOTAL VEHICLE MILES TRAVELED, 1938-1998 (In Billions)

Year	Rural	Urban	Total	% Change
1998	1,033	1,592	2,625	3.7%
1997	985	1,547	2,532	2.0
1996	960	1,522	2,482	2.5
1995	933	1,489	2,422	2.7
1994	909	1,449	2,358	2.7
1993	887	1,410	2,297	2.2
1992	884	1,363	2,247	3.4
1991	884	1,289	2,173	1.2
1990	870	1,277	2,147	1.9
1989	849	1,258	2,107	3.0
1988	818	1,208	2,026	5.5
1987	780	1,141	1,921	4.7
1986	748	1,087	1,835	3.4
1985	730	1,044	1,774	3.1
1984	718	1,002	1,720	4.1
1983	701	952	1,653	3.6
1982	689	906	1,595	2.7
1981	686	867	1,553	1.7
1980	672	855	1,527	-0.2
1979	676	854	1,530	-0.9
1978	682	862	1,544	5.2
1977	651	816	1,467	4.6
1976	625	777	1,402	5.6
1975	602	726	1,328	3.8
1974	585	695	1,280	-2.5
1973	606	707	1,313	4.2
1972	590	670	1,260	6.9
1971	573	606	1,179	6.3
1970	539	570	1,109	4.5
1969	524	537	1,061	4.4
1968	506	510	1,016	5.4
1967	481	483	964	4.1
1966	476	450	926	4.3
1965	464	424	888	4.0
1964	441	405	846	5.1
1963	420	385	805	4.0
1962	399	368	767	3.9
1961	398	340	738	2.6
1960	387	332	719	2.6
1959	377	324	701	5.4
1958	358	307	665	2.8
1957	350	297	647	2.5
1956	344	287	631	4.1
1955	331	275	606	7.8
1954	314	248	562	3.3
1953	308	236	544	6.0
1952	289	224	513	4.5
1951	268	223	491	7.2
1950	240	218	458	8.0
1949	219	205	424	6.5
1948	199	199	398	7.3
1947	187	184	371	8.8
1946	171	170	341	36.4
1944	102	111	213	2.4
1942	130	138	268	-19.8
1940	152	150	302	6.0
1938	135	136	271	0.4

Selected Travel Data by State

TRAVEL DATA BY STATE, 1998

State	Resident Population in Thousands	Population Per Vehicle	Annual Miles Traveled		Public Road and Street Mileage			State Gasoline Tax Rate
			Per Vehicle	Per Licensed Driver	Rural	Urban	Total	
Alabama	4,352	1.13	14,306	16,076	73,598	20,630	94,228	18.0¢
Alaska	614	1.12	8,269	9,877	10,870	1,809	12,679	8.0
Arizona	4,669	1.59	15,450	14,219	36,650	17,319	53,969	18.0
Arkansas	2,538	1.45	16,159	14,779	85,123	9,987	95,110	18.6
California	32,667	1.28	11,189	13,973	82,414	83,537	165,951	18.0
Colorado	3,971	1.15	11,334	13,334	71,271	14,001	85,272	22.0
Connecticut	3,274	1.21	10,857	12,483	8,985	11,742	20,727	32.0
Delaware	744	1.21	13,308	15,026	3,749	1,983	5,732	23.0
District of Columbia	523	2.29	14,459	9,476	0	1,421	1,421	20.0
Florida	14,916	1.32	12,193	11,432	67,079	48,337	115,416	13.0
Georgia	7,642	1.11	14,076	18,252	86,183	27,369	113,552	7.5
Hawaii	1,193	1.69	11,348	10,692	2,346	1,873	4,219	16.0
Idaho	1,229	1.10	12,006	15,584	42,191	3,916	46,107	25.0
Illinois	12,045	1.29	10,882	13,151	102,057	35,905	137,962	19.0
Indiana	5,899	1.10	12,820	17,316	73,484	19,860	93,344	15.0
Iowa	2,862	0.94	9,470	14,827	103,346	9,465	112,811	20.0
Kansas	2,629	1.24	12,772	14,638	123,745	10,081	133,826	18.0
Kentucky	3,936	1.38	16,374	17,643	62,611	11,024	73,635	16.4
Louisiana	4,369	1.27	11,754	14,739	46,818	13,929	60,747	20.0
Maine	1,244	1.34	14,565	14,846	20,009	2,630	22,639	19.0
Maryland	5,135	1.37	12,891	15,212	15,954	14,235	30,189	23.5
Massachusetts	6,147	1.19	10,046	11,795	12,191	23,060	35,251	21.0
Michigan	9,817	1.21	11,554	13,807	91,745	29,737	121,482	19.0
Minnesota	4,725	1.13	11,879	17,304	115,440	15,747	131,187	20.0
Mississippi	2,752	1.22	15,166	19,460	65,371	7,924	73,295	18.4
Missouri	5,439	1.24	14,742	16,992	106,480	16,367	122,847	17.0
Montana	880	0.89	9,703	14,821	67,405	2,485	69,890	27.0
Nebraska	1,663	1.09	11,506	14,817	87,612	5,132	92,744	23.5
Nevada	1,747	1.43	14,173	13,880	29,719	5,692	35,411	24.75
New Hampshire	1,185	1.14	11,144	12,760	12,194	2,930	15,124	19.5
New Jersey	8,115	1.40	11,160	11,596	11,709	24,212	35,921	10.5
New Mexico	1,737	1.09	13,916	18,433	53,769	6,144	59,913	18.5
New York	18,175	1.74	11,838	11,690	71,701	40,823	112,524	22.65
North Carolina	7,546	1.29	14,549	15,411	75,518	23,091	98,609	21.6
North Dakota	638	0.95	10,910	16,116	84,768	1,835	86,603	20.0
Ohio	11,209	1.12	10,451	13,211	82,755	33,464	116,219	22.0
Oklahoma	3,347	1.15	14,399	18,235	99,366	13,158	112,524	17.0
Oregon	3,282	1.10	11,199	13,808	57,791	10,690	68,481	24.0
Pennsylvania	12,001	1.34	11,127	11,887	85,143	34,138	119,281	25.9
Rhode Island	988	1.38	11,165	11,705	1,345	4,705	6,050	29.0
South Carolina	3,836	1.33	14,801	15,978	54,286	10,608	64,894	16.0
South Dakota	738	0.96	10,536	15,135	81,432	1,980	83,412	18.0
Tennessee	5,431	1.22	13,999	15,360	69,011	17,593	86,604	20.0
Texas	19,760	1.48	15,462	15,464	214,295	82,286	296,581	20.0
Utah	2,100	1.37	13,882	15,269	34,094	7,249	41,343	24.5
Vermont	591	1.19	13,294	13,272	12,881	1,371	14,252	20.0
Virginia	6,791	1.17	12,149	14,766	51,032	18,828	69,860	17.5
Washington	5,689	1.18	10,764	12,730	62,575	17,651	80,226	23.0
West Virginia	1,811	1.31	13,547	14,571	32,638	3,192	35,830	25.35
Wisconsin	5,224	1.24	13,479	15,271	95,721	16,231	111,952	25.4
Wyoming	481	0.86	14,367	22,370	26,180	2,278	28,458	14.0
Total	**270,296**	**1.28**	**12,406**	**14,193**	**3,064,650**	**841,654**	**3,906,304**	

SOURCE: U.S. Department of Commerce, Bureau of the Census, and U.S. Department of Transportation.

State Highway Agency Capital Outlay and Maintenance

STATE HIGHWAY AGENCY CAPITAL OUTLAY AND MAINTENANCE, 1997-1998(In Thousands)

	Capital Outlay		Maintenance		Total		Percent Change
	1997	1998	1997	1998	1997	1998	
Alabama	$439,077	$535,282	$217,042	$156,151	$656,119	$691,433	5.4
Alaska	251,881	224,607	31,260	38,600	283,141	263,207	-7.0
Arizona	554,517	649,427	52,495	61,684	607,012	711,111	17.1
Arkansas	518,915	491,817	105,090	110,496	624,005	602,313	-3.5
California	2,756,830	2,669,580	364,447	421,279	3,121,277	3,090,859	-0.0
Colorado	424,974	609,823	127,731	122,558	552,705	732,381	32.5
Connecticut	580,509	502,141	58,822	64,831	639,331	566,972	-11.3
Delaware	213,453	248,521	26,456	41,722	239,909	290,243	20.0
District of Columbia	92,060	115,387	23,247	18,971	115,307	134,358	16.5
Florida	2,130,221	2,448,044	277,768	305,411	2,407,989	2,753,455	14.3
Georgia	602,530	1,111,114	219,716	114,047	822,246	1,225,161	49.0
Hawaii	252,040	194,746	37,862	21,958	289,902	216,704	-25.2
Idaho	196,543	209,119	15,992	19,591	212,535	228,710	7.6
Illinois	1,471,094	1,472,402	217,445	246,118	1,688,539	1,718,520	1.8
Indiana	719,607	785,505	201,807	277,513	921,414	1,063,018	15.4
Iowa	488,070	505,566	72,008	64,752	560,078	570,318	1.8
Kansas	679,469	637,165	85,760	97,955	765,229	735,120	-3.9
Kentucky	728,340	777,719	165,979	173,109	894,319	950,828	6.3
Louisiana	486,455	643,033	96,586	115,656	583,041	758,689	30.1
Maine	217,011	187,691	80,095	71,902	297,106	259,593	-12.6
Maryland	688,734	588,224	88,862	91,314	777,596	679,538	-12.6
Massachusetts	1,446,495	1,853,968	56,336	63,280	1,502,831	1,917,248	27.6
Michigan	781,918	965,723	158,921	146,161	940,839	1,111,884	18.2
Minnesota	558,716	561,994	179,252	168,688	737,968	730,682	-0.0
Mississippi	545,366	564,335	58,250	57,605	603,616	621,940	3.0
Missouri	835,254	791,672	219,579	216,997	1,054,833	1,008,669	-4.4
Montana	205,288	211,567	44,365	52,625	249,653	264,192	5.8
Nebraska	308,147	271,469	39,264	38,247	347,411	309,716	-10.9
Nevada	226,552	218,907	49,326	60,099	275,878	279,006	1.1
New Hampshire	146,780	168,936	72,009	57,500	218,789	226,436	3.5
New Jersey	787,710	775,648	158,612	183,675	946,322	959,323	1.4
New Mexico	290,917	269,662	49,555	44,447	340,472	314,109	-7.7
New York	2,202,119	2,551,865	343,154	361,628	2,545,273	2,913,493	14.5
North Carolina	1,164,850	1,355,164	423,729	521,001	1,588,579	1,876,165	18.1
North Dakota	192,878	189,898	34,696	20,139	227,574	210,037	-7.7
Ohio	1,244,508	1,464,561	302,255	194,925	1,546,763	1,659,486	7.3
Oklahoma	384,539	459,816	127,032	125,657	511,571	585,473	14.4
Oregon	385,392	450,821	136,426	154,756	521,818	605,577	16.1
Pennsylvania	1,792,605	1,546,071	714,218	893,197	2,506,823	2,439,268	-2.7
Rhode Island	125,747	180,173	27,901	27,780	153,648	207,953	35.3
South Carolina	451,008	465,434	137,945	130,578	588,953	596,012	1.2
South Dakota	232,287	203,678	30,793	27,452	263,080	231,130	-12.1
Tennessee	690,327	772,521	239,191	213,654	929,518	986,175	6.1
Texas	2,194,642	2,368,058	744,930	769,766	2,939,572	3,137,824	6.7
Utah	563,934	820,138	64,887	69,718	628,821	889,856	41.5
Vermont	98,883	99,873	14,906	27,115	113,789	126,988	11.6
Virginia	1,116,381	1,244,314	607,566	589,488	1,723,947	1,833,802	6.4
Washington	781,896	692,370	86,350	95,906	868,246	788,276	-9.2
West Virginia	610,464	499,433	198,309	249,047	808,773	748,480	-7.5
Wisconsin	694,843	709,128	82,308	84,921	777,151	794,049	2.2
Wyoming	168,652	200,559	58,219	65,574	226,871	266,133	17.3
Total	$35,721,428	38,534,669	8,026,754	8,347,244	43,748,182	46,881,913	7.2

SOURCE: U.S. Department of Transportation, Federal Highway Administration.

Motor Vehicle and Equipment Manufacturing Employment by State

MOTOR VEHICLE AND EQUIPMENT MANUFACTURING EMPLOYMENT BY STATE, 1997

State	Motor Vehicles	Truck and Bus Bodies	Parts & Accessories	Truck Trailers	Motor Homes	Total Motor Vehicles and Parts (SIC 371)
Alabama	*	*	6,901	2,086	*	11,381
Alaska	*	*			*	*
Arizona	*	*	6,277	*	*	6,837
Arkansas	*	*	6,703	*	*	8,994
California	6,295	2,784	18,444	1,045	2,514	31,082
Colorado	*	61	2,025	*	*	2,911
Connecticut	*	*	*	*	*	*
Delaware	*	*	*	*	*	*
District of Columbia	*	*	*	*	*	*
Florida	*	*	3,306	495	*	7,449
Georgia	*	1,655	6,429	*	*	16,819
Hawaii	*	*	*	*	*	*
Idaho	*	*	*	*	*	496
Illinois	10,021	*	18,963	2,130	*	32,404
Indiana	6,891	4,517	66,278	4,733	5,850	88,269
Iowa	*	1,363	5,873	*	*	11,600
Kansas	*	*	*	*	*	7,745
Kentucky	16,705	*	14,387	*	*	32,078
Louisiana	*	46	143	*	*	*
Maine	*	*	*	*	*	*
Maryland	*	*	*	23	*	3,284
Massachusetts	*	186	648	*	*	1,041
Michigan	62,308	883	116,450	261	962	180,864
Minnesota	*	*	*	*	*	5,613
Mississippi	*	817	8,059	*	*	9,115
Missouri	*	446	*	595	*	33,233
Montana	*	*	*	*	*	*
Nebraska	*	2,657	*	*	3,795	
Nevada	*	*	393	*	*	435
New Hampshire	*	*	*	*	*	*
New Jersey	*	253	1,481	*	*	6,244
New Mexico	*	*	64	*	*	*
New York	*	777	22,120	*	*	23,663
North Carolina	*	3,420	16,827	*	*	24,966
North Dakota	*	*	*	*	*	*
Ohio	36,425	2,556	64,596	*	*	104,884
Oklahoma	*	386	4,139	421	*	9,198
Oregon	2,494	476	1,871	184	1,680	6,705
Pennsylvania	*	4,173	9,673	976	*	16,920
Rhode Island	*	*	*	*	*	*
South Carolina	3,332	*	9,423	*	*	12,961
South Dakota	*	*	626	768	*	1,541
Tennessee	15,817	*	23,806	805	*	41,107
Texas	*	1,145	6,672	1,988	*	13,778
Utah	*	*	*	*	*	2,015
Vermont	*	*	*	*	*	*
Virginia	*	*	*	*	*	11,559
Washington	*	*	1,576	*	*	*
West Virginia	*	*	*	*	*	473
Wisconsin	*	2,496	12,645	*	*	24,095
Wyoming	*	*	*	*	*	*
Total	**237,580**	**40,009**	**491,760**	**28,648**	**17,515**	**815,513**

CONTINUED ON NEXT PAGE

*Omission of data for individual state is due to either the absences of such business from the state or the necessity of withholding the data to avoid disclosure of individual firm's data.
SOURCE: U.S. Department of Commerce, Bureau of the Census.

Motor Vehicle and Equipment Manufacturing Employment by State

MOTOR VEHICLE AND EQUIPMENT MANUFACTURING EMPLOYMENT BY STATE, 1997 — continued

State	Automotive Stampings	Other Equipment**	Total Motor Vehicle and Equipment Manufacturing	Total State Manufacturing Employment	Motor Vehicle and Equipment Percent of Total State Manufacturing Employment	Facilities (SIC 371)
Alabama	*	8,627	20,008	377,476	5.3%	107
Alaska	*	*	*	13,524	*	1
Arizona	172	453	7,290	212,284	3.4%	83
Arkansas	*	2,650	11,644	245,549	4.7%	70
California	1,669	10,992	42,074	1,922,850	2.2%	658
Colorado	*	309	3,220	194,419	1.7%	72
Connecticut	505	1,018	*	289,670	*	40
Delaware	*	*	*	62,700	*	6
District of Columbia	*	*	*	12,181	*	1
Florida	720	2,371	9,820	480,959	2.0%	186
Georgia	1,461	5,620	22,439	599,516	3.7%	131
Hawaii	*	*	*	16,329	*	3
Idaho	*	978	1,474	73,390	2.0%	15
Illinois	5,098	11,879	44,283	988,416	4.5%	213
Indiana	13,358	23,847	112,116	664,319	16.9%	350
Iowa	*	5,486	17,086	252,077	6.8%	88
Kansas	*	3,005	10,750	206,885	5.2%	66
Kentucky	3,434	1,437	33,515	310,568	10.8%	92
Louisiana	*	239	*	180,160	*	23
Maine	*	*	*	88,600	*	11
Maryland	*	*	*	186,492	*	38
Massachusetts	*	660	1,701	455,951	0.4%	51
Michigan	52,400	12,954	193,818	968,905	20.0%	532
Minnesota	*	*	*	436,321	*	91
Mississippi	*	2,633	11,748	236,045	4.0%	66
Missouri	1,407	2,257	35,490	427,435	8.3%	184
Montana	*	*	*	23,027	*	10
Nebraska	*	1,249	5,044	116,199	4.3%	39
Nevada	*	*	*	40,346	*	25
New Hampshire	*	*	*	105,550	*	11
New Jersey	*	743	6,987	523,740	1.3%	78
New Mexico	*	*	*	44,983	*	18
New York	*	4,996	28,659	897,238	3.2%	167
North Carolina	*	9,477	34,443	835,919	4.1%	182
North Dakota	*	*	*	23,691	*	18
Ohio	30,059	17,381	122,265	1,089,980	11.2%	336
Oklahoma	*	10,657	19,855	172,748	11.5%	86
Oregon	77	2,428	9,133	238,923	3.8%	87
Pennsylvania	2,836	13,385	30,305	929,187	3.3%	180
Rhode Island	*	*	*	80,316	*	14
South Carolina	1,602	1,459	14,420	368,678	3.9%	66
South Dakota	*	*	*	46,933	*	23
Tennessee	2,032	9,410	50,517	511,650	9.9%	164
Texas	*	2,251	16,029	1,061,689	1.5%	288
Utah	*	647	2,662	119,706	2.2%	38
Vermont	*	*	*	45,625	*	6
Virginia	*	470	12,029	399,767	3.0%	83
Washington	*	*	*	362,346	*	95
West Virginia	*	*	*	77,898	*	14
Wisconsin	*	3,577	27,672	602,971	4.6%	130
Wyoming	*	*	*	10,565	*	10
Total	**126,712**	**249,880**	**1,065,393**	**18,632,696**	**5.7%**	**5,346**

*Omission of data for individual state is due to either the absence of such business from the state or the necessity of withholding the data to avoid disclosure of individual firm's data.
**Carburetors, pistons, vehicular lighting, tires, and other related manufacturing industries.
SOURCE: U.S. Department of Commerce, Bureau of the Census.

U.S. Motor Vehicle and Related Industries Employment

U.S. EMPLOYMENT IN MOTOR VEHICLE AND RELATED INDUSTRIES, 1997

Industry	Establishments	Employees	Payrolls(000)
Motor Vehicle and Equipment Manufacturing			
Motor vehicles and equipment	5,346	815,513	$35,774,637
Miscellaneous transportation equipment	1,246	60,739	1,829,336
Automotive stampings	809	126,712	5,676,880
Carburetors, pistons, piston rings, and valves	144	18,290	691,207
Vehicular lighting equipment	105	16,689	634,932
Storage batteries	137	23,131	792,506
Electrical equipment for internal combustion engines	569	52,885	1,631,220
Tires and inner tubes	163	63,699	2,752,587
Cold-rolled steel sheet, strip, and bars	195	14,447	654,661
Sub-total	**8,714**	**1,192,105**	**$50,437,966**
Motor Freight Transportation and Related Services			
Trucking and courier services, except by air or by the U.S. Postal Service	121,111	1,811,597	52,279,581
Trucking Terminal Facilities	20	190	7,834
Arrangement of transportation of freight and cargo	15,994	143,126	5,028,577
Truck rental and leasing, without drivers	4,886	46,566	1,396,030
Miscellaneous services incidental to transportation	2,396	45,744	2,396
Sub-total	**144,407**	**2,047,223**	**$58,714,418**
Petroleum Refining and Wholesale Distribution			
Petroleum Refining	248	67,023	4,023,680
Asphalt paving mixtures and blocks	1,169	13,324	586,644
Lubricating oils and greases	415	12,086	490,814
Petroleum bulk stations and terminals	8,885	110,645	3,479,808
Petroleum and petroleum products wholesalers, except bulk stations and termi	3,674	35,220	1,385,504
Sub-total	**14,391**	**238,298**	**$9,966,450**
Passenger Transportation			
Local and suburban transportation	10,234	227,926	4,559,857
Taxicabs	3,224	28,185	403,453
Intercity and rural bus transportation	410	15,654	390,476
Bus charter service	1,562	31,500	556,681
School buses	4,332	147,704	1,853,250
Arrangement of passenger transportation	33,878	230,663	5,957,543
Passenger car rental	4,344	103,202	2,162,050
Passenger car leasing	863	8,807	343,756
Utility trailer and recreational vehicle rental	402	2,156	56,452
Automobile parking	9,835	77,509	1,013,154
Recreational vehicle parks and campsites	4,140	17,067	297,775
Sub-total	**73,224**	**890,373**	**$17,594,447**
Automotive Sales and Servicing			
Retail automotive dealers (New and Used)	26,208	1,067,841	36,367,848
Retail automotive dealers (used only)	23,395	93,227	2,216,077
Auto and home supply stores	41,755	326,014	6,459,152
Gasoline service stations	95,847	720,628	9,270,657
Recreational vehicle dealers	3,031	30,223	841,510
Wholesale trade in motor vehicles	47,729	550,141	15,902,244
Automotive repair shops	144,068	638,579	15,075,783
Automotive services, except repair	28,942	230,246	3,069,252
Sub-total	**384,767**	**2,589,058**	**52,834,675**
Total of Motor Vehicle and Related Industries	**625,503**	**6,957,057**	**189,547,956**
U.S. Total*	**6,894,869**	**105,299,123**	**$3,047,907,469**
Motor Vehicle Percent of U.S. Total	**9.1%**	**6.6%**	**6.2%**

*data for employees of establishments totally exempt from FICA are excluded, as are self-employed persons, domestic service workers, railroad employees, agricultural production workers and most government employees.
SOURCE: U.S. Department of Commerce, Bureau of the Census.

New-Car Dealerships

FRANCHISED NEW-CAR DEALERSHIPS BY STATE, 1999

State	Establish-ments*	Sales (Millions)	Paid Employees	Payrolls (Millions)	State	Establish-ments*	Sales (Millions)	Paid Employees	Payrolls (Millions)
Alabama	357	$8,454	15,325	$540	Nebraska	242	3,515	7,056	230
Alaska	43	1,016	2,127	90	Nevada	99	$4,235	7,403	$350
Arizona	214	12,101	21,830	900	New Hampshire	176	3,449	6,626	260
Arkansas	291	511	8,786	280	New Jersey	644	20,455	30,572	1,370
California	1,628	68,451	118,787	5,380	New Mexico	133	3,020	6,625	230
Colorado	270	10,796	18,375	760	New York	1,291	29,768	49,528	2,010
Connecticut	341	7,956	14,321	630	North Carolina	709	17,295	31,281	1,180
Delaware	69	1,783	3,727	140	North Dakota	120	1,492	3,304	100
Florida	979	42,105	66,901	2,730	Ohio	1,072	28,296	49,660	1,790
Georgia	602	20,553	33,504	1,320	Oklahoma	321	7,121	13,441	440
Hawaii	61	1,729	3,654	140	Oregon	281	7,128	14,316	560
Idaho	137	2,560	5,234	190	Pennsylvania	1,313	26,674	52,235	1,830
Illinois	1,100	24,885	45,125	1,830	Rhode Island	73	1,543	2,964	110
Indiana	594	13,464	23,879	870	South Carolina	327	7,362	14,246	510
Iowa	442	6,100	12,943	430	South Dakota	138	1,638	3,552	120
Kansas	302	5,735	11,331	410	Tennessee	418	12,250	22,564	870
Kentucky	338	6,782	14,290	470	Texas	1,346	50,074	82,104	3,320
Louisiana	332	8,793	17,445	600	Utah	138	4,195	8,294	300
Maine	166	2,350	5,086	170	Vermont	99	1,287	2,742	90
Maryland	348	11,921	23,035	910	Virginia	564	15,376	30,666	1,160
Massachussetts	531	14,006	23,598	970	Washington	385	10,610	12,120	870
Michigan	862	28,312	42,795	1,850	West Virginia	197	3,135	6,866	200
Minnesota	499	11,730	20,483	760	Wisconsin	646	12,425	24,056	810
Mississippi	253	4,567	8,915	310	Wyoming	76	844	2,088	70
Missouri	533	11,884	22,447	850	Dist. of Columbia	5	124	328	10
Montana	143	1,638	3,718	110	**Total**	**22,250**	**608,093**	**1,081,300**	**424,600**

*Establishment data are NADA estimates for January 1, 2000.

DEALERSHIPS' TOTAL SERVICE AND PARTS SALES
(Billions of Dollars)

	Amount	% Change
1999	67.84	6.7
1998	63.56	1.7
1997	62.93	3.6
1996	60.76	7.4
1995	56.57	2.6
1994	55.12	7.4
1993	51.31	4.6
1992	49.07	4.4
1991	47.00	-2.8
1990	48.34	6.3
1989	45.50	4.9

DEALERSHIPS' SERVICE AND PARTS SALES, 1998-1999
(Millions of Dollars)

Service Labor Sales	1998	1999	Percent Change	Parts Sales	1998	1999	Percent Change
Customer mechanical	$11.06	$12.3	11.2	Customer mechanical	$8.80	$9.83	11.7
Customer body	3.66	3.94	7.9	Customer body	3.01	3.16	5.1
Warranty	5.23	5.41	3.5	Wholesale	11.00	11.25	2.3
Sublet	2.71	2.83	4.3	Counter	2.05	2.12	3.2
Internal	3.48	3.73	7.4	Warranty	6.50	6.92	6.4
Other	1.79	1.9	6.1	Internal	2.79	2.91	4.3
				Other	1.49	1.53	2.6
Total Service Labor	**$27.92**	**$30.12**	**7.9**	**Total Parts**	**$35.64**	**$37.72**	**5.8**

SHARE OF TOTAL DEALERSHIP SALES DOLLARS BY DEPARTMENT, 1999

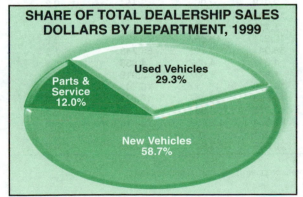

Used Vehicles 29.3%
Parts & Service 12.0%
New Vehicles 58.7%

PROFILE OF THE FRANCHISED DEALERSHIP'S SERVICE AND PARTS OPERATION, 1999

	Average Dealership	All Dealers
Total service and parts sales	$3,048,821	$67.8 Billion
Total gross profit as percent of service and parts sales	44.5%	—
Total net profit as percent of service and parts sales	6.0%	—
Total number of repair orders written	9,808	218 Million
Total service and parts sales per customer repair order	$178	—
Total service and parts sales per warranty repair order	$199	—
Number of technicians	11.6	258,800
Number of service bays (excluding body)	16.6	369,350
Total parts inventory	$222,700	$5.0 Billion
Average customer mechanical labor rate	$57	—

SOURCE: National Automobile Dealers Association.

Personal Income of Motor Vehicle and Equipment Manufacturing Employees by State

PERSONAL INCOME OF MOTOR VEHICLE AND EQUIPMENT MANUFACTURING EMPLOYEES, 1996-1998[1]

	Personal Income (In Millions)						1998 Motor Vehicle & Equipment Percent of Total Manufacturing
	Motor Vehicle and Equipment Manufacturing Employees			All Manufacturing Employees			
	1996	1997	1998	1996	1997	1998	
Alabama	$671	$614	$719	$13,209	$13,489	$13,754	5.2%
Alaska	0	*	*	605	598	566	*
Arizona	274	249	282	8,924	9,733	10,710	2.6
Arkansas	320	293	317	7,575	7,790	8,114	3.9
California	1,736	1,623	1,703	88,845	96,313	102,939	1.7
Colorado	105	113	118	8,630	9,276	9,915	1.2
Connecticut	163	204	217	15,501	16,448	17,311	1.3
Delaware	328	353	420	4,375	4,320	3,843	10.9
District of Columbia	7	6	*	963	965	942	*
Florida	313	284	298	18,897	19,557	20,490	1.5
Georgia	891	885	977	21,100	21,963	23,645	4.1
Hawaii	2	*	2	793	799	716	0.3
Idaho	37	36	38	2,990	3,111	3,242	1.2
Illinois	2,053	1,834	1,959	45,138	47,783	48,996	4.0
Indiana	5,367	4,832	5,403	30,533	30,921	31,921	16.9
Iowa	492	472	504	9,419	9,967	10,357	4.9
Kansas	493	426	421	7,718	8,263	8,676	4.9
Kentucky	1,892	1,848	2,107	12,016	12,444	12,938	16.3
Louisiana	225	176	*	8,204	8,564	9,191	*
Maine	15	16	17	3,213	3,364	3,481	0.5
Maryland	311	284	259	7,970	8,428	8,617	3.0
Massachusetts	78	76	78	22,625	23,910	24,678	0.3
Michigan	24,354	21,206	23,699	56,591	54,899	59,880	39.6
Minnesota	339	332	362	18,968	19,961	20,818	1.7
Mississippi	191	178	211	7,136	7,256	7,610	2.8
Missouri	2,055	1826	1,872	17,437	18,068	18,045	10.4
Montana	7	7	8	834	863	950	0.8
Nebraska	141	139	145	3,912	4,135	4,260	3.4
Nevada	12	12	19	1,464	1,577	1,735	1.1
New Hampshire	24	36	56	4,531	4,895	5,180	1.1
New Jersey	447	405	437	25,948	26,798	28,890	1.5
New Mexico	47	51	52	1,721	1,857	1,852	2.8
New York	2,231	1,977	2,038	47,006	48,272	50,072	4.1
North Carolina	1,292	1,161	1,353	29,457	30,426	31,220	4.3
North Dakota	55	51	57	697	756	816	7.0
Ohio	7,181	6,732	6,917	51,493	52,317	53,091	13.0
Oklahoma	652	592	537	7,001	7,322	8,152	6.6
Oregon	415	395	480	10,083	10,899	11,152	4.3
Pennsylvania	923	866	879	41,734	43,457	45,775	1.9
Rhode Island	30	31	26	2,978	3,069	3,154	0.8
South Carolina	648	634	742	13,050	13,415	13,813	5.4
South Dakota	55	51	59	1,418	1,536	1,695	3.5
Tennessee	2,363	2,109	2,128	19,341	19,567	20,153	10.6
Texas	780	733	842	53,041	56,712	54,748	1.5
Utah	305	288	300	4,581	4,837	4,955	6.1
Vermont	24	24	24	1,823	1,897	2,019	1.2
Virginia	646	608	665	15,470	16,117	16,446	4.0
Washington	278	256	310	16,298	18,117	18,811	1.6
West Virginia	27	15	27	3,375	3,337	3,394	0.8
Wisconsin	1,434	1,297	1,396	23,874	25,157	26,116	5.3
Wyoming	2	3	2	391	402	445	0.4
Total	62,731	56,639	61,482	820,896	855,927	890,289	6.9

*Withheld to avoid disclosure; estimates are included in the U.S. total.
(1) Personal Income is measured as the of wage and salary disbursements, other labor income, proprietors' income, rental income, personal dividend income and personal interest income.
SOURCE: U.S. Department of Commerce, Bureau of Economic Analysis.

Automotive Employment and Compensation

HOURLY COMPENSATION OF AUTOMOTIVE PRODUCTION EMPLOYEES IN SELECTED COUNTRIES, 1995-1996

| Country | Exchange Rate | | Hourly Compensation | | | | 1996 Percent of U.S. Earnings |
| | National Currency | National Currency Per U.S. Dollar | National Currency | | U.S. Currency | | |
			1995	1996	1995	1996	
Canada	Dollar	1.364	28.47	28.73	20.74	21.06	77
France	Franc	5.115	105.59	108.13	21.18	21.14	78
Germany	Mark	1.505	62.03	64.69	43.32	42.98	158
Ireland	Pound	0.625	10.12	10.42	16.22	16.66	61
Italy	Lira	1,543.404	28032	29016	17.21	18.8	69
Japan	Yen	108.817	2748	2814	29.25	25.86	95
Korea	Won	804.450	8367	9943	10.85	12.36	45
Mexico	Peso	7.593	16.11	18.68	2.51	2.46	9
Spain	Peseta	126.694	2103	2150	16.87	16.97	62
Taiwan	Dollar	27.466	187.09	188.69	7.06	6.87	25
United Kingdom	Pound	0.641	10.45	10.72	16.5	16.73	61
United States	Dollar	1.000	26.55	27.23	26.55	27.23	100

U.S. MOTOR VEHICLE AND EQUIPMENT MANUFACTURING EMPLOYMENT, 1970-1999

| Year | All Employees (000) | Production Workers | | |
		Number (000)	Percent of Total Employees	Average Hourly Earnings
1999	1,000.1	762.4	76.2	$18.41
1998	989.8	760.3	76.8	17.86
1997	985.6	779.1	79.1	18.04
1996	962.5	760.3	79.0	17.75
1995	933.1	758.9	81.3	17.36
1994	898.6	703.9	78.3	17.02
1993	836.6	642.0	76.7	16.10
1992	812.5	621.9	76.5	15.45
1991	788.8	601.5	76.3	15.23
1990	812.1	617.1	76.0	14.56
1989	858.5	663.8	77.3	14.25
1988	856.4	667.4	77.9	13.99
1987	865.9	673.1	77.7	13.53
1986	871.8	670.2	76.9	13.45
1985	883.1	684.5	77.5	13.39
1984	861.5	663.9	77.1	12.73
1982	699.3	511.9	73.2	11.62
1980	788.8	575.4	72.9	9.85
1978	1,004.9	781.7	77.8	8.50
1976	881.0	682.4	77.5	7.09
1974	907.7	687.5	75.7	5.87
1972	874.8	676.0	77.3	5.13
1970	799.0	605.3	75.8	4.22

NOTE: These figures are annual averages for the Motor Vehicle and Equipment Manufacturing Industry (SIC 371) as defined by the Standard Industrial Classification System. Many others are employed in manufacturing automotive components which are classified in other industries.
SOURCE: U.S. Department of Labor, Bureau of Labor Statistics.

U.S. MOTOR VEHICLE AMD EQUIPMENT MANUFACTURING EMPLOYMENT, 1986-1999

Industrial Production and Capacity Utilization

INDUSTRIAL PRODUCTION INDEX FOR MOTOR VEHICLE AND PARTS MANUFACTURERS, 1988-1999

	Industrial Production Index			
	Total		Motor Vehicle and Parts	
Year	Index	Percent Change	Index	Percent Change
1999	142.3	4.3	151.0	6.6
1998	136.4	4.8	141.7	0.8
1997	130.1	8.9	140.6	12.5
1996	119.5	4.5	132.6	3.2
1995	114.4	4.9	128.5	-0.9
1994	109.1	5.4	129.7	14.1
1993	103.5	3.5	113.7	13.7
1992	100.0	3.1	100.0	12.0
1991	97.0	-1.9	88.5	-7.1
1990	98.9	-0.2	95.3	-5.8
1989	99.1	1.7	101.2	0.0
1988	97.4	4.5	100.2	5.6

NOTE: "Industrial Production" is an index benchmarked to 1992=100.
SOURCE: Board of Governors of the Federal Reserve System.

CAPACITY UTILIZATION FOR MOTOR VEHICLE AND PARTS MANUFACTURING, 1988-1999

Year	All Manufacturing	Percent Change	Vehicle & Parts Mfg.	Percent Change
1999	79.8	-1.4	82.0	6.1
1998	80.9	-1.8	77.3	-2.8
1997	82.4	1.2	79.5	4.2
1996	81.4	-1.6	76.3	-0.8
1995	82.7	0.2	76.9	-7.9
1994	82.5	2.5	83.5	8.0
1993	80.5	1.3	77.3	10.6
1992	79.5	2.1	69.9	9.2
1991	77.9	-4.3	64.0	-10.6
1990	81.4	-2.6	71.6	-9.9
1989	83.6	-0.2	79.5	-2.1
1988	83.8	3.1	81.2	5.7

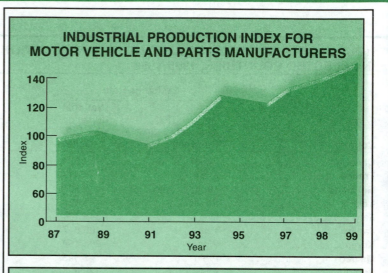

INDUSTRIAL PRODUCTION INDEX FOR MOTOR VEHICLE AND PARTS MANUFACTURERS

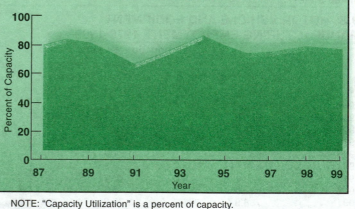

CAPACITY UTILIZATION FOR MOTOR VEHICLE AND PARTS MANUFACTURING

NOTE: "Capacity Utilization" is a percent of capacity.
SOURCE: Board of Governors of the Federal Reserve System.

AUTO AND TRUCK OUTPUT, 1987-1999 (Dollars in Billions)

Year	Auto Output	Auto Percent of GDP	Truck Output	Truck Percent of GDP	Total Motor Vehicle Output	Percent of GDP	Gross Domestic Product (GDP)
1999	$126.9	1.4	$215.5	2.3	$342.4	3.7	$9256.1
1998	130.5	1.5	182.8	2.1	313.3	3.6	8,759.9
1997	127	1.5	166.4	2.0	293.4	3.5	8,300.8
1996	126.1	1.6	149.5	1.9	275.6	3.5	7,813.2
1995	130.5	1.8	139.8	1.9	270.3	3.7	7,400.5
1994	133.3	1.9	129.0	1.8	262.3	3.7	7,054.3
1993	121.9	1.8	105.0	1.6	226.9	3.4	6,642.3
1992	111.7	1.8	89.2	1.4	200.9	3.2	6,318.9
1991	102.3	1.7	72.4	1.2	174.7	2.9	5,986.2
1990	113.1	1.9	77.0	1.3	190.1	3.3	5,803.5
1989	121.8	2.2	81.8	1.5	203.6	3.7	5,489.1
1988	121.6	2.4	75.4	1.5	197.0	3.9	5,108.3
1987	118.7	2.5	68.0	1.4	186.7	3.9	4,742.5

SOURCE: U.S. Department of Commerce, Bureau of Economic Analysis.

Corporate Profits and Research and Development Spending

SELECTED AUTOMOBILE MANUFACTURERS' REVENUES/NET INCOME, 1955-1999 (U.S. Dollars in Millions)

	DaimlerChrysler*		Ford		General Motors		Toyota		Volkswagen	
	Revenues	Net Income	Revenues	Net Income	Revenues	Net Income	Revenues	Net Income	Revenues	Net Income
1999	$151,035	$5,785	$162,558	$7,237	$152,635	$6,002	$100,990	$3,747	$75,525	$2,534
1998	154,615	5,656	144,416	22,071	161,315	2,956	88,473	3,442	80,395	1,343
1997	61,147	2,805	153,627	6,920	178,174	6,698	99,730	3,143	63,664	765
1996	61,397	3,529	146,991	4,446	164,013	4,963	101,177	2,426	64,491	437
1995	53,195	2,025	137,137	4,139	160,254	6,881	89,715	1,458	61,168	233
1994	52,235	3,713	128,439	5,308	154,951	4,901	91,317	1,227	50,930	95
1993	43,596	-2,551	108,521	2,529	138,676	2,466	95,063	1,643	44,774	-1,134
1992	36,897	723	100,132	-7,385	132,429	-23,498	80,128	1,875	53,977	93
1991	29,370	-795	88,286	-2,258	123,056	-4,453	71,731	3,140	48,826	713
1990	30,620	68	97,650	860	124,705	-1,986	59,962	2,878	45,429	725
1989	35,186	359	96,146	3,835	126,932	4,224	61,440	2,652	37,606	597
1988	34,421	1,050	92,446	5,300	123,642	4,856	—	—	—	—
1987	28,353	1,290	79,893	4,625	114,870	3,551	—	—	—	—
1986	24,569	1,389	69,695	3,285	115,610	2,945	—	—	—	—
1985	22,738	1,610	57,616	2,515	106,656	3,999	—	—	—	—
1984	19,717	2,373	56,323	2,907	93,145	4,517	—	—	—	—
1983	13,240	701	44,500	1,867	74,582	3,730	—	—	—	—
1982	10,040	170	37,067	-658	60,026	963	—	—	—	—
1981	9,971	-476	38,247	-1,060	62,698	333	—	—	—	—
1980	9,225	-1,710	37,086	-1,543	57,729	-763	—	—	—	—
1979	12,002	-1,097	43,514	1,169	66,311	2,893	—	—	—	—
1978	13,618	-205	42,784	1,589	63,221	3,508	—	—	—	—
1977	16,708	163	37,842	1,673	54,961	3,338	—	—	—	—
1976	15,537	423	28,840	983	47,181	2,903	—	—	—	—
1975	11,598	-260	24,009	323	35,700	1,253	—	—	—	—
1974	10,860	-52	23,621	361	31,550	950	—	—	—	—
1973	11,667	255	23,015	907	35,800	2,398	—	—	—	—
1972	9,641	221	20,194	870	30,435	2,163	—	—	—	—
1971	7,999	84	16,400	657	28,264	1,936	—	—	—	—
1970	7,000	-8	14,980	516	18,752	609	—	—	—	—
1969	7,052	99	14,756	547	24,295	1,711	—	—	—	—
1968	7,445	291	14,100	627	22,755	1,732	—	—	—	—
1967	6,213	200	10,516	84	20,026	1,627	—	—	—	—
1966	5,650	189	12,240	621	20,209	1,793	—	—	—	—
1965	5,300	233	11,537	703	20,734	2,126	—	—	—	—
1964	4,287	214	9,670	506	16,997	1,735	—	—	—	—
1963	3,505	162	8,743	489	16,495	1,592	—	—	—	—
1962	2,378	65	8,090	481	14,640	1,459	—	—	—	—
1961	2,127	11	6,709	410	11,396	893	—	—	—	—
1960	3,007	32	5,238	428	12,736	959	—	—	—	—
1959	2,643	-5	6,649	451	11,233	873	—	—	—	—
1958	2,165	-34	4,130	116	9,522	634	—	—	—	—
1957	3,565	120	5,771	283	10,990	844	—	—	—	—
1956	2,676	20	4,647	237	10,796	847	—	—	—	—
1955	3,466	100	5,594	437	12,443	1,189	—	—	—	—

Note: Figures are U.S. dollars in millions * Results prior to 1998 are for Chrysler Corp. only. Source: Ward's Research and company annual reports.

RESEARCH & DEVELOPMENT EXPENDITURES FOR SELECTED MANUFACTURERS, 1975-1999 (U.S. Dollars In Millions)

Year	Daimler-Chrysler*	Ford	General Motors	Toyota	Volkswagen	Year	Daimler-Chrysler*	Ford	General Motors	Toyota	Volkswagen
1999	7,628	7,100	6,800	4,771	3,806	1988	866	2,930	4,754	—	—
1998	7,853	6,300	7,900	3,367	3,343	1987	773	2,514	4,361	—	—
1997	1,714	6,327	8,200	3,723	2,555	1986	732	2,305	4,158	—	—
1996	1,602	6,821	8,900	—	—	1985	609	2,018	3,625	—	—
1995	1,420	6,624	8,200	—	—	1984	452	1,915	3,076	—	—
1994	1,303	5,811	6,900	—	—	1983	365	1,751	2,602	—	—
1993	1,230	5,618	6,030	—	—	1982	307	1,764	2,175	—	—
1992	1,053	4,332	5,917	—	—	1981	250	1,718	2,250	—	—
1991	955	3,728	5,887	—	—	1980	278	1,675	2,225	—	—
1990	908	3,558	5,342	—	—	1979	358	1,720	1,950	—	—
1989	958	3,167	5,248	—	—	1975	161	748	1,114	—	—

*Data reflects DaimlerChrysler for 1998.
SOURCE: Compiled by Ward's Communications from company annual reports.

Use of Tax Revenues by State

STATE MOTOR USE TAX REVENUES, 1999 (In Thousands)

State	Total State Tax Revenue	State Tax on Motor Vehicle Fuel	State License Tax on Motor Vehicles	State License Tax on Motor Vehicle Operators	Total Motor Vehicle Fuel and License Taxes	Percent Motor Vehicle of Total Taxes
Alabama	$6,038,302	$497,582	$184,383	$16,622	$715,209	11.8
Alaska	1,249,160	38,011	33,914	0	71,925	5.8
Arizona	7,317,902	584,747	143,723	12,955	741,425	10.1
Arkansas	4,271,768	379,832	106,722	7,459	494,013	11.6
California	71,305,372	3,034,046	1,662,753	141,105	4,837,904	6.8
Colorado	6,211,234	515,768	165,363	11,944	693,075	11.2
Connecticut	9,891,899	544,667	224,864	29,651	799,182	8.1
Delaware	2,086,583	103,122	30,285	143	133,550	6.4
Florida	23,707,350	1,576,708	873,346	112,714	2,562,768	10.8
Georgia	12,204,273	566,402	217,606	40,305	824,313	6.8
Hawaii	3,344,734	73,566	64,164	329	138,059	4.1
Idaho	2,166,514	212,489	103,110	5,665	321,264	14.8
Illinois	20,820,075	1,328,723	780,471	59,341	2,168,535	10.4
Indiana	10,264,490	663,942	139,874	0	803,816	7.8
Iowa	5,057,287	340,767	314,536	10,621	665,924	13.2
Kansas	4,894,475	325,898	143,440	12,027	481,365	9.8
Kentucky	7,492,580	444,701	183,227	6,632	634,560	8.5
Louisiana	6,404,654	536,584	103,613	8,740	648,937	10.1
Maine	2,495,530	172,975	62,930	5,540	241,445	9.7
Maryland	9,678,002	680,055	177,557	21,215	878,827	9.1
Massachusetts	15,257,055	636,551	234,115	59,312	929,978	6.1
Michigan	22,843,459	1,088,370	771,003	43,568	1,902,941	8.3
Minnesota	12,114,167	580,831	591,777	27,623	1,200,231	9.9
Mississippi	4,573,838	395,007	109,473	21,395	525,875	11.5
Missouri	8,658,489	663,397	251,376	21,487	936,260	10.8
Montana	1,402,547	179,790	50,819	5,492	236,101	16.8
Nebraska	2,772,898	263,648	79,211	8,317	351,176	12.7
Nevada	3,399,450	237,491	111,190	11,768	360,449	10.6
New Hampshire	1,062,016	119,653	61,378	8,269	189,300	17.8
New Jersey	16,432,755	483,234	363,167	31,553	877,954	5.3
New Mexico	3,764,153	247,188	132,605	7,398	387,191	10.3
New York	38,072,393	505,232	576,800	84,600	1,166,632	3.1
North Carolina	14,605,146	1,145,969	400,422	81,795	1,628,186	11.1
North Dakota	1,135,579	104,893	39,831	3,310	148,034	13.0
Ohio	18,578,721	1,370,698	586,501	39,215	1,996,414	10.7
Oklahoma	5,582,018	383,588	577,425	6,835	967,848	17.3
Oregon	5,264,274	396,960	332,309	20,438	749,707	14.2
Pennsylvania	21,723,798	746,779	735,840	51,859	1,534,478	7.1
Rhode Island	1,878,543	119,404	52,576	414	172,394	9.2
South Carolina	5,984,617	350,998	99,528	15,033	465,559	7.8
South Dakota	877,885	107,323	32,486	1,352	141,161	16.1
Tennessee	7,367,237	769,912	215,321	36,721	1,021,954	13.9
Texas	25,935,474	2,592,251	882,192	98,548	3,572,991	13.8
Utah	3,641,096	312,711	73,249	5,790	391,750	10.8
Vermont	1,008,456	56,622	33,640	3,754	94,016	9.3
Virginia	11,102,230	794,798	286,701	27,580	1,109,079	9.0
Washington	12,432,442	717,813	273,290	27,653	1,018,756	8.2
West Virginia	3,171,765	237,110	81,190	4,470	322,770	10.2
Wisconsin	11,741,206	909,076	276,103	27,330	1,212,509	10.3
Wyoming	901,108	62,617	47,136	2,382	112,135	12.4
Total	$500,186,997	$28,330,413	$13,672,480	$1,260,931	$43,263,824	8.6

NOTE: 1999 is preliminary
SOURCE: U.S. Department of Commerce, Bureau of the Census.

New Car Corporate Average Fuel Economy

NEW CAR CORPORATE AVERAGE FUEL ECONOMY, 1974-2000 MODEL YEARS
(Sales Weighted Combined City/Highway Miles Per Gallon)

Manufacturer	Final Sales Basis									Preliminary Sales Basis		
	1974	1983	1985	1987	1989	1991	1993	1995	1997	1998	1999	2000
DOMESTIC FLEETS												
Chrysler	13.9	26.9	27.8	27.5	28.0	27.5	27.8	28.4	27.6	28.8	27.5	27.7
Ford	14.2	24.3	26.6	26.9	26.6	27.6	28.8	27.7	27.2	27.8	27.2	28.0
General Motors	12.1	24.0	25.8	26.9	27.3	27.1	27.4	27.4	28.2	27.8	27.7	28.1
Honda	—	—	—	—	—	—	—	—	28.5	32.7	33.5	35.3
Mazda	—	—	—	—	—	—	29.7	30.3	27.2	27.8	27.2	28.0
Toyota	—	—	—	—	—	—	—	—	28.5	28.8	28.0	28.3	33.3
IMPORT FLEETS												
Alfa Romeo	—	25.8	27.7	25.5	26.9	25.2	—	—	—	—	—	—
AMC-Renault	—	32.0	28.6	33.0	—	—	—	—	—	—	—	—
BMW	19.5	26.2	26.4	24.9	22.2	23.2	25.2	25.3	25.7	25.4	25.4	25.0
Chrysler	—	34.5	36.2	33.4	30.3	28.7	31.0	28.6	25.7	25.4	26.3	25.1
Ford	—	35.4	25.2	24.2	31.7	33.2	26.7	34.0	31.3	28.9	30.1	27.2
Fuji(Subaru)	25.7	33.0	32.6	31.0	32.5	28.4	29.6	28.9	28.3	27.8	27.5	28.0
General Motors	—	—	47.9	39.0	40.4	32.4	30.5	36.7	32.1	29.4	27.9	24.8
Honda	31.1	36.0	34.5	33.2	31.6	30.7	32.5	32.7	32.4	28.1	29.4	29.0
Hyundai	—	—	—	34.8	33.4	32.9	31.3	31.2	31.4	30.9	31.4	30.7
Isuzu	—	31.4	34.2	38.8	35.8	34.9	34.8	—	—	—	—	—
Kia	—	—	—	—	—	—	—	31.0	30.9	31.2	29.8	
Mazda	13.6	29.4	30.3	29.6	29.8	30.5	31.0	31.4	31.3	28.9	30.1	27.2
Mercedes-Benz	15.3	27.2	23.6	22.3	21.4	22.3	22.9	24.7	25.2	27.2	—	—
MG-TREaguar	21.3	19.0	19.3	19.3	20.8	—	—	—	—	—	—	—
Mitsubishi	—	30.8	31.9	31.7	31.4	30.3	29.4	29.9	30.0	31.5	29.6	29.4
Nissan	24.0	33.4	30.1	29.7	30.4	29.2	29.4	29.5	29.9	30.7	29.9	27.9
Peugeot	19.0	25.6	25.2	24.1	25.5	26.3	26.2	—	—	—	—	—
Saab	19.8	26.6	26.4	26.2	26.6	—	—	—	—	—	—	—
Suzuki	—	—	58.7	50.4	36.9	43.2	45.6	40.8	35.2	35.9	35.5	35.5
Toyota	22.5	33.3	33.5	33.4	32.1	30.9	29.1	30.4	30.1	30.7	29.9	28.5
Volvo	19.4	26.5	27.2	26.4	25.0	25.3	25.9	26.0	25.8	25.6	26.2	—
VW-Audi	25.9	30.7	30.5	30.1	30.4	29.9	27.2	29.0	29.0	29.0	28.2	28.0
Yugo	—	—	—	33.7	33.6	34.6	—	—	—	—	—	—

NOTE: After 1979, domestic fleet excludes captive imports.
SOURCE: U.S. Department of Transportation.

NEW CAR CORPORATE AVERAGE FUEL ECONOMY, 1974-2000 (Sales Weighted Combined City/Highway Miles Per Gallon)

Model Year	Federal Standard	Domestic Fleet	Import Fleet	Total Fleet
1974	None	13.2	22.2	14.2
1976	None	16.6	25.4	17.5
1978	18.0	18.7	27.3	19.9
1980	20.0	22.6	29.6	24.3
1982	24.0	25.0	31.1	26.6
1984	27.0	25.6	32.0	26.9
1985	27.5	26.3	31.5	27.6
1986	26.0	26.6	31.6	28.2
1987	26.0	27.0	31.2	28.5
1988	26.0	27.4	31.5	28.8
1989	26.5	27.2	30.8	28.4
1990	27.5	26.9	29.9	28.0
1991	27.5	27.3	30.1	28.4
1992	27.5	27.0	29.2	27.9
1993	27.5	27.8	29.6	28.4
1994	27.5	27.5	29.7	28.3
1995	27.5	27.7	30.3	28.6
1996	27.5	28.1	29.6	28.5
1997	27.5	27.8	30.1	28.7
1998 (prelim.)	27.5	28.6	29.2	28.8
1999 (prelim.)	27.5	27.9	29.0	28.3
2000 (prelim.)	27.5	28.7	28.0	28.4

NOTE: After 1979, domestic fleet excludes captive imports.
SOURCE: U.S. Department of Transportation.

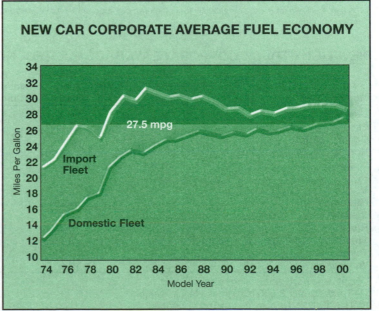

NEW CAR CORPORATE AVERAGE FUEL ECONOMY

New Light Truck Corporate Average Fuel Economy

NEW LIGHT TRUCK[1] FUEL ECONOMY PERFORMANCE, 1979-2000 (Sales Weighted Combined City/Highway Miles Per Gallon)

	2-Wheel Drive			4-Wheel Drive		
	Federal Standard	Sales Weighted Average Domestic*	Import	Federal Standard	Sales Weighted Average Domestic*	Import
1979	17.2	17.9	20.9	15.8	16.5	25.5
1981	16.7	18.6	28.3	15.0	17.1	24.3
1983**	19.5	19.6[2]	27.1[2]	17.5	19.6[2]	27.1[2]
1985**	19.7	19.9	27.4	18.9	19.6	24.7
1987**	21.0	20.4	27.5	19.5	19.4	25.3
1988**	21.0	20.6[2]	24.6[2]	19.5	20.6[2]	24.6[2]
1989**	21.5	20.4[2]	23.5[2]	19.0	20.4[2]	23.5[2]
1990**	20.5	20.3[2]	23.0[2]	19.0	20.3[2]	23.0[2]
1991**	20.7	20.9[2]	23.0[2]	19.1	20.9[2]	23.0[2]

	Federal Standard	Other[3]	Captive Import[4]	Total Fleet
1992	20.2	20.8	21.0	20.8
1993	20.4	21.0	24.3	21.0
1994	20.5	20.8	—	20.8
1995	20.6	20.5	—	20.5
1996	20.7	20.7	—	20.8
1997	20.7	20.4	—	20.6
1998	20.7	20.8	—	21.1
1999	20.7	—	—	20.7
2000	20.7	—	—	21.2

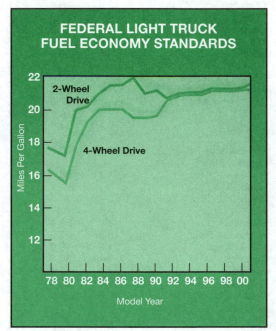

FEDERAL LIGHT TRUCK FUEL ECONOMY STANDARDS

*Captive imports are excluded.
**Manufacturers may elect to meet a single combined corporate fleet average of 19 mpg in 1983, 20 mpg in 1984, 19.5 mpg in 1985, 20 mpg in 1986, 20.5 mpg in 1987-89, 20 in 1990, and 20.2 in 1991.
(1) Light truck defined as 0-6,000 lbs. In 1979 and 0-8,500 lbs. in subsequent years.
(2) Combined 2-wheel and 4-wheel drive fleet average.
(3) Not a captive import light truck; 2 and 4 wheel drive combined.
(4) A light truck which is not domestically manufactured but imported by a manufacturer whose principal place of business is the United States; 2 and 4 wheel drive combined.
SOURCE: U.S. Department of Transportation.

NEW LIGHT TRUCK CORPORATE AVERAGE FUEL ECONOMY, 1993-2000[1] (Miles Per Gallon)

Manufacturer	1993 Model Year Combined	1995 Model Year Combined	1997 Model Year Combined	1998 Model Year Combined	1999 Model Year Combined	2000 Model Year Combined
Chrysler*	21.2	20.1	20.2	20.6	20.7	21.2
Ford*	20.9	20.8	20.0	20.4	20.4	20.8
General Motors*	20.2	20.1	20.5	21.2	20.0	21.0
Honda	—	—	26.9	26.9	26.1	25.3
Isuzu	21.8	20.3	19.6	21.4	21.5	20.8
Kia	—	24.4	23.7	24.4	24.2	23.5
Mazda	23.6	20.9	20.5	20.4	20.4	20.8
Mitsubishi	21.3	20.2	22.3	22.9	22.3	21.5
Nissan	23.7	22.4	22.3	22.3	21.2	21.4
Rover	15.5	16.3	17.2	17.2	17.0	17.0
Suzuki	28.9	28.1	27.4	27.4	23.8	23.8
Toyota	22.3	21.2	22.6	23.5	22.9	21.7
Volkswagen	21.0	19.6	18.5	—	19.1	19.2

* Captive imports are excluded.
(1) Trucks under 8,500 lbs. gross vehicle weight
SOURCE: U.S. Department of Transportation.

Gas Guzzler Tax Receipts, Automotive Fuel Prices and New Car Quality Improvements

NEW CAR GAS GUZZLER TAXES

Miles Per Gallon* At Least-Less Than	1980	1981	1982	1983	1984	1985	1986-90	1991 & Later
0-12.5	$550	$650	$1,200	$1,550	$2,150	$2,650	$3,850	7,700
12.5-13.0	550	650	950	1,550	1,750	2,650	3,200	6,400
13.0-13.5	300	550	950	1,250	1,750	2,200	3,200	6,400
13.5-14.0	300	550	750	1,250	1,450	2,200	2,700	5,400
14.0-14.5	200	450	750	1,000	1,450	1,800	2,700	5,400
14.5-15.0	200	450	600	1,000	1,150	1,800	2,250	4,500
15.0-15.5	0	350	600	800	1,150	1,500	2,250	4,500
15.5-16.0	0	350	450	800	950	1,500	1,850	3,700
16.0-16.5	0	200	450	650	950	1,200	1,850	3,700
16.5-17.0	0	200	350	650	750	1,200	1,500	3,000
17.0-17.5	0	0	350	500	750	1,000	1,500	3,000
17.5-18.0	0	0	200	500	600	1,000	1,300	2,600
18.0-18.5	0	0	0	350	600	800	1,300	2,600
18.5-19.0	0	0	0	350	450	800	1,050	2,100
19.0-19.5	0	0	0	0	450	600	1,050	2,100
19.5-20.0	0	0	0	0	0	600	850	1,700
20.0-20.5	0	0	0	0	0	500	850	1,700
20.5-21.0	0	0	0	0	0	500	650	1,300
21.0-21.5	0	0	0	0	0	0	650	1,300
21.5-22.0	0	0	0	0	0	0	500	1,000
22.0-22.5	0	0	0	0	0	0	500	1,000
22.5 & Over	0	0	0	0	0	0	0	0

NOTE: New car purchaser pays tax if car's combined city/highway fuel economy rating is lower than standard.
*Combined city/highway rating.
SOURCE: 26 U.S. Code 4064.

GAS GUZZLER TAX RECEIPTS

Dollars in Millions

Fiscal Year	1990	1991	1992	1993	1994	1995	1996	1997	1998	1999
	103.2	118.4	144.2	111.6	64.1	73.5	52.6	48.2	47.7	68.3

U.S. CITY AVERAGE RETAIL PRICES FOR AUTOMOTIVE FUEL, 1980-1999
(Cents Per Gallon, Including Taxes)

Year	Unleaded Regular	Unleaded Premium	All Types[1]	Diesel
1999	116.5	135.7	122.1	112.0
1998	105.9	125.0	111.5	104.5
1997	120.0	138.1	124.5	120.0
1996	123.1	141.3	128.8	123.6
1995	114.7	133.6	120.5	110.9
1994	111.2	130.5	117.4	112.0
1993	110.8	130.2	117.3	114.8
1992	112.7	131.6	119.0	114.5
1991	114.0	132.1	119.6	124.3[2]
1990	116.4	134.9	121.7	134.3
1989	102.1	119.7	106.0	110.0
1988	94.6	110.7	96.3	104.6
1987	94.8	109.3	95.7	106.3
1986	92.7	108.5	93.1	99.9
1985	120.2	134.0	119.6	129.5
1980	124.5	N.A.	122.1	112.4

N.A.-Not available.
(1) Includes types of motor gasoline not shown separately.
(2) Price changed from "Full Service" to "Self Service."

AVERAGE RETAIL PRICE INCREASES FOR NEW CAR QUALITY IMPROVEMENTS, 1968-2000

Model Year	Requirements (Adjusted to 1999 Dollars) Safety	Emissions*	Other**	Total
1968	$81.64	$44.06	-$1.93	$123.77
1969	37.95	0.00	-35.24	2.71
1970	19.75	14.49	86.92	121.16
1971	0.00	48.05	-63.22	-15.17
1972	5.10	15.31	30.63	51.04
1973	218.06	70.56	26.75	315.37
1974	259.43	3.38	21.46	284.26
1975	23.75	264.55	0.00	288.30
1976	27.96	15.86	-11.27	32.55
1977	13.78	28.36	75.15	117.29
1978	0.00	18.40	73.91	92.31
1979	9.81	20.65	48.64	79.10
1980	20.99	186.41	173.99	381.39
1981	6.39	695.24	89.26	790.89
1982	0.00	121.37	59.68	181.05
1983	0.00	90.34	88.58	178.92
1984	-16.42	79.97	85.93	149.49
1985	0.00	26.41	172.86	199.27
1986	34.61	0.00	200.79	235.40
1987	0.00	0.00	57.41	57.41
1988	78.12	0.00	215.12	293.24
1989	27.11	0.00	187.08	214.19
1990	205.26	0.00	44.41	249.66
1991	239.60	0.00	0.00	239.60
1992	37.68	0.00	244.77	282.45
1993	0.00	0.00	94.59	94.59
1994	188.94	40.50	143.81	373.26
1995	120.36	53.74	0.00	174.0:
1996	16.31	87.23	86.90	190.44
1997	8.97	20.45	153.35	182.78
1998	0.00	51.73	177.27	229.01
1999	0.00	76.61	408.25	484.86
2000	15.26	0.00	0.00	15.26

*Includes changes to improve fuel economy and emissions control.
**Includes improved warranties, corrosion protection and changes in standard equipment.
SOURCE: U.S. Department of Labor, Bureau of Labor Statistics.

Federal Exhaust Emission Standards for Cars and Light Trucks

FEDERAL EXHAUST EMISSION STANDARDS FOR CONVENTIONALLY FUELED PASSENGER CARS AND LIGHT TRUCKS, 1991-2003 (Grams Per Mile)

Vehicle Type and Model Year	Useful Life	Percent of Fleet	NMHC	CO	CO Cold Start	NOx Gasoline	NOx Diesel	Particulates (PM-10)
LIGHT-DUTY VEHICLES(0-6,000 LBS. GROSS VEHICLE WEIGHT RATING)								
Passenger Cars								
1991-3	5/50	100	0.41[e]	3.4	—	1.0	1.0	0.20
1994	5/50	40	0.25[d]	3.4	10.0	0.4	1.0	0.08
1994	10/100	40	0.31	4.2	—	0.6	1.25	0.10
1995	5/50	80	0.25[d]	3.4	10.0	0.4	1.0	0.08
1995	10/100	80	0.31	4.2	—	0.6	1.25	0.10
1996-2000	5/50	100	0.25[d]	3.4	10.0[b]	0.4	1.0	0.08
1996-2000	10/100	100	0.31	4.2	—	0.6	1.25	0.10
1999-2003 "NLEV"	10/100	100	0.075	3.4	3.4[b]	0.2	—	0.08
Light-Duty Trucks(0-3,750 lbs. Loaded Vehicle Weight)								
1991-3	5/50	100	0.80[e]	10.0	—	1.2	1.2	0.20
1994	5/50	40	0.25[d]	3.4	10.0	0.4	1.0	0.08
1994	10/100	40	0.31	4.2	—	0.6	1.25	0.10
1995	5/50	80	0.25[d]	3.4	10.0	0.4	1.0	0.08 (40%)
1995	10/100	80	0.31	4.2	—	0.6	1.25	0.10 (40%)
1996-2000	5/50	100	0.25[d]	3.4	10.0[b]	0.4	1.0	0.08 (80%)[c]
1996-2000	10/100	100	0.31	4.2	—	0.6	1.25	0.10 (80%)[c]
1999-2003 "NLEV"	10/100	100	0.075	3.4	3.4[b]	0.2	—	0.08
Light-Duty Trucks(3,751 - 5,750 lbs. Loaded Vehicle Weight)								
1991-3	11/120	100	0.80[e]	10.0	—	1.7	1.7	0.13
1994	5/50	40	0.32[d]	4.4	12.5	0.7	1.7	—
1994	10/100	40	0.4	5.5	—	0.0	0.97	0.13
1995	5/50	80	0.32[d]	4.4	12.5	0.7	1.7	0.08 (40%)
1995	10/100	80	0.4	5.5	—	0.0	0.97	0.10 (40%)
1996-2000	5/50	100	0.32[d]	4.4	12.5	0.7	1.7	0.08 (80%)[c]
1996-2000	10/100	100	0.4	5.5	—	0.0	0.97	0.10 (80%)[c]
1999-2003 "NLEV"	11/120	100	0.1	4.4	—	0.4	—	0.10
LIGHT-DUTY TRUCKS (6,001-8,500 LBS. GROSS VEHICLE WEIGHT RATING)								
Light-Duty Trucks (3,751-5,750 lbs.Test Weight)								
1991-3	11/120	100	0.80[e]	10.0	—	1.7	1.7	0.13
1994	11/120	100	0.80[e]	10.0	12.5 (40%)	1.7	1.7	0.13
1995	11/120	100	0.80[e]	10.0	12.5 (80%)	1.7	1.7	0.13
1996	5/50	50	0.32[d]	4.4	12.5 (100%)	0.7	—	—
1996	11/120	50	0.46	6.4	—	0.0	0.98	0.10
1997-2003	5/50	100	0.32[d]	4.4	TBD	0.7	—	—
1997-2003	11/120	100	0.46	6.4	—	0.0	0.98	0.10
Light-Duty Trucks (Over 5,750 lbs. Test Weight)								
1991-3	11/120	100	0.80[e]	10.0	—	1.7	1.7	0.13
1994	11/120	100	0.80[e]	10.0	12.5 (40%)	1.7	1.7	0.13
1995	11/120	100	0.80[e]	10.0	12.5 (80%)	1.7	1.7	0.13
1996	5/50	50	0.39[d]	5.0	12.5 (100%)	1.1	—	—
1996	11/120	50	0.56	7.3	—		1.53	1.53	0.12
1997-2003	5/50	100	0.39[d]	5.0	TBD	1.1	—	—
1997-2003	11/120	100	0.56	7.3	—		1.53	1.53	0.12

NMHC-Nonmethane (reactive) hydrocarbons.
TBD-To be determined by EPA at level equivalent to car standard.
Test Weight = (GVWR + curb weight) / 2.

5/50   5 year/50,000 miles.
10/100   10 year/100,000 miles. In-use compliance is 7/75,000.
11/120   11 year/120,000 miles. In-use compliance is 7/90,000.

(a) The voluntary NLEV (National Low Emission Vehicle) program begins in nine of the thirteen states in the Northeast Trading Region (NTR) in the 1999 Model Year and begins in the rest of the country (37 states) in the 2001 Model Year.
(b) If by June 1997, six or more areas have a CO design value equal to or greater than 9.5ppm, then standards of 3.4 for cars, 4.4 for light trucks up to 6,000 lbs. GVWR, and a level of comparable stringency for LDTs equal to or greater than 6,000 lbs. GVWR, under cold start requirements shall apply beginning Model Year 2002.
(c) 100% in 1997 and thereafter.
(d) A set of intermediate in-use standards also applies during thephase-in period 1994-1997 for passenger cars and small light-duty trucks and 1996-1998 for larger light-duty trucks.
(e) Total hydrocarbons.
SOURCE: U.S. Environmental Protection Agency.

Federal Motor Vehicle Safety Standards

FEDERAL MOTOR VEHICLE SAFETY STANDARDS (FMVSS)

FMVSS NUMBER	Car	MPV	Truck	Bus	Equip.
100 SERIES Crash Avoidance					
101 Controls, Location & Identification	•	•	•	•	
102 Transmission Shift Lever Sequence	•	•	•	•	
103 Windshield Defrosting & Defogging	•	•	•	•	
104 Windshield Wiping & Washing System	•	•	•	•	
105 Hydraulic Brake System(1)	•	•*	•*	•*	
106 Brake Hoses	•	•	•	•	•
108 Lights & Reflectors	•	•	•	•	
109 New Tires for Passenger Cars(2)					•
110 Tire Selection & Wheels for Passenger Cars	•				
111 Rearview Mirrors	•	•	•	•	
113 Hood Latch System	•	•	•	•	
114 Theft Protection	•	•	•	•	
115 Vehicle Identification Number (Location)	•	•	•	•	
116 Hydraulic Brake Fluids	•	•	•	•	•
117 Retreaded Tires					•
118 Power Operated Window Systems	•	•	•		
119 New Tires for Trucks , Buses, etc					•
120 Tire Selection & Wheels for Trucks, Buses, etc.		•	•	•	
121 Air Brake Systems			•	•	
122 Motorcycle Brake System					•
123 Motorcycle Controls, Displays					•
124 Accelerator Control Systems	•	•	•	•	
125 Warning Devices					•
126 Truck-Camper Loading					•
129 Non-pneumatic Tires					•
131 School Bus Pedestrian Safety Devices				•	
135 Passenger Car Brake Systems(1)	•				
200 SERIES Occupant Protection					
201 Occupant Protection in Interior Impacts	•	•*	•*	•*	
202 Head Restraints	•	•*	•*	•*	
203 Steering Wheel Impact Protection	•	•*	•*	•*	
204 Steering System Rearward Movement	•	•*	•*	•*	
205 Glazing Materials	•	•	•	•	•
206 Door Locks & Hinges	•	•	•		
207 Anchorage of Seats	•	•	•	•	
208 Occupant Restraints	•	•	•	•	•
209 Seat Belt Assemblies(2)					•
210 Seat Belt Anchorages	•	•	•	•	

FMVSS NUMBER	Car	MPV	Truck	Bus	Equip.
212 Windshield Mounting	•	•*	•*	•*	
213 Child Restraint Systems					•
214 Side Door Strength	•	•	•		
216 Roof Crush Resistance	•*	•	•	•	
217 Bus Window Strength & Emergency Release				•	
218 Motorcycle Helmets					•
219 Windshield Zone Intrusion	•	•*	•*	•*	
220 School Bus Rollover Protection				•*	
221 School Bus Body Joint Strength				•*	
222 School Bus Seats				•*	
223 Rear Impact Guards					•
300 SERIES Post Crash Protection					
301 Fuel System Integrity	•	•*	•*	•*	
302 Flammability of Interior Materials	•	•	•	•	
303 Fuel System Integrity-CNG	•	•*	•*	•*	
304 CNG Fuel Container Integrity	•	•	•	•	
49CFR PART NO. - Code of Federal Regulation (CFR) Parts					
— Importation of Motor Vehicles & Equipment	•	•	•	•	•
541 Theft Prevention	•*				
565 Vehicle Identification Number (Content)	•	•	•	•	
566 Manufacturers Identification	•	•	•	•	
567 Certification	•	•	•	•	
568 Vehicles Manufactured in 2 or More Stages	•	•	•	•	
569 Regrooved Tires					•
572 Anthropomorphic Dummy (Test Equipment)					•
573 Defect Reports	•	•	•	•	
574 Tire Identification & Record Keeping	•	•	•	•	
575 Consumer Information					
103 Truck Camper Loading			•		
104 Uniform Tire Quality Grading					•
105 Utility Vehicle			•		
577 Defect Notification	•	•	•	•	
579 Defect & Non-Compliance Responsibility	•	•	•	•	
580 Odometer Disclosure Requirements	•	•	•	•	
581 Bumper Damage Limits	•				
582 Insurance Cost Information .	•				
583 Automobile Parts Content Labeling					•
595 Retrofit On-Off Switches for Air Bags					•

(1) Passenger cars may comply with either FMVSS or 135 until September 1, 2000 when FMVSS 135 becomes mandatory.
(2) Vehicle application is implied or is specified in other FMVSS.
* Application or requirements vary for specific vehicle types or Gross Vehicle Weight Ratings (GVWR).
PASSENGER CAR: Motor vehicle with motive power, except a multipurpose passenger vehicle, motorcycle or trailer designed for carrying 10 persons or less.
MULTIPURPOSE PASSENGER VEHICLE: Motor vehicle with motive power, except a trailer, designed to carry 10 persons or less which is constructed either on a truck chassis or with special features for occasional off-road operation.
TRUCK: Motor vehicle with motive power, except a trailer, designed primarily for the transportation of property or special purpose equipment.
BUS: Motor vehicle with motive power, except a trailer, designed for carrying more than 10 persons.
EQUIPMENT: Individual vehicle components or systems whether installed on a new vehicle or provided as a replacement.
SOURCE: Compiled by Ward's Communications.

Motor Vehicle Deaths by Type of Accident and Death Rates

MOTOR VEHICLE DEATHS BY TYPE OF ACCIDENT AND DEATH RATES, 1913-1999

Year	Total Motor Vehicle Deaths	Pedes-trians	Other Motor Vehicles	Rail-road Trains	Pedal cycles	Animal drawn Veh. or Animal	Fixed Objects	Deaths from Non-collision Accidents	Per 10,000 Motor Vehicles	Per 100,000,000 Vehicle Miles	Per 100,000 Popu-lation
1999*	41,300	5,800	18,800	300	900	100	11,100	4,300	1.89	1.54	15.1
1998**	41,800	5,900	18,500	400	700	100	12,000	4,200	1.94	1.59	15.5
1997**	43,458	5,900	19,900	371	800	100	12,000	4,400	2.05	1.70	16.2
1996	43,649	6,100	19,600	373	800	100	12,100	4,600	2.07	1.76	16.5
1995	43,363	6,400	19,000	514	800	100	12,100	4,400	2.11	1.79	16.5
1994	42,524	6,300	18,900	549	800	100	11,500	4,400	2.11	1.80	16.3
1993	41,893	6,400	18,300	553	800	100	11,500	4,200	2.12	1.82	16.3
1992	40,982	6,300	17,600	521	700	100	11,700	4,100	2.11	1.83	16.1
1991	43,536	6,600	18,200	541	800	100	12,600	4,700	2.26	2.00	17.3
1990	46,814	7,300	19,900	623	900	100	13,100	4,900	2.43	2.18	18.8
1989	47,575	7,800	20,300	720	900	100	12,900	4,900	2.48	2.26	19.3
1988	49,078	7,700	20,900	638	1,000	100	13,400	5,300	2.60	2.42	20.1
1987	48,290	7,500	20,700	554	1,000	100	13,200	5,200	2.63	2.51	19.9
1986	47,865	8,900	20,800	574	1,100	100	3,300	13,100	2.63	2.60	19.9
1985	45,901	8,500	19,900	538	1,100	100	3,200	12,600	2.59	2.59	19.2
1984	46,263	8,500	20,000	630	1,100	100	3,200	12,700	2.69	2.69	19.6
1983	44,452	8,200	19,200	520	1,100	100	3,100	12,200	2.62	2.68	19.0
1982	45,779	8,400	19,800	554	1,100	100	3,200	12,600	2.77	2.88	19.7
1981	51,385	9,400	22,200	668	1,200	100	3,600	14,200	3.13	3.30	22.4
1980	53,172	9,700	23,000	739	1,200	100	3,700	14,700	3.29	3.50	23.4
1979	53,524	9,800	23,100	826	1,200	100	3,700	14,800	3.35	3.50	23.8
1978	52,411	9,600	22,400	986	1,200	100	3,600	14,500	3.41	3.39	23.6
1977	49,510	9,100	21,200	902	1,100	100	3,400	13,700	3.33	3.35	22.5
1976	47,038	8,600	20,100	1,033	1,000	100	3,200	13,000	3.28	3.33	21.6
1975	45,853	8,400	19,550	979	1,000	100	3,130	12,700	3.33	3.45	21.3
1974	46,402	8,500	19,700	1,209	1,000	100	3,100	2,800	3.44	3.59	21.8
1973	55,511	10,200	23,600	1,194	1,000	100	3,800	15,600	4.28	4.24	26.3
1972	56,278	10,300	23,900	1,260	1,000	100	3,900	15,800	4.60	4.43	26.9
1971	54,381	9,900	23,100	1,378	800	100	3,800	15,300	4.68	4.57	26.3
1970	54,633	9,900	23,200	1,459	780	100	3,800	15,400	4.92	4.88	26.8
1965	49,163	8,900	20,800	1,556	680	120	2,200	14,900	5.36	5.54	25.4
1960	38,137	7,850	14,800	1,368	460	80	1,700	11,900	5.12	5.31	21.2
1955	38,426	8,200	14,500	1,490	410	80	1,600	12,100	6.12	6.34	23.4
1950	34,763	9,000	11,650	1,541	440	90	1,300	10,600	7.07	7.59	23.0
1943-47ave.	28,458	10,570	7,490	1,660	490	120	820	7,120	8.60	10.52	20.8
1938-42ave.	33,549	12,430	9,500	1,624	748	140	1,048	7,848	10.41	11.49	25.4
1933-37ave.	36,313	14,484	8,630	1,598	540	214	1,034	9,464	13.50	15.55	28.6
1928-32ave.	31,050	12,300	5,700	1,850	—	274	700	9,100	12.10	15.60	25.3
1923-27ave.	21,800	—	—	1,200	—	—	—	—	11.10	18.20	18.8
1918-22ave.	12,700	—	—	—	—	—	—	—	13.90	—	11.9
1913-17ave.	6,800	—	—	—	—	—	—	—	23.80	—	6.8

* Preliminary.
** Revised.
SOURCE: National Safety Council.

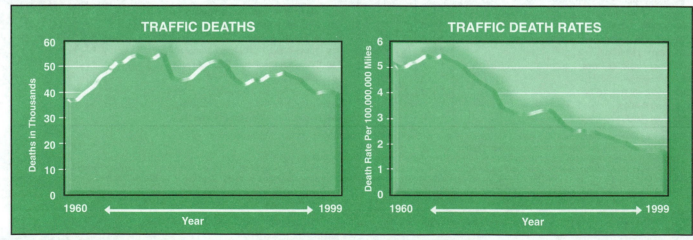

Motor Vehicle Traffic Deaths and Traffic Death Rates by State

MOTOR VEHICLE TRAFFIC DEATHS AND TRAFFIC DEATH RATES BY STATE, 1994-1999

| State | Traffic Deaths | | | | | | Traffic Deaths Per 100,000,000 Vehicle Miles | |
	1994	1995	1996	1997	1998	1999	1998	1999
Alabama	1,083	1,111	1,142	1,181	1,069	1,107	2.0	2.0
Alaska	85	86	80	77	72	76	1.6	1.7
Arizona	915	1,040	993	961	980	1,024	2.2	2.2
Arkansas	611	631	615	660	625	602	2.2	2.1
California	4,226	4,165	3,972	3,377	3,161	3,204	1.1	1.1
Colorado	585	645	434	516	524	N.A.	1.4	N.A.
Connecticut	310	318	310	337	329	301	1.1	1.0
Delaware	112	123	120	147	115	103	1.4	1.2
Dist. of Columbia	N.A.	N.A.	N.A.	N.A.	58	46	1.7	1.4
Florida	2,735	2,812	2,813	2,847	2,804	2,920	2.0	2.1
Georgia	1,438	1,494	1,578	1,584	1,580	1,514	1.7	1.5
Hawaii	122	127	145	131	120	98	1.5	1.2
Idaho	249	263	258	259	265	278	2.0	2.0
Illinois	1,554	1,589	1,475	1,404	1,392	1,456	1.4	1.4
Indiana	979	960	981	N.A.	978	1,019	1.4	1.5
Iowa	478	527	465	468	444	489	1.6	1.7
Kansas	442	438	491	483	493	532	1.8	1.9
Kentucky	791	856	844	865	868	819	1.9	1.7
Louisiana	838	880	809	840	812	923	2.0	2.2
Maine	188	189	168	192	184	179	1.4	1.3
Maryland	656	682	614	609	606	598	1.3	1.2
Massachusetts	440	448	417	443	406	414	0.8	0.8
Michigan	1,419	1,537	1,505	1,446	1,367	1,386	1.5	1.4
Minnesota	644	597	576	598	650	626	1.3	1.2
Mississippi	792	868	811	861	948	926	2.9	2.7
Missouri	1,089	1,110	1,148	1,192	1,169	1,094	1.8	1.7
Montana	202	215	198	265	237	220	2.5	2.2
Nebraska	271	254	293	302	315	295	1.8	1.6
Nevada	294	312	348	347	360	350	2.2	2.0
New Hampshire	119	118	134	125	129	141	1.1	1.2
New Jersey	761	776	818	N.A.	755	665	1.2	1.0
New Mexico	447	485	481	484	424	461	1.9	2.0
New York	1,658	1,668	1,562	1,625	1,405	1,473	1.1	1.2
North Carolina	1,431	1,438	1,492	1,484	1,574	1,506	1.9	1.7
North Dakota	88	74	85	105	92	119	1.3	1.6
Ohio	1,371	1,357	1,393	1,439	1,421	1,430	1.3	1.3
Oklahoma	695	674	775	842	769	740	1.8	1.7
Oregon	491	572	524	521	538	413	1.6	1.2
Pennsylvania	1,441	1,480	1,470	1,562	1,485	1,549	1.5	1.5
Rhode Island	63	69	69	75	74	88	1.0	1.1
South Carolina	847	882	930	903	1,001	1,064	2.4	2.4
South Dakota	154	158	175	148	165	150	2.0	1.8
Tennessee	1,214	1,240	1,211	1,223	1,208	1,282	2.0	2.0
Texas	3,142	3,172	3,738	3,476	3,516	3,517	1.7	1.7
Utah	343	321	321	367	346	360	1.7	1.7
Vermont	77	106	88	96	104	92	1.6	1.4
Virginia	930	900	869	981	934	877	1.3	1.2
Washington	641	654	690	659	665	637	1.3	1.2
West Virginia	356	376	344	372	351	395	1.9	2.1
Wisconsin	712	739	759	721	709	745	1.3	1.3
Wyoming	144	170	143	137	154	189	2.0	2.3
Total*	42,524	43,363	43,649	42,400	41,800	41,300	1.6	1.5

N.A.-Not available.
*Total includes both traffic and nontraffic motor vehicle related deaths.
SOURCE: National Safety Council.

Traffic Accidents and Fatalities

MOTOR VEHICLE TRAFFIC DATA, 1988-1999

Year	Crashes	Injuries	Fatalities
1999 ...	N.A.	N.A.	41,753
1998 ...	6,498,000	3,251,000	41,480
1997 ...	6,764,000	3,399,000	42,013
1996 ...	6,842,000	3,511,000	42,065
1995 ...	6,699,000	3,465,000	41,817
1994 ...	6,496,000	3,266,000	40,716
1993 ...	6,106,000	3,149,000	40,150
1992 ...	6,000,000	3,070,000	39,250
1991 ...	6,117,000	3,097,000	41,508
1990 ...	6,471,000	3,231,000	44,599
1989 ...	6,653,000	3,284,000	45,582
1988 ...	6,887,000	3,416,000	47,087

TRAFFIC FATALITIES BY AGE AND SEX OF VICTIM, 1999

Age of Victim	Male	Female	Total
4 & under ...	406	330	736
5-9	463	336	799
10-15	837	570	1,407
16-20	3,989	1,943	5,932
21-24	2,943	952	3,895
25-34	5,022	1,822	6,844
35-44	4,732	2,011	6,743
45-54	3,426	1,496	4,922
55-64	2,088	1,160	3,248
65-74	1,816	1,262	3,078
75-98	2,272	1,771	4,043
Unknown ...	81	25	106
Total	28,075	13,678	41,753

TRAFFIC FATALITIES BY AGE AND PERSON TYPE, 1999

Age of Victim	Drivers	Passengers	Pedestrians	Pedalcyclists	Other	Total
4 & under	0	558	163	6	9	736
5-9	4	510	194	82	9	799
10-15	144	912	211	126	14	1,407
16-20	3,488	2,064	275	73	32	5,932
21-24	2,544	1,060	231	36	24	3,895
25-34	4,778	1,334	623	75	34	6,844
35-44	4,604	1,058	912	149	20	6,743
45-54	3,319	794	698	96	15	4,922
55-64	2,130	581	486	43	8	3,248
65-74	1,887	689	450	46	6	3,078
75-98	2,352	1,023	641	18	9	4,043
Unknown	21	31	50	3	1	106
Total	25,271	10,614	4,934	753	181	41,753

TRAFFIC FATALITIES BY HOUR OF DAY AND DAY OF WEEK, 1998

Hour of Day	Sun.	Mon.	Tues.	Wed.	Thurs.	Fri.	Sat.	Total
12 to 3 am	1,208	400	322	380	506	530	1,218	4,564
3 to 6 am	641	269	256	267	332	329	630	2,724
6 to 9 am	382	569	554	560	518	503	494	3,580
9 am to noon ..	479	543	560	526	494	558	611	3,771
noon to 3 pm ..	645	719	681	705	701	803	716	4,970
3 to 6 pm	885	840	887	822	894	1,015	869	6,213
6 to 9 pm	848	685	721	710	821	984	1,028	5,797
9 pm to 12 am .	581	561	575	593	678	1,099	1,047	5,135
Total	5,734	4,608	4,595	4,593	4,985	5,864	6,686	37,081

SOURCE: U.S. Department of Transportation, National Highway Traffic Safety Administration.

Traffic Deaths in Selected Countries and Countries with Safety Belt Use Laws

STATES WITH STANDARD/PRIMARY SEAT BELT ENFORCEMENT LAWS*

Alabama	Maryland
California	Michigan
Connecticut	New Mexico
District of Columbia	New York
Georgia	North Carolina
Hawaii	Oklahoma
Indiana	Oregon
Iowa	Texas
Louisiana	

*The safety belt use law may be enforced independent of another violation.
SOURCE: National Highway Traffic Safety Administration.

TRAFFIC DEATHS IN SELECTED COUNTRIES, 1996-1998

				Traffic Fatalities	
				Per 100,000 Registered Motor Vehicles	Per 100 Million Vehicle Miles Traveled
	1996	1997	1998		
Austria	1,027	1,105	963	20.8	N.A.
Belgium	1,356	1,364	1,500	28.5	1.5
Canada	3,082	3,064	2,884	16.4	N.A.
Denmark	514	489	499	22.8	1.8
Finland	404	438	400	17.3	1.4
France	8,080	7,989	8,437	26.1	1.1
Germany	8,758	8,549	7,792	16.9	2.2*
Hong Kong	263	241	N.A.	N.A.	3.7
Italy	6,193	6,226	5,857	19.5	14.9*
Japan	9,942	9,640	9,211	12.9	2.0*
Korea, South	12,653	11,603	N.A.	N.A.	27.8*
The Netherlands	1,180	1,163	1,066	16.1	1.6
Norway	255	303	352	15.9	2.2
Poland	6,359	7,310	7,080	108.2	7.4
Portugal	2,100	1,939	1,865	44.0	3.4*
Romania	2,845	2,863	2,778	95.5	12.5
Sweden	537	541	531	12.8	1.3
Switzerland	616	587	597	16.3	1.9
Turkey	5,428	5,125	4,935	95.7	15.9
United Kingdom	3,740	3,743	3,581	14.2	1.4*
United States	43,649	42,400	41,800	19.8	1.6

N.A. - Not available.
*1997 Data
Note: Data varies significantly between countries both definitionally and quantitatively.
SOURCE: Compiled by Ward's Communications from various sources.

COUNTRIES WITH SAFETY BELT USE LAWS

Country	Effective Date	Country	Effective Date
Australia	1/72	Colorado	7/1/87
Austria	7/76	Connecticut	1/1/86
Belgium	6/75	Delaware	5/22/91
Brazil	6/72	Dist. of Col.	12/12/85
Bulgaria	1976	Florida	7/1/86
Canadian Provinces		Georgia	9/1/88
Alberta	7/87	Hawaii	12/16/85
British Columbia	10/77	Idaho	7/1/86
Manitoba	4/84	Illinois	7/1/85
Newfoundland	7/82	Indiana	7/1/87
New Brunswick	11/83	Iowa	7/1/86
Nova Scotia	1/85	Kansas	7/1/86
Ontario	1/76	Kentucky	7/15/94
Prince Edward Island	1/88	Louisiana	7/1/86
Quebec	7/76	Maine	12/27/95
Saskatchewan	7/77	Maryland	7/1/86
Czechoslovakia	1/69	Massachusetts	2/1/94
Denmark	1/76	Michigan	7/1/85
Finland	7/75	Minnesota	8/1/86
France	10/79	Mississippi	3/20/90
Germany	1/76	Missouri	9/28/85
Greece	12/79	Montana	1/1/88
Hong Kong	10/83	Nebraska	1/1/93
Hungary	7/77	Nevada	7/1/87
Iceland	10/81	New Hampshire	
Ireland	2/79	New Jersey	3/1/85
Israel	7/75	New Mexico	1/1/86
Ivory Coast	1970	New York	12/1/84
Japan	12/71	North Carolina	10/1/85
Jordan	12/83	North Dakota	6/94
Luxembourg	6/75	Ohio	5/6/86
Malaysia	4/79	Oklahoma	2/1/87
Netherlands	6/75	Oregon	12/7/90
New Zealand	6/72	Pennsylvania	11/23/87
Norway	9/75	Puerto Rico	1/1/74
Poland	1/84	Rhode Island	6/18/91
Portugal	1/78	South Carolina	7/1/89
Singapore	7/81	South Dakota	1/1/95
South Africa	12/77	Tennessee	4/21/86
Spain	10/74	Texas	9/1/85
Sweden	1/75	Utah	4/28/86
Switzerland	1/76	Vermont	7/1/93
Turkey	10/84	Virginia	1/1/88
United States and Territories		Washington	6/11/86
Alabama	7/18/91	West Virginia	9/1/93
Alaska	9/90	Wisconsin	12/1/87
Arizona	12/31/90	Wyoming	6/8/89
Arkansas	7/15/91	United Kingdom	1/83
California	1/86	USSR	1/76
		Zimbabwe	7/80

SOURCE: University of Michigan Transportation Research Institute and the American Automobile Manufacturers Association.

INDEX

INDEX

Publications Order Form
All prices valid through December 31, 2000

Newsletters

Ward's Automotive Reports®*
- ❏ One year (52 issues) with **Yearbook** - **$1,215**
  (airmail overseas, add $50)
- ❏ 13-week trial - **$235**
  (airmail overseas, add $12.50)

Ward's Engine and Vehicle Technology Update®*
- ❏ One year (24 issues) with **World Engines database** - **$850**
  (airmail overseas, add $25)
- ❏ Half-year (12 issues) - **$460** *(airmail overseas, add $12.50)*
- ❏ **World Engines database** (separately)** - **$350**

Ward's Automotive International®*
- ❏ One year (24 issues) with the **2000 World Automakers** wall chart and book set - **$595**
  (airmail overseas, add $30)

Ward's Focus On China®*
- ❏ One year (12 issues) - **$385** *(airmail overseas, add $20)*

Special Reports

General Motors in the Twentieth Century**
- ❏ **Regular Price: $100** Please add $5 shipping per book within the U.S. and Canada, or $30 for airmail overseas

- ❏ **Special Price for Facts & Figures subscribers: $75** Please add $5 shipping per book within the U.S. and Canada, or $30 for airmail overseas

Magazines

Ward's Auto World® One year (12 issues)*
- ❏ **$55** U.S. and Mexico
- ❏ **$68** Canada
- ❏ **$85** Airmail Overseas

Ward's Dealer Business® One year (12 issues)*
- ❏ **$40** U.S. and Mexico
- ❏ **$58** Canada
- ❏ **$85** Airmail Overseas

Reference Annuals

Ward's Automotive Yearbook®**
- ❏ 1999 Yearbook - **$385**
- ❏ 2000 Yearbook - **$425**
  (airmail overseas, add $30)

"How the World's Automakers** Are Related" Chart**
- ❏ 2000 Wall chart and book set - **$75**
  (airmail overseas, add $10.00)

*Subject to sales tax in AL, CO, FL, GA, IN, KS, KY, MO, SC, TN and Canada
**Subject to sales tax in AL, AK, CA, CO, CT, FL, GA, IL, IN, KS, KY, MA, MI, MN, MO, MS, NE, NJ, NY, OH, PA, SC, TN, TX, WI and Canada

- -

Please make checks payable to: **Ward's Communications** in U.S. funds, drawn on a U.S. bank.

Payment enclosed $ _____ **Signature** _____

Bill to my: ❏ VISA   ❏ Mastercard   ❏ AmEx   ❏ Discover

Card number _____ **Exp. Date** _____

Name/Title (Please print) _____

Company/Division _____   **FF0800**

Street Address _____

City _____   **State/Prov.** _____

Zip/Postal Code _____   **Country** _____

Phone _____   **Fax** _____

3000 Town Center, Suite 2750, Southfield, MI 48075 USA • Phone: (248) 357-0800; FAX: (248) 357-0810
Mail, Fax or Phone in Your Order Today!

71528